Advocates and Adversaries

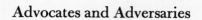

ROBERT R. ROSE, circa 1922
when he ran for U.S. Representative from Wyoming

Courtesy of Ms. Virginia Rose and Judge Robert R. Rose, Jr.

The Lakeside Classics

ADVOCATES
AND ADVERSARIES

*The Early Life and Times
of Robert R. Rose*

By Robert R. Rose

EDITED BY
GENE M. GRESSLEY

The Lakeside Press

R. R. DONNELLEY & SONS COMPANY
CHICAGO
Christmas, 1977

PUBLISHERS' PREFACE

IN 1914, a young lawyer from Denver, Robert R. Rose, arrived in Kemmerer, Wyoming to hang up his shingle and commence the practice of his profession. As a small town lawyer, he became closely acquainted with the activities of the county, and was directly involved in many of them. The story of his eight years in Kemmerer, never before published, makes up the seventy-fifth annual edition of *The Lakeside Classics*, "Advocates and Adversaries," which is subtitled, "The Early Life and Times of Robert R. Rose." The book reflects the economic development of a western twentieth century frontier community with an economic base of petroleum, livestock, and mining industries. It is peopled with several colorful citizens, frequently given fictitious names, whose activities sometimes required an attorney well versed in criminal law.

The manuscript is in the Western History Research Center at the University of Wyoming, and was suggested by Dr. Gene M. Gressley, who also serves as Editor. Publication was made possible by the cooperation of Judge Robert R. Rose, Jr., and Virginia Rose, children of the author.

Dr. Gressley is a noted professor of American history as well as the author of numerous books and articles on the subject. He has been associated with the University of Wyoming for twenty years. For eight years he was Director of the University's School of American Studies. He now is Assistant to the President, American Heritage Center, and is active in many historical associations, both regional and national.

Robert Williams has again made the final drawings for the map which clarifies the locale of the book. Mr. Williams, a Chicago artist and calligrapher, worked from a basic map provided by the Donnelley Cartographic Services. The Donnelley Creative Services Division contributed design, typographic assistance, and technical editorial service.

Once again the Donnelley Electronic Graphics® service has generated the type pages using their computerized electronic equipment. The volume was printed by offset lithography and bound on modern high-speed binding lines, both in our Crawfordsville (Indiana) Division. The entire production of this 1977 edition, from type generation through printing and binding, was accomplished with equipment and techniques of the electronic age. These methods continue the philosophy of Thomas E. Donnelley who initiated *The Lakeside Classics* in 1903 to demonstrate the advantages of machine-made books over expensive hand-made volumes. Mr. Donnelley was a forward-looking President of our Company who believed even at the beginning of the century that a machine-made book could be attractive and easy to read. Methods of the 1970s continue to prove him right.

IN THE PUBLISHERS' PREFACE of last year's edition of *The Lakeside Classics*, we mentioned the increase in sales and income as the year of 1976 progressed. Fortunately, this trend continued through 1977. Thus the comparable increases for the first six months of 1977 were quite dramatic, and those for the last six months were more modest, but making for a good year overall. We enjoyed higher activity in all major product categories, but especially in magazines and catalogs, and this, with improved productivity, resulted in another high record in earnings and continued our steady earnings growth. For the seventh consecutive year, the Board of Directors increased the annual dividend.

Late in 1976, after our book for that year had been distributed, the Chicago South Plant was given to, and accepted by, the City of Chicago. We had unsuccessfully sought a constructive use for this large, modern building since LIFE magazine ceased publication in 1972. Our good neighbor, McCormick Place Exhibition Center, requires much needed additional exhibit space with high floor loading and a rail siding. This will enable it to accommodate exhibits which have outgrown its facilities or require a much different type of building. With this gift our Company's vital interest in the City of Chicago and our immediate neighborhood is well served. In appreciation of its value to the City, the late Mayor Richard J. Daley recommended that the building be named Donnelley Hall in honor of Thomas E.

Donnelley, son of our founder and the originator of *The Lakeside Classics*.

In the past we have referred to short supplies of certain grades of coated papers used mainly for magazines and catalogs, followed by excessive inventories during the recent recession. Lately we have seen evidences of renewed current shortages and even a more serious situation in the future. This has resulted from a hesitancy of paper companies to expand sufficiently in these grades to accommodate expected growth. Now there are indications that certain paper manufacturers are contemplating added capacity, and we are cautiously optimistic.

Also we have expressed our concern over the adequacy of energy supplies, especially natural gas which we use in large quantities for drying presswork. Since there is no economically feasible substitute for gas, we have where possible arranged for gas wells dedicated to our exclusive use and have provided standby liquid propane and fuel oil for all our plants. While this is expensive both as an insurance and operating cost, it stood us in very good stead during the energy crisis last winter. While other plants had to shut down or curtail their operations, we were able to continue full production with very few minor exceptions. Thus we avoided loss of production; our people enjoyed full employment; and our customers were fully supplied. In fact, we had additional activity because we were able to produce.

Our Company is planning and executing plans for future growth. Capital expenditures will probably reach a new high this year, as will even higher appropriations for future capital projects. A significant portion is for pollution control, which brings no return, but actually increases operating costs.

All divisions continue to make capital additions necessary to remain a leader in new technology and to have modern facilities. Major capital expansion programs are under way in Gallatin, Warsaw, and Mattoon with new press and binding facilities, and in Lancaster East where we have installed a highly sophisticated computer composition system. The start-up costs of these new projects will be high, as they have been in the past, and will be a significant drain on earnings, but the alternative, the failure to meet the challenges of our future, is unthinkable.

As a service business, our success is very much dependent on close relationships with our customers. In recognition of this, we are positioning more of our sales representatives in offices in major cities spread across the United States from coast to coast and from north to south.

To accommodate the continuing growth, adjustments in organization naturally evolve. On the one hand, our manufacturing divisions are tending to concentrate on the preparation of printing surfaces, presswork, and binding. On the other hand, we are developing a series of centers to concentrate mainly on composition and preliminary work, prior to preparation of printing surfaces. We expect this trend to continue, perhaps even accelerate. Some are now linked by coaxial cable and microwave, and a network of communications employing satellites is quite conceivable.

All these plans and objectives are hardly realistic without a strong group of intelligent and dedicated people. These we are proud to say we have in great measure. They are ever adapting and increasing their skills to meet the challenges of the future.

With their continued support and that of many other friends among our customers, suppliers, and the communities in which we operate, we face the future with optimism.

The Company published in 1977 a book entitled *To Be a Good Printer*. The book was written by Gaylord Donnelley after his retirement. Gaylord, the grandson of our founder, served our Company for forty-three years in many capacities including President and Chairman of the Board. The book analyzes what we believe are the factors underlying our strength and growth.

To all, warm greetings of the season, and very best wishes for the year ahead.

THE PUBLISHERS

Christmas, 1977

CONTENTS

xiv   *Contents*

ILLUSTRATIONS

The Wyoming
of Robert R. Rose

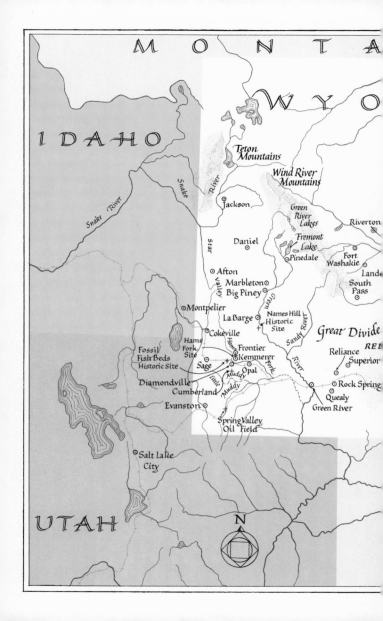

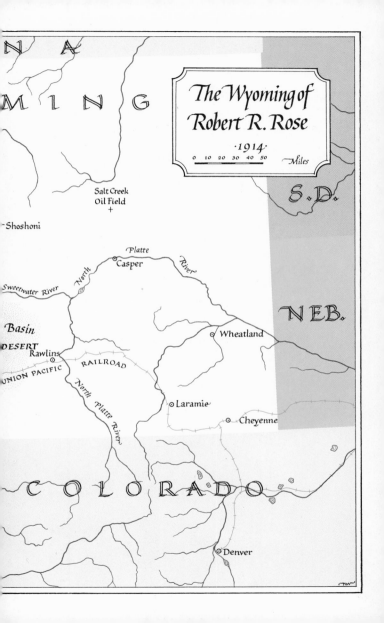

The Wyoming of
Robert R. Rose

·1914·

0 10 20 30 40 50

Miles

S. D.

MONTANA

WYOMING

Salt Creek
Oil Field
+

Shoshoni

Platte
Casper

River

North

Sweetwater River

NEB.

Basin

DESERT

Rawlins

RAILROAD

Wheatland

UNION PACIFIC

North Platte River

Laramie

Cheyenne

COLORADO

Denver

HISTORICAL INTRODUCTION

O^F ALL the literary landscapes depicting the twentieth century West, Robert R. Rose's autobiography is and will remain a classic of Americana. The excruciatingly poignant opening chapter, which so graphically and quickly immerses the readers in the loneliness, scenic beauty and small town society, possesses a never-to-be-forgotten power. Here is a Rolvaaglike image of a Western frontier town. With a deceptively simple, Lincolnesque style, young Bob Rose forcefully evokes his emotions, reactions and, above all, his wonderment at having committed his future to a Western society, whose very meagerness, economically and socially, seemed so evident with each early morning walk downtown.

Yet the anguish of those first self-doubts, the knifelike emptiness of being forsaken all evaporated with amazing alacrity. For Bob Rose possessed a personable quality that quickly made him one with any society—legal, economic, political, social—he selected. Simply stated, Bob Rose liked people, and those he met sensed this trait immediately and reciprocated. Recalling those years of warmth and steady friendships was why, more than any other motivation, Bob Rose could look back after three decades and regard his early days at Kemmerer as his golden age. Fundamentally, he loved his neighbor, and his neighbor was known to have loved him.

What made up Kemmerer, that gray spring day of 1914, when young Bob Rose alighted from the Oregon Short Line passenger car? Any one could have, and probably did, tell the young attorney that Kemmerer resulted from a coupling of the economic vision of a Western entrepreneur, P. J. Quealy, and the investment of an Eastern financier, Mahlon Kemmerer.[1] The anticipated economic return was based on the richness of the nearby coal seams— how rich no one at that point could be certain; but then speculation was and continues to be the major ingredient of all natural resource development. The town of Kemmerer soon stabilized, and a group of small satellite communities—Frontier, Diamondville, and Quealy, grew up around it. Later petroleum could be the natural resource wealth of this wild and beautiful country. Though less dramatic and frequently forgotten, the livestock industry was always present in the surrounding terrain, contributing a steadying influence on the economy. Indeed Cokeville, a small town thirty-five miles northwest of Kemmerer boasted, for a brief spell in its history,

[1]Those aficionados of Kemmerer will enjoy and profit from Glen Barrett's description of early Kemmerer in *Kemmerer, Wyoming. The Founding of an Independent Coal Town, 1897-1902* (Kemmerer, 1972); although published too late to be utilized by the editor, *A Tale of Two Towns*, edited by Dorise Marx Housley, Betty Carpenter Pfaff and Wanda Sims Vasey (n.p., 1977) is highly recommended.

of being the wealthiest community—on a per capita basis—of any town in the United States—a wealth built on thousands of lazily grazing herefords and Rambouillets.[2]

Finally, Kemmerer achieved an economic significance as a mercantile and distributing point for the surrounding hinterland, a significance which declined somewhat with the coming of the Model T. One longtime resident of Kemmerer told the editor, "If you couldn't buy what you wanted in Kemmerer, you might go to Rock Springs, or perhaps even Evanston, but most likely, if it were a major purchase, you headed for Salt Lake." In those pioneering years of Robert Rose's residence in Kemmerer, few excursions were undertaken to Salt Lake. Some of the local citizenry trudged down to the "Golden Rule" store, which the J. C. Penney Company, Incorporated has labeled on its façade—the "No. 1" store. Others, Penney clerks and residents alike, simply refer to it as the "mother" or first store of the Penney chain.

Almost simultaneously with Attorney Rose's appearance on the Kemmerer streets, occurred, if not the most significant economic event in Kemmerer's history, at least the one producing the most promotion, the greatest publicity, and the highest expectations. On March 4, 1914, the Kemmerer *Camera* let its readers in on an exciting bit of news. One

[2]Anges Wright Spring (ed.), *Wyoming, A Guide to Its People* (New York, 1941), p. 250.

Charles Lackey, drilling on the Fred Beck place on North Piney Creek, "opened up a pocket of oil bearing sand, with some gas at a depth of about fifty-five feet which raises to the surface several gallons of petroleum."

From that histrionic moment on, Bob Rose was not, much to his later chagrin, free of the obsessions which recent oil news might bring, that is until he left Kemmerer. Not that the 1914 Lackey announcement took Kemmerer by storm. Far from it—the petroleum potential of the Dry Piney, La Barge and Spring Valley areas had been known of as far back as a half-century.[3] (In the early years of the twentieth century) the United States Geological Survey had published several reports on the Dry Piney and La Barge fields.[4]

All of Kemmerer knew there was nothing to that infectious talk in John Griff's "Belmont," or in the lobby of the Kemmerer Hotel about a "mother pool" under the La Barge field. That is, all of Kemmerer knew, except the increasingly sizeable groups of men who clustered around the "newest" geologist from Salt Lake, Denver or Tulsa to hear those exceptionally learned treatises about the mysteries

[3]F. J. H. Merrill, "The Spring Valley Oilfield in Southwestern Wyoming," *Mining and Scientific Press*, January 27, 1912, p. 162; T. H. Harrison to S. H. Keoughan, August 20, 1923, Petroleum History and Research Center, University of Wyoming, Laramie.

[4]W. R. Calvert, "Report on Part of the Spring Valley Oil Field, Unita County, Wyoming," Petroleum History and Research Center.

under the earth's crust.[5] That Jonah and the Whale were both present did not bother these would-be millionaires till later.

For three years after Bob Rose first viewed the Kemmerer Town Hall, seldom was published an issue of the *Camera* which missed shouting an announcement of some new shooting well, a recently formed company or a party of visiting investors seeking a place to sink their surplus wealth.

Singular were the Kemmerer residents, who withstood for long the explosive enthusiasms engendered by such headlines as: "Kemmerer May Soon Be the Center of the State's Next Big Oil Boom;" "Spudding In 'Witnessed' by Hundreds;" "Two More Big Companies to Drill in Lincoln County."[6] Some solid citizens kept their feet on the ground and their hands over their pocket books. Mrs. Roy Mason refused to allow her husband to put his money into the earth; but then, she ruefully admits, years later, to having invested their life savings in silver fox farms—with disastrous results.[7]

As an indication of the frenetic atmosphere on Kemmerer sidewalks in 1916, all one has to read is

[5] "Lincoln County Being Sized up Favorably as an Oil Field," Kemmerer *Camera*, February 14, 1917.

[6] "Kemmerer May Soon Be Center of State's Next Big Oil Boom," Kemmerer *Camera*, November 29, 1915; "Spudding In 'Witnessed' by Hundreds," Kemmerer *Camera*, September 26, 1917; "Two More Big Companies to Drill in Lincoln County," Kemmerer *Camera*, October 31, 1917.

[7] Interview with Mrs. Roy A. Mason, November 4, 1976.

an article in the *Camera* for November 29th. Casting restraint aside, the editor asked his readers to imagine—"Kemmerer, a city of 6,000! Kemmerer, the Center of Wyoming's ever-increasing Oil Interests; Kemmerer, the headquarters for a company that represents millions!" After weaving through that article, a *Camera* reader would have to be well-inoculated, indeed, against the speculative urge not to dash out the next minute and sink all he possessed in penny oil stocks.

The *Camera* reporter then went on to paint, in less intense hues, the actual facts of the petroleum development as he saw them. *Camera* subscribers were reliably informed that the Plains Oil Company of Kansas City, Missouri, would spend "a 'cool' half a million" within a few months exploiting the La Barge field. According to contracts already signed by Plains Oil with leasors, twenty wells would be drilled in the La Barge field within the coming year. The Ohio Oil Company, under the dynamic and shrewd leadership of Jack McFadyen had "pronounced it (La Barge field) as one of the most promising ones in the state."[8] Had the Kemmererites been in the mood (which they were not) to critically assess the *Camera's* phrases, a sentence of warning was embedded in gushing prose: "Many Eastern fields have shown a tendency to weaken, and it is now feasible to begin working on fields that are a considerable distance from a rail-

[8]Kemmerer *Camera*, November 29, 1916.

road."[9] The dearth of transportation and market had beviled and limited the Western petroleum operator long before the La Barge-Dry Piney boom. But Kemmerer found even slight hints of caution as traitorous.

The rhapsody continued in Kemmerer over their soon-to-be-millionaire status, "old heads have studied the lay of the land. The question that is bothering the minds of this particular aggregation [a group of Denver capitalists] is just which one of Lincoln county's prospective oil fields is THE one." But never mind, "Oil men who know the game have systems of their own," the *Camera* knowingly declared to its readers. For instance, if "a well were sunk to a great depth in the Fossil field and oil was struck, the scientific oil man would know where to strike next."[10]

That the residents of Kemmerer went to bed with visions of oil wells dancing in their heads is not exactly astonishing. Frontier towns the West over from the first settlement wave in the nineteenth century until the present time have espoused boomerism, seeing themselves as the next Chicago or Denver. What was astonishing about the Kemmerer oil boom was that it lasted so long (1916–1921) with so little substance. Not even one truly magnificent bonanza well! True, the La Barge field did slowly evolve into a respectable, if modest, production.

[9] *Ibid.*
[10] *Ibid.*, February 14, 1917.

But no one even in Kemmerer could compare La Barge and Salt Creek.

That Kemmerer savored its boom as long as it did, as Attorney Rose makes clear, was due to the mesmerizing presence of amazing Charles Lackey. A charming and persistent promoter, Lackey possessed just enough geological knowledge to be dangerous both to himself and others. In a room full of promoters in Henning Hotel in Casper, Lackey would not have been singled out from the crowd. What did distinguish Lackey from his fellow breed, was his unrivalled ability to inject credibility into his smooth flowing and dramatically spiced conversation. Lackey, one must concede, probably himself believed what he told others! For undeniably he had a deep fundamentalist faith in the Dry Piney field. Few promoters would have traveled over Western Wyoming for a decade with so little to show for their endeavours. Lackey told his listeners, as long as they would listen, that they would be rich on the morrow; and privately he knew he would be!

We will probably never know what motivated Lackey, for his background, motives and aspirations remain as enigmatic in 1977, as his smile was in 1916.[11] The corporate vehicle that accommodated Lackey's petroleum trances, and ensnared Bob Rose, went under the geologically respectable and

[11]Bits and pieces of Lackey's background show up in the Kemmerer *Camera* articles, for example see: March 4, 1914; November 14, 28, 1917; October 30, 1918; July 23, 1919.

significantly sounding name of the Cretaceous Oil Company.[12] From the spring of 1917, through the summer of 1921, the press of Kemmerer dutifully at first, then slowly and more reluctantly, recorded the spontaneous activities of the Cretaceous Oil Company, and the goings and comings of Charles Lackey.

Big Piney residents looked with wonderment when, in April of 1917, a "huge Keystone Drill moved into operation on the Cretaceous holdings in the Dry Piney field."[13] By that autumn Lackey had convinced himself and others that the most advantageous aggrandizement of the Cretaceous leases would come with the incorporation of an operating company to drill their leases. So *tout de suite*, following this tried and true promoter practice, Lackey requested that his friend and fellow Cretaceous officer, Robert Rose, organize the Lackey Oil Company—with a modest, but not untypical, capitalization of $1,000,000. The elected officers, some of whom held their high responsibilities with increasing uneasiness, were: Charles Lackey, Big Piney, President; C. P. Budd, Marbleton, Vice-President; N. H. Jensen, Secretary-Treasurer, and R. R. Rose, Counsel.[14]

[12]"Pushing Oil Project," Kemmerer *Camera*, September 20, 1916.

[13]"Cretaceous Begins Active Work," Kemmerer *Camera*, April 25, 1917.

[14]"Big Oil Company to Develop Upper La Barge Field," Kemmerer *Camera*, November 14, 1917.

Simultaneously with the announcement of the latest company to originate from Lackey's fertile imagination came a report that Lackey had struck a shallow well at the depth of 835 feet. Supposedly this news so stimulated C. R. Bender, editor of the *Mining and Oil Record* of Salt Lake City, that he immediately rushed over to the Dry Piney field to take a look for himself. Bender graciously confessed that "Like any one who has had much to do with oil and mining, I at first was skeptical about the reports that were brought from the Piney fields." But once Bender walked over the field all his skepticism left him, inspired by Lackey's faith, and "the first well" situated on the La Barge anticline. Bender also observed the non sequitur that during Lackey's four-year interest in Dry Piney fifty-six water wells had been drilled.[15]

Outside of providing Lackey with a platform for future promotional orations, Bender did give a hint about the background of Mr. Lackey, in fact the only information we have as to Lackey's previous association with the petroleum industry. And according to Bender, Lackey had been sent to Wyoming by the famous firm of Guffey and Galey of Spindletop discovery fame. His mission—to investigate the La Barge field. Lackey was intrigued by what he discovered and stayed on, to the eventual grief of Cretaceous investors. Since Lackey's experience was incorporated in Bender's recitation almost

[15]La Barge File, Petroleum History and Research Center.

as an afterthought, one might give some credence to Bender's comments.

Two weeks after the announcement of the formation of the Lackey Oil Company, Lackey placed an advertisement in the *Camera,* offering unwary readers stock in the Lackey Oil Company at the bargain price of fourteen cents a share.[16] For this modest investment in their future, shareholders would participate in a company which controlled 920 acres in the Dry Piney field, and a company which would soon acquire more sections, plus having the management of Charles Lackey.

Eight days before Christmas of 1917, the *Camera* noted that four hundred acres adjacent to the Cretaceous holdings in the Dry Piney field were about to be drilled by a group of Idaho capitalists. Then the article concluded with one of the most delightful observations of the entire odyssey of the Cretaceous company, "Certainly the finding of oil at a depth of 835 feet by the Cretaceous Co., together with the indication that Charles Lackey has found every water well he has sunk, gives encouragement to every prospective holder in the Dry Piney district. Of course, the drilling of any well is more or less a speculation."[17] Investors take note—oil and water do mix!

[16]"Lackey Oil at 14 Cents," Kemmerer *Camera*, November 28, 1917.

[17]"Another Oil Corporation," Kemmerer *Camera*, December 19, 1917.

In April of 1918, the *Camera* conceded that "Conjecture, which has been rife as to the probable production of the Cretaceous well drilled in the Shannon sands by Charles Lackey last year, will soon be replaced with fact, for according to Mr. Lackey, the well is to be shot early in April."[18] In bold type the admission was made that in reality neither Lackey nor his investors had yet to see any sustained production from the 835 foot well. However, the article ended with the assurance "that the well will establish the Dry Piney field as one of the most promising of any Lincoln county fields drilled to date."

So it went through the year of 1918, with gossip and news about the latest Lackey success permeating Kemmerer society. First, the Lincoln-Idaho Oil Company, "of obvious and known prosperity,"[19] leased some Dry Piney acreage of the Cretaceous. Then as winter came on Lackey busily started the four wells in the Dry Piney field with the unshakable conviction that all that rested between Lackey, associates, and prosperity was a load of well casing.

The year 1919 opened auspiciously for the Cretaceous Oil Company. On the evening of April 15, "a rumor was circulated on the streets of Kemmerer late last night to the effect that a gusher had been

[18]"Cretaceous Well," Kemmerer *Camera*, March 27, 1918.
[19]"Important Oil Deal," Kemmerer *Camera*, April 24, 1918.

brought in in the Cretaceous oil field. . . ."[20] The new "gusher" turned out to be a short, explosive shot of oil from an old well—which had been cleaned out. Then disaster struck Lackey and the Cretaceous. As Lackey was splicing a cable, he part way fell into the well, fracturing his leg. He was immediately transported to the Kemmerer Hospital, where his stay was prolonged to the discomfort of patients and staff.[21]

Silence settled about the Cretaceous wells for the rest of 1919. With the breaking of Spring in 1920, Lackey returned to his old haunts, bringing with him a new star rig financed by the Hubert V. Utterbach "Syndicate."[22] Evidently Utterbach's attention was diverted from the potential wealth of Dry Piney, for in August, Lackey launched another hunt for investors. Astoundingly, in San Francisco, he located American Producers and Refiners Corporation of California, who promised to erect a refinery at Dry Piney—doubtlessly to be prepared for the enormous production to gush forth from the mother pool.[23] The cowboys in and around the Dry

[20]"Cretaceous Well Shoots Skyward About 40 Feet—the Highest Grade Oil Known to the World Today," Kemmerer *Camera*, April 16, 1919.

[21]"Lackey Injured at Baum Well," Kemmerer *Camera*, July 23, 1919.

[22]"Petrogas Oil Corporation Moving Oil Outfit to the Dry Piney Oil Fields," Kemmerer *Camera*, March 24, 1920.

[23]"Oil Refinery for the Dry Piney Field," Kemmerer *Camera*, August 18, 1920.

Piney field never saw the refinery, and thus another Lackey air castle blew away in the Wyoming wind.

All of a sudden, or so the Cretaceous directors thought, the land titles of their leases came under a heavy legal barrage. For most of 1920, Robert Rose, now in his twin capacities as President and General Counsel of the Cretaceous, spent his time defeating the fairy-tale imaginations of a family who claimed prior rights to the Cretaceous land on the basis of coal land titles.[24]

Two years later, the oil excitement in Kemmerer had trickled down to whispers; and the most fervent believers in the futures of Cretaceous Oil and Mr. Charles Lackey conceded that the business obituaries for both would soon inscribe *finis*. And so be it! The *Camera* published a remarkable story full of resignation, more than a touch of humor. It wrote the end to Cretaceous, Lackey and, one suspects, all immediate petroleum promotion in general. On June 14th, the *Camera* announced: "Coupled with other signs of the times are the silent goings and comings of Charles Lackey, well known oil operator of this county and discoverer of the Dry Piney field. Since returning to Lincoln county in anticipation of the development work for the present year, less than a month ago, Lackey has made five round

[24]"Cretaceous Land Contest," Kemmerer *Camera*, December 15, 1920; "Keenan Loses Contest for Cretaceous Ground," Kemmerer *Camera*, August 24, 1921.

trips to Big Piney . . . several trips to Salt Lake and
other Utah points and back, all presumably on business in connection with Cretaceous Oil Company,
of which he is the founder. 'I am staging a comeback
that will be surprising and pleasing to my many
friends and my acquaintances here,' said Lackey
in response to questions submitted by the *Camera*
with a view to publishing something definite in connection with the Lackey plans. 'Further than this I
do not wish to be quoted at this time. All I can say
now is that you keep your eyes and ears open and I
believe that you will see much real oil news
now.' "[25]

Though Robert Rose, Sr., never found the wealth
he daydreamed of in 1914, the Rose family today
receives a miniscule royalty check annually—the
only tangible evidence of their father's encounter
with the Cretaceous Oil Company and the theatri-
cal Charles Lackey.

While the petroleum commotion of 1915–1920
dominated the hearts and minds of Kemmererites,
the oil flurry shouldn't disguise the solid economic
progress in other phases of Kemmerer's growth.
The two banks prospered in these years, the livestock industry continued to mature; and above all
coal production remained the foundation for Kemmerer's economic base. Some longtime residents insist that Kemmerer has always been a community in

[25]"Here to Stage Comeback Says Charles Lackey," Kemmerer *Camera*, June 14, 1922.

search of an economic future. And so it may have
seemed to many. Yet in 1977, with its mineral resources, primarily coal, with an assured market,
Kemmerer has come of age—economically speaking, although more than a few Kemmerer residents,
despite the certainty of their economic future, now
debate with new anxiety the inherent problems of a
boom town economy. Especially worrisome are
the examples of other Wyoming communities such
as: Rock Springs and Gillette, who have undergone
similar and recent economic transformations from
small villages to communities with all night neon
lights. Other residents of Western Wyoming nod in
agreement, but quickly concede that they would
rather opt for regional prosperity with problems,
than poverty with peace.

Against this economic tableau of the Rose years
in Kemmerer, what was it like to walk down the
streets, go to church, and in general live in this
Western "Our Town?" One conclusion is easily
reached; the cultural life of the community revolved
around the churches (although some Kemmererites
would vigorously dissent on behalf of the bars). Besides James Mythen's fondness for the spirits, and
respect for the spirit, he is most engraved in Kemmerer memories as the one who taught the "Fox
Trot" and "Charleston" to his members (and perhaps even a Lutheran or two) in the Episcopal
church basement.[26] It is doubtful though that the

[26]Interview with Mrs. Helen Mason Gernert and Mrs. Roy

small group of devout Episcopalians, who met on the porch of the Roy Mason home to organize their church, had dancing below the sanctuary in mind. But once the edifice was erected, Sunday worshippers enthusiastically joined in this mid-week extracurricular activity. Church socialization obviously was not restricted to the "Fox Trot;" if anything, churches over-regulated the social life of the community. Mrs. Mason recalls the ladies club, "The Knitters"—knitted more with their vocal cords than their hands.[27]

Religion also enveloped the town because of the heavy foreign extraction of the miners. All you have to do today to realize the historic number of foreign immigrants to Kemmerer is to run your hand down the current telephone directory; names of Finnish, Italian, Slovene, Polish, Scandinavian, and Oriental origins pop out at you. The Slovenski Dom in Diamondville developed into a community hall, where marriage and funerals competed with activities which provided the reputation for the hall's sacrilegious name, "Bucket of Blood."

Funerals for the miners were both a time of mourning and a time of celebration. Perhaps they might be interpreted best as a serio-tragic Irish wake! That is, if any occasion could merit that appellation. On a funeral day, miners dressed in their finest; sometimes entire outfits of new clothes

Mason, November 4, 1976.
[27] *Ibid.*

would be purchased for their children. Then in wavering, erratic lines, the mining community would march down Pine Avenue to the Cemetery. Mrs. Helen Mason Gernert told of her father's lifelong memory of the band playing for a funeral on the first day he saw Kemmerer in 1900.[28]

Major social events which always prompted high revelry were the special holidays—the Fourth of July and "First Footing."[29] In fact, Independence Day in Kemmerer took on some of the characteristics of Christmas observances in the Midwest of the same vintage. Candy, nuts and fruit were passed out wholesale to the town's bib-overall set. Extending over two days, the town turned out for hotly contested baseball games, ice cream socials and, above all, horse races. The horse tracks were laid out for a three-eighths-of-a-mile, a quarter-of-a-mile and three hundred yards. In one quarter-of-a-mile race in 1914's Fourth, "Boogerboo," belonging to a B. H. Smith of Salt Lake, won over the local favorite, "Hippy," entered by Al Hileman.[30]

New Year's Eve holds another special place of joy in memories of early Kemmererites. Mrs. Helen Mason Gernert tells of her mother and father's participation in "First Footing"—a Scottish tradition for the advent of the New Year—complete with

[28] *Ibid.*

[29] Memorandum to Gene M. Gressley from Helen Mason Gernert, November 5, 1976.

[30] "Saturday Racing," Kemmerer *Camera*, July 8, 1914.

dinner parties, music and dancing. Furthermore, Mrs. Gernert emphasized, "All with no liquor of any kind!"

When reviewing Kemmerer's social and cultural life, one dominant, and overriding consideration which few could escape, although some tried, was the intimacy of a small town atmosphere. Everyone not only knew everyone else, they usually were aware of what their neighbors had done yesterday, and were planning for the morrow. In view of the chatter time at organizations like the "Knitters" and bridge tables, one wonders if the newspapers, featuring their "About Town" columns, were not superfluous. For undoubtedly the news spread rapidly without the benefit of print. Many found the constant recognition in public places of private faces a deeply satisfying part of living a Kemmerer life. Others, especially those who had experienced broader and deeper cultural resources in a distant metropolitan setting, found Kemmerer's limited cultural opportunities as extremely stultifying. Both Virginia and Robert R. Rose, Jr., remember their mother as being less than totally enchanted with the small world of Kemmerer.[31] The lively bridge group in Kemmerer must have been a pleasurable experience for Mrs. Rose; she was totally and fervently addicted to the game! At age eighty-five, she was known, Wyoming over, for her fantastic skill

[31]Interviews with Judge Robert R. Rose, Jr., October 18, 1976; Ms. Virginia Rose, November 4, 1976.

as an accomplished duplicate bridge player. Nevertheless, Virginia Rose, in retrospect, recalls her mother visibly shuddering whenever her father retold some of the famous cases, or referred to an intriguing incident from the Kemmerer years. "Thank goodness," Mrs. Rose's shudders telegraphed, "that was all in the past."

The warm glow from conversations with friends, the lazy, pleasant summer afternoons, the friendly downtown exchanges between clerks and shoppers, all provided the sunlight and twilight side of growing up in Kemmerer. A darker and more sinister side exploded all too prevalently in crime and violence. A contemporary reader of the Kemmerer *Camera* can not help but be impressed with the numbers of banners and headlines on murder, attempted murder, mayhem, rustling, suicides, bootlegging and robbery.

The accumulative effect, with the objectivity lent by fifty years of distance, is that violence claimed an inherent place in Kemmerer's life. How many Western communities, in one judicial session, had three murder cases appealed to their state supreme courts? The hard side of Kemmerer life ran just below the surface, threatening to flare (at any given moment) whenever tempers erupted. Yet as with most interpretations of the past, the coloration of life can easily be murkier or more luminescent depending on who holds the candle. Without an intensive quantitative investigation of the West, or even Wyoming, it would be impossible to say with any degree of credence that Kemmerer life contained more violence than elsewhere. We do know that as a new, raw, frontier community Kemmerer had a susceptibility for violence—susceptibility that readily attracted publicity for a town of less than a thousand.

If you probe the Kemmerer residents' consciousness as to why the late teens and early twenties were (or presumably were) crime-ridden years you receive a standard reply—prohibition. True, Kemmerer had a widespread reputation then (and since) of being an island awash in a sea of moonshine, a veritable bootleggers' heaven, where stills could be hid in the hills, safe from discovery or demolition. Kemmerer inhabitants with occasionally the barest hint of suppressed pride would tell visitors that in the twenties and thirties their town had the name of "Little Chicago." Yet Western bootlegging never acquired the Eastern entrepreneurial organization of Al Capone.[32] Westerners, individualistic to the core, even about their liquor, saw no rationale for joining up with anybody. After all, a small investment and a thin piece of copper brought surprisingly large rewards (no matter how you defined the word).

[32]The editor has followed (with a few excursions chartered by Kemmererites) Glen Barrett's interpretation of Kemmerer's era of "prohibition." See *Kemmerer, Wyoming, The Founding of An Independent Coal Town, 1897–1902* (Kemmerer, 1972), pp. 71–75.

As in many communities, East or West, on the final evening before prohibition, June 30, 1919, Kemmererites gathered in the town Triangle to commiserate with each other and watch a hearse carrying the coffin of "John Barleycorn." The band, we are told, played appropriate music—funeral dirges. The next day dawned brightly for the bootlegger in Kemmerer and the nation.

The subsequent decade of Kemmerer's history was filled with announcements of the confiscations of casks of wine, bottles of bathtub gin, and several strongly scented brandy kegs. One Kemmerer resident recalled that the pouring out of the brandy, by the prohibition agents, as "wanton, malicious and unjustified vandalism!" Soon the town hall, the Hamsfork bridge, the hills behind Kemmerer, the Frontier Supply store, were all granted memorial trust status in the community as one after another of these spots became the sorrowful site of a gurgling waste disposal.[33]

Prohibition also provoked one of the most strikingly vitriolic editorials that ever appeared under the masthead of Robert Rose during his ownership of the *Camera*. The righteous wrath of the *Camera* pinpointed two targets, the honorable T. Hunter Salmon, Mayor, and his support by the Kemmerer *Republican*. The *Camera* editor told his readers that, like the swallows returning to Capistrano, every time Mayor Salmon wanted to divert the atten-

[33]Kemmerer *Camera*, August 19, November 3, 1920.

tion of the town from more serious affairs, he would begin to campaign for a new purified water supply. Why? The *Camera*, under the subtle headline of "Water, Booze and Camouflage" explained that the perennial agitation of the water question this year arrived a little earlier than usual. "The reason is interesting," stated the *Camera* editorial, "About two months ago, the *Camera* began, mildly enough, it will be admitted, to expose the shocking manner in which the liquor laws are not being enforced. . . . No effort whatever is being made, or ever has been made by our belligerent and boozy mayor to enforce the laws. Alcohol is King, and the roulette wheel is his handmaiden! Every form of vice flourishes under the indulgent eye of Tricky Tom, while he bravely proclaims his holy determination to fight to the ditch for a pure water supply."[34]

The *Camera* went on in a similar vein, reminiscent of the prose of a territorial editor of the likes of Bill Nye, M. C. Barrow, or an E. A. Slack, to peel the figurative hide off the mayor and his adherents. The water campaign, insisted the *Camera*, represented a mere subterfuge for covering up political and governmental maleficence. Evidently the cover-up was somewhat successful, for toward the conclusion of the *Camera's* polemic came the words, "The water question has been used as a camouflage for the booze question, and behind that screen the am-

[34]"Water, Booze and Camouflage," Kemmerer *Camera*, December 10, 1919.

munition has been fired which has defeated the efforts of the citizens of the community to secure a decent city government."

Neither prosecutor nor editor Rose (in this instance they held the same identity) could defeat the forces of evil—prohibition in Kemmerer "flourished." And violence continued to be part of the Kemmerer scene. While historians have had a preoccupation, bordering at times on morbidity about violence on the nineteenth century frontier, the Kemmerer experience, plus similar community incidences elsewhere, would suggest that historians might well inquire into causation of violence in the early twentieth century West. Kemmerer may have been, because of ethnicity and as a bootlegging Shangri-la, more receptive to corruption, but until we have further historical research our knowledge will be as vaporous as the fumes of the moonshiner's still.

This then is a kaleidoscopic panorama of Kemmerer in the early twentieth century; the Kemmerer that young Bob Rose knew so intimately and loved so long. What was Rose's basis for this strong personal attachment to Kemmerer? Probably it reduced to that Rose personality trait—once a friend, always a friend—friends with the names of E. L. Smith, who found it impossible to converse without telling a humorous story, expressing a witticism, or just providing a limerick; Roy Mason, banker and Deacon of the Episcopal Church, who told his fellow worshipper, Bob Rose, to stay clear of the smell of oil; fellow attorney, Ivan Jones, who insisted that whether he wanted to or not, he "all too often" found himself on Rose's side of the legal fence; Charles Lackey, who absorbed so much of Rose's capital, but who, as he hobbled away in the Casper Hotel, earned Rose's eternal respect. The list could be extended indefinitely for it read as a "Who's Who" of Kemmerer—bottom and top.

Young Bob Rose's very youth may have been part of his infatuation with the people he met on the Triangle. Life is bright when you are young, hope is high, people are warm and friendly (for you have not lived long enough to have found them otherwise); there is, in sum, with your fellow man a closeness that may never be yours again. Helen Mason Gernert, "cause I am getting older and can look back on all of this," treasures her youth in Kemmerer as those "star-lit" years.[35] Bob Rose would have agreed. Neither his family, nor his friends, ever heard him mention carrying his autobiography through the Casper period—life had changed, perhaps along with his advancing age so had some of the drama and the fun.

So we return to the question: what kind of man was Bob Rose? To his children, Virginia and Robert, Jr., he retains an unforgettable place as an enormously kind and generous father, a father, who is

[35]Interview with Mrs. Helen Mason Gernert, November 4, 1976.

locked in their memories as a talented musician, who played the piano by the hour, as one who always had time for them.[36] In some respects, Bob Rose led a very disciplined and circumscribed life which revolved around his family, law practice, church and politics—in that order. Understandably, children have an intense affection for their parents. But the Rose siblings go beyond a reverence of respect to a devotion of love.

What emotionally moves the outside observer, perhaps even astounds, is the enormous admiration which Bob Rose achieved among his friends; and that after three decades his friends still memorialize him. Red Fenwick, columnist, editor and story teller relates that one "of the truly great happenings of the day for Bob Rose was when a member of his family would telephone him at the office. Instantly, he'd shove back everything on his desk, whoop and laugh and holler like a kid hearing from Santa Claus."[37]

Virginia Rose, in her mind, most often sees her father at the piano, where he would play for hours, primarily a classical repertoire; but he could at a moment's notice change moods and notes. Virginia also recalls her father and mother sitting before the fire playing gin rummy evening after evening. Virginia Rose sensed that her mother (an intense, bril-

[36]Interview with Judge Robert R. Rose, Jr., October 18, 1976; and Ms. Virginia Rose, November 4, 1976.

[37]R. W. Fenwick to Gene M. Gressley, November 1, 1976.

liant bridge player) uncovered more pleasure at the card table than her father. Virginia also remembers her father reading "westerns" for relaxation, but then she admitted he read everything—"mostly non-fiction." As to where her father found his remarkable literary style, "I have no idea, except that he wrote as he spoke."[38]

His son, Judge Robert R. Rose, Jr., of the Wyoming State Supreme Court, shares his sister's memories of paternal affection and generosity. One gray October afternoon of 1976, Judge Rose, in his pleasant chambers in Cheyenne, thought back on his father. "He was a very kind individual," Judge Rose emphasized. "He truly cared about the little man, he really did."[39]

Mortal men are not molded as saints. Robert Rose in the courtroom epitomized the adversary's adversary. Tough, shrewd, brilliant and an excellent orator, Rose, to use the hoary cliche, gave no quarter nor did he expect the opposing attorney to bestow kindness. Rose considered that he was in that courtroom to uphold the law and to espouse his client's cause; his rival attorneys argued that Rose could be confused on which came first. However, you could not be a successful advocate and avoid animosity. Bob Rose acquired enemies; but seldom did he gain rancor sans respect.

[38] Interview with Ms. Virginia Rose, November 4, 1976.
[39] Interview with Judge Robert R. Rose, Jr., October 18, 1976.

Judge Rose buttresses the opinions of his father's friends and rivals. "Massively prepared, tough, quick, smart," are the words that come tumbling from Judge Rose in reminiscing about his father.[40] Perpetually aggressive and combative in the courtroom, once Rose left the courthouse, he totally lost interest in the adversary process. He did not bring his work home in the sense that he relived his day in law at the family dining table. Those were different worlds for Bob Rose, and for the most part he kept them separated.

Attracted to the cause of the forgotten man, Judge Rose never concerned himself with the affluence of his clients. Many of his clients could not or would not pay their bills; when Rose passed away his office ledgers were a roll call of philanthropy. Another reason Rose's law practice did not evolve into a profitable business derived from his preoccupation with the law versus clients. In common with many lawyers, Bob Rose could easily be seduced by a fascinating technical legal puzzle that would absorb his total energies for days or even weeks on end. Meanwhile the rest of his client load slipped by unattended.[41]

As a further indication of the economic limitations of his practice, Rose specialized in the field of criminal and negligence law. In the final assessment, Rose was a people's lawyer. The only corpo-

[40] *Ibid.*
[41] *Ibid.*

rate client that Judge Rose can recall his father had was the Chicago, Northwestern Railway Company.

A less tangible wealth, of course, originates in the steadfast friendships that Rose formed all over Wyoming. Friends who knew him as an able attorney, also recognized him as a strong humanitarian. One anecdote Judge Robert R. Rose, Jr. tells can only be recounted today, as two decades ago, with amazement; in fact, bizarre would be a more accurate description. During his Casper period, Rose found himself in front of the judge's bench time and again in confrontation with another Casper attorney. Judge Rose recalls that he listened to unending depictions of father's legal foe as a despicable individual. Bitterness between the two counsels became so intense that they refused, outside the courtroom, to speak to each other. Rose's *bête noir* had a son, physically handicapped and of whom he was very fond. Suddenly, the son died, and the father was unconsolable. The only person the bereaved parent wanted to see was his reputed enemy, Bob Rose. Of course, Rose went to visit his adversary and expressed his sympathy. But his lawyer-opponent would not let him leave. So Rose phoned his wife and stayed a couple of days and nights doing his best to offer what compassion he could. Finally, Rose returned home; the next time that he encountered the grief-stricken attorney on the street, the lawyer refused to speak or recognize him. In fact, the man never said another word, outside the courthouse, to Rose the rest of his life. Personal tragedy and law did not mix![42]

Fortunately, not all of Rose's humanitarian gestures were rebuffed so quickly or permanently. Red Fenwick tells of the time he went to Rose about a widowed mother—with several children, who desperately needed money for food and rent. In fact, her landlord was about to evict her. "Give her this $50.00," Rose said, "but don't tell her where it came from." Then Rose added, "Keep in touch with her, please, and let me know how she gets along."[43]

These tales of humanitarian impulses of Robert Rose are again not related as an attempt at canonization, but they are offered as verification of what his friends knew about the man, and what even his enemies suspected. Rose's public altruism was disclosed when he honored the request of Governor Hunt to act as Wyoming's counsel, in the enormously complex water case of *Nebraska v. Wyoming*.[44] The case dragged on for four or five years at significant physical, mental and emotional exploitation of Rose. This was in addition to the financial liability he suffered from hours away from his office and clients.

The same qualities of organization, perseverance

[42]*Ibid.*
[43]R. W. Fenwick to Gene M. Gressley, November 1, 1976.
[44]State of Nebraska v. State of Wyoming, *et al.* "325 U.S. 589, pp. 1332-73.

and intensive application that Bob Rose brought to the practice of law he transferred to the political arena. One of Judge Rose's most vivid assessments of his father's thought and action reduces to the fact that Bob Rose was a "political animal." Rose's love of politics and people showed up first in his Kemmerer career when he ran for County Prosecuting Attorney and won in November of 1916.[45] Whether or not Rose's purchase of the Kemmerer *Camera* in June of 1916[46] was in anticipation of the furtherance of his local political career, with an especial eye set on the prosecutor's race, is unknown. If Rose did buy the *Camera* to advance his political future, he would not have been the first nor the last to use the press for such a motivation. A brief review of the Wyoming press (particular territorial) will document the premise that more than one editor was the captive of a party or party chieftain.

Rose won the County Prosecutor's race in 1916 by a small margin. Four years later, upon the death of the incumbent in the office, he received an appointment to the very same office.[47] Bob Rose's first major entrance into the Wyoming political scene occurred in 1922, when he decided to challenge incumbent Charles Winter for the lone Congressional seat. The indefatigability Rose had so often displayed in his legal and political careers was om-

[45]Kemmerer *Camera*, November 20, 1916.
[46]*Ibid.*, June 6, 1916.
[47]Kemmerer *Camera*, October 13, 1920.

nipresent in the House race of 1922.[48] Criss-crossing
Wyoming, Rose carried his message of the development of Wyoming resources and the necessity for a
Wyoming voice on the national scene to every town
and hamlet that he could reach in a five-month
campaign. In a "Republican year," Rose lost by a
little more than 2,000 votes out of 40,000 votes
cast.[49] Rose could take some satisfaction in the fact
that hundreds of Wyoming voters who had never
heard of, or about Bob Rose, now not only recognized his physical presence but knew the sound of
his voice.

One of Bob Rose's most potent weapons, whether
he was addressing a jury or the Democratic Central
Committee, was his oratorical ability. Those who
heard Rose for the first time never forgot the experience. A young correspondent for the Greybull
(Wyoming) *Standard* never lost the memory of his
first encounter with Rose the orator. Rose had come
to Greybull, in the nineteen thirties, to make a political address. He began by looking over his audience, and saying, "I am a lawyer. I deal with facts.
And I have brought the facts with me." Lifting his
thick briefcase to the rostrum, Rose started his
speech, an address that lasted for an hour and forty-
five minutes, concluding to cries from the audience
of "keep going, keep going." The reporter in the
hall that night recalled Rose as "the master of rhet-

[48]Kemmerer *Camera*, July 12, 1922.
[49]Kemmerer *Camera*, November 8, 1922.

oric, of the fine art of argumentation and persua-
siveness, and he was gifted with a singular command of the King's English. All of this combined
with a good strong voice, excellent enunciation, a
physical presence which offset his rather small stature, made Robert R. Rose a commanding figure on
the speaker's platform."[50]

After 1922, Wyoming knew Robert Rose, and
Robert Rose knew Wyoming. Sometime in the autumn of 1922, Rose decided to leave Kemmerer,
sell the *Camera*, and settle in Casper.[51] Just what
impelled him in the total sense to seek his future
elsewhere, as with many facets of his life, remains
obscure. We know that his wife, Eleanor Virginia
Bronaugh Rose, whom he had married on July 25,
1913, found Kemmerer confining and limiting socially and culturally. He may have felt that after the
1922 race, if he desired a political career, he required a larger population base. Or Rose may have
been weary of a small town practice. Although eter-
nally stimulating in some phases, such a practice
was also perpetually repetitious in other aspects.
The immediate push to depart Kemmerer came
from his friend and newly-elected Governor, William B. Ross. Ross offered Rose the District Judgeship of the recently created Eighth Judicial District.

Robert R. Rose left Kemmerer for Casper on

[50]R. W. Fenwick to Gene M. Gressley, November 8, 1976.
[51]"R. R. Rose Announces His Retirement from Management of Paper," Kemmerer *Camera*, December 27, 1922.

February 22, 1923, never to return only for the briefest of visits.[52] What deep sadness and regret enshrouded him as he drove down Pine street for the last time—we will never know. We do know of the tremendous fondness he had for this Western coal community and its people, for his affection shines through every page of Rose's autobiography. The Kemmerer years were the most impressionable of his life. He had arrived at E. L. Smith's home in 1914, a neophyte lawyer, with few friends and an unknown future. He departed Kemmerer that wintery Thursday morning of 1923, with an enviable reputation as an astute attorney, more friends than he ever knew existed, and what most of Wyoming's populace would have assessed as a bright political career close at hand.

Once in Casper, Rose rapidly expanded his legal and political horizons. After a year on the District bench, Rose resigned to run for the United States Senate against the venerable and formidable, Francis E. Warren. As his correspondence testifies, in letter after letter, Warren never forgot that Wyoming was home, or that the populace at the grass roots required perpetual and loving cultivation. By 1924, Senator Warren had held his Senate seat continuously for twenty-nine years, building the most potent political machine ever fashioned in the state of Wyoming. Although Rose campaigned vigorous-

[52]"Owner and Publisher of the *Camera* Picks Casper as a Future Home," Kemmerer *Camera*, February 28, 1923.

ly, again visiting every hill and dale of Wyoming
which he could possibly reach, he lost the election
by about 7,000 votes. Considering the Republican
party's dominance in Wyoming and the popularity
of Senator Warren, most political observers thought
that Rose made a good race.

That Senatorial defeat might have prompted
Rose, upon reflection, to come to the same conclusion that his political contemporary, Milward Simpson, did after hearing some fatherly advice. Senator
Simpson, who has been labelled Wyoming's "Fiery
Petrel" told that when he was twenty-one and about
to cast his first vote, his father, a staunch Democrat,
informed him, ". . . that Democrats are fine, but
Republicans always win, so I registered as a Republican. I have stayed on that side of the fence
ever since because I like the GOP philosophy."[53]

If Rose ever wistfully thought of switching parties, he never registered such heresy with his friends
or family. Instead, he did what many defeated poli-
ticians do, returning in 1925, with a vengeance, to
his law practice. Typically, the cases that presented
intricate legal perplexities were the ones that fascinated and absorbed his time and energy. In one
murder case argued in Rawlins, Rose had the entire
front of the courtroom dismantled and reconstruct-
ed the site of the murder.

[53]Olga Curtis, "Milward Simpson: Wyoming's 'Fiery Petrel' is still Afire," Empire Section, Denver *Post*, October
31, 1976.

As immersed as Rose was in his legal practice, politics would always be the fire bell that rang in the night. Perpetually the "political animal" that his son remembered, Rose soon found a local and strong state following in the Democratic party. As a political campaigner, Rose, his friend Fenwick remembers, was not the "blustery, extrovert type politician, who went out and shook hands or spent hours in smoke-filled rooms." On the other hand he was "indefatigable, consistent, and intensely persistent, a stickler for detail, and he preferred to work behind the scenes, composing advertising material, meeting with a few individuals at home or his office in the Con Roy Building in Casper, writing speeches—sometimes for others—and planning the party overall strategy,"[54]—all, it would eventually be apparent, at a tremendous physical cost.

Bob Rose, in essence, became Wyoming's Jim Farley. A powerful, disciplined campaigner, and a dedicated organizer, Rose sat in the high councils of the Democratic party for two decades. He achieved an enviable prestige as one who could elect Democrats. Although he had the depression era with the upsurge of the Democrats to assist him, he never took an election for granted, and the November returns were expressive affirmation of that belief.

In 1934, Rose created a legend in the Democratic party, when under his tutelage, the party won five state offices: Leslie A. Miller, Governor; Lester C.

[54]R. W. Fenwick to Gene M. Gressley, November 1, 1976.

Hunt, Secretary of State; William "Scotty" Jack, auditor; J. Kirk Baldwin, treasurer; and Jack R. Gage, Superintendent of Public Instruction. Never before or since has the Wyoming Democratic Party made such a clean sweep of elective positions. At the national level, Joseph C. O'Mahoney won a term as a U. S. Senator; Paul E. Greever beat Rose's old nemesis, Charles E. Winter.

Rose reveled in his party victory at the polls. His office, always a mecca where friends and the party faithfuls exchanged political gossip, increasingly took on the scene of that forgotten smoke-filled room. A battery of secretaries and young and old political pros puffed away on cigars and cigarettes, producing a loud roar of confusion and smarting eyes. Those who comment on the political Rose of the thirties and forties, invariably mention Rose's propensity and ability at gathering the young "turks" of the party about himself. Not only did he personally find the presence of their company invigorating, but he discerned that the future of Democracy in Wyoming was in their hands.

After his defeat by Warren in 1924, Rose avoided directly entering the political arena, preferring to manipulate backstage to operating front and center. He managed several campaigns, particularly those of his friend and partner H. H. Schwartz, who was elected U. S. Senator in 1936. There are friends of Rose today who insist that had Schwartz retired in 1942, Rose would have been elected the Senator, instead of Schwartz's opponent, E. V. Robertson. Political speculation aside, not until 1946 did Rose enter another political contest, this time for non-partisan judgeship on the Wyoming State Supreme Court.[55] He lost to the incumbent Judge Fred H. Blume.

Had Bob Rose been blessed with a genie-like perception into the future, he would have taken considerable satisfaction in his son's appointment to the Wyoming Supreme Court in 1975, and his subsequent election in 1976. Judge Rose is convinced that his father, after his defeat in 1924, aspired to the U. S. District Judgeship. Due to Judge T. Blake Kennedy's long tenure, the fulfillment of this ambition was denied him. As far as realizing his own goals, Rose suffered frustration politically, although any pangs he may have endured over his successive defeats may have also been assuaged by the endowment he presented to the victories of his friends.

When his first angina pectoris attack struck in 1945, Rose decided as a form of relaxation to write the account of his Wyoming beginnings that you are about to read. So evening after evening, sometimes during the day in the office, he would draft and read what he had written to his friends and family. Then after absorbing their comments, he would rewrite the manuscript. A decade ago, when

[55]"Rose Enters Race for State Court," *Wyoming State Tribune*, June 3, 1946.

I first picked up the Rose narrative from Paul Schubert, and began to read it, I was almost hypnotized by the eloquence of Rose's literary style. Simple, direct, decent, with a soft quality of humanity engrained on every page, the narrative left a haunting memory. Perhaps for some readers, the experience was analogous to their reaction when they first heard "Madame Butterfly," or when they finished reading, *A Tale of Two Cities*, or first saw Thornton Wilder's "Our Town."

With a mixture of poetic emotion and a deep love for his friends, family and the raw land that was Wyoming, Bob Rose left an unforgettable legacy—of one place at a time, that he passed through— few men have done more.

On a vacation trip to see his brother in Muskogee, Oklahoma, on March 17, 1948, Bob Rose was stricken with a heart attack in Wheatland, Wyoming; he died in Casper on March 29th.[56] He left more friends than he ever knew about, and a storied reputation that one still hears recalled in a filling station in Shoshoni, Wyoming, or at the New Grand Cafe in Rock Springs.

Gene M. Gressley

The University of Wyoming
Laramie, Wyoming, 1977

[56]"Judge Rose dies here following heart seizure," Casper *Tribune-Herald*, March 31, 1948.

ACKNOWLEDGMENTS

OVER A DECADE AGO, Paul Schubert of Shell, Wyoming brought to the editor's attention through the kindness of Vandi Moore, a mutual friend and author, the manuscript of a remarkable Wyoming gentleman—Robert R. Rose, by name. Schubert, a long time writer and contributor to the *Saturday Evening Post* had been given the manuscript by the author's son and fellow board member of the Wyoming Division of the American Cancer Society at one of the Board's meetings. Paul Schubert immediately recognized the narrative power and historical value of the Rose memoir as capturing for all time, one place and one moment in the history of the twentieth century West.

Upon a first reading, the editor enthusiastically endorsed Paul Schubert's judgment. We are fortunate that the publishers of *The Lakeside Classics*, R. R. Donnelley & Sons Company, joined in our appreciation for what can only be identified as an enduring page of Americana.

As editor it becomes a distinct pleasure and a privilege to acknowledge, with gratitude, the help received along the way. Obligations in any venture of this nature are incurred with amazing rapidity, seldom to be adequately repaid. First and foremost the children of Robert and Eleanor Rose, Virginia and Robert R. Rose, Jr. were consistently gracious, supportive and helpful in providing numerous insights into that multi-faceted man—their father—an amazingly warm and talented human being and a brilliant lawyer. Without the willingness of Virginia Rose and Judge Robert R. Rose, Jr. to answer countless questions, and their diligent review and suggestions on the editorial portions of the manuscript, this book would have never appeared. The words "thank you" are as inexpressive as they are insufficient to cover such cooperation.

My sincerest gratitude to Mrs. Roy A. Mason and her daughter Mrs. Helen Mason Gernert, long time residents of Kemmerer, now of Casper, who were extremely helpful in offering their reminiscences of life in Western Wyoming of five decades ago. As intimate friends of the Rose family they were able to provide a personal view of Robert R. Rose's contribution to life in Kemmerer.

R. W. "Red" Fenwick, one of the voices of that vociferous "Voice of the Rockies", *the Denver Post*, wrote an astoundingly detailed and perceptive letter analyzing his colleague, friend and political mentor, Robert R. Rose.

Several librarians and former residents of Wyoming produced that specific bit of information which made the manuscript richer and fuller, but at an obvious exploitation of their own time. Again "thank you" is not enough recognition. These individuals include: Ms. Judith Austin of the Idaho State Historical Society; Mrs. Joyce Dayton of the

Cokeville (Wyoming) Library; and Mrs. Hortense Allerd, formerly of Afton, Wyoming. Of especial assistance was Mrs. Jacob Antilla of Kemmerer whose research on early twentieth century Western Wyoming will become a permanent part of the historical heritage of the Western History Research Center.

Finally, Dr. Glen Barrett of Boise State College willingly gave of his deep knowledge of Western Wyoming, regardless of how mundane the question, or obvious the answer.

G.M.G.

Advocates and Adversaries

Chapter One

IT WAS MIDAFTERNOON of a gray day in early Spring (1914) almost thirty-five years ago. For hours I had been staring out of the Pullman car window of a Union Pacific train moving rapidly westward. I had once heard the expression "the land that God forgot." This seemed to me to be that land. No other words could describe it. Since early morning, but for two or three widely separated little towns, I had seen nothing but wilderness. Nowhere was there a human habitation, except at long intervals an occasional sectionhouse, usually with two, or three, or four shabby little urchins in front of it staring at the passing train. I wondered whether in their endless days anything more interesting ever happened. Numberless jackrabbits scurried away, dodging in and out among the sagebrush; and now and then a lean coyote would lope a hundred yards or so from the track and turn to watch the train go by, just as the shabby little urchins had done. Here and there were patches of snow in the bottoms of the deep ravines which cut into the range of barren hills lying to the south of the track; and an occasional tree, dwarfed and gnarled and bent, clung to a patch of ground where each spring the late melting snow watered its roots and kept it alive.

I was traveling to a life that would be filled with adventure in Western Wyoming. There would be thrills, comedy, tragedy; stimulating activity; an energetic, intelligent, interesting people; majestic mountains; clear streams alive with trout; pine forests groaning in the wind; and opportunity beckoning from a thousand directions. But I didn't know it, and couldn't have believed that life in such a country could possibly hold anything interesting, or even endurable.

I fell to wondering, wondering what strange and unreasoning impulse had led me to leave a pleasant home, good friends and agreeable surroundings, to be traveling to a little town in this desolate country. In my garden, when I had last seen it the day before, the blossoms had already faded from the jonquils, hyacinths and tulips bloomed in profusion, and the grass was ready for its second cutting. Here in this endless waste there was no sign of grass, the hills were as barren as they could have been in the dead of winter, and surely no flowers would ever bloom.

The train moved on. Each revolution of its flying wheels carried me farther from everything that made life worth living. Now we passed an isolated coal mine, and then another, each with a little cluster of dirty yellow houses nearby where I supposed the miners lived with their families. Or did they have families? Could any sane man bring his wife and children to live in such utter loneliness? I remembered Emerson's essay on "Compensation," and wondered what possible compensation there could be for living far out here on this desert, isolated from every interest in life except that of watching the trains go by.

Now we were approaching Rock Springs,[1] which I had pictured as a veritable oasis in the desert with clear cool waters bubbling from gravel-bottomed springs, with trees shading gently sloping lawns, and flowers and shrubs growing in profusion. But none of these were to be seen, though just before entering the town we passed a little stream half covered with ice, with high banks of loose dirt which would make the water muddy later on when the ice had melted. There were trainloads upon trainloads of coal on a half dozen tracks stretching away until they curved out of sight, and scores of men on their way home from the pits with miner's lamps on their caps. But the streets were sloppy, and the half melted snow that covered the railroad yards was black with cinders.

A few miles farther west we came to Green River

[1]One historian claimed that for years after its birth (circa, 1870), Rock Springs was widely known as a 'one-horse town.' The name, so this Wyoming Clio argued, was appropriate as Rock Springs did possess one horse and one wagon. The two belonged to Beckwith-Quinn Company, which opened the first coal mine and also established a company store, the first mercantile concern in the Rock Springs community. For decades the primary economic base of Rock Springs has rested on the Union Pacific coal mines. In 1977, the Rock Springs region has one of the most diversified economies of any area in Wyoming—trona, coal, petroleum, recreation and tourism. I. S. Bartlett, *History of Wyoming* (Chicago, 1918) I, p. 600.

City,[2] sheltered by a wall of fantastically shaped rock that rose immediately north of it to a height of several hundred feet looking like the crumbled ruins of some ancient city with its magnificent castle still proudly lifting its battered tower above the surrounding desolation. It was good to see lawns and trees on either side of the depot, though neither yet showed a sign of green. But this place was much smaller than Rock Springs, and I shuddered at the thought that Kemmerer, the town to which I was going to live, and perhaps raise my family, was smaller still, much smaller, and perhaps even less inviting.

Two hours later the train came to a stop. On the north side of the track stood a very long low frame building that housed a post office and general store. I wondered where the trade could come from that would justify so large an establishment. A few rods away was a two-story structure of the same material with "saloon and hotel" painted in large letters

[2] As with many of the communities in Southern Wyoming, Green River owes its existence to the arrival of the Union Pacific railroad. Although at first the builders of the Union Pacific ignored the nascent town (begun in July, 1868), Green River later became heavily dependent on Union Pacific economic policies. T. S. Taliaferro, an able attorney, described the barbeque celebrating the founding of Green River as a wonderful success "without the annoyances of the Volsteads." Today, like its neighbor, Rock Springs, Green River is enjoying (or suffering through, depending on to whom one addresses the question) an economic boom. Green River *Star*. June 15, 1923.

across the front. Around these two buildings a half dozen small frame dwelling houses were scattered in a haphazard manner. Two or three cowboys lounged lazily on the platform in front of the store, while a half dozen saddle horses were tied to the hitching pole outside the saloon. Just west of the railroad station was a large corral with loading chutes leading to a string of cattle cars standing on a side track.

As the train pulled out after only a moment's stop I noticed the word "Opal"[3] painted on the station house. Looking at the timetable I observed that we were only eighteen miles from Kemmerer, my journey's end. My journey's end—the unspoken words struck with a stunning physical impact. The few hundred miles in a Pullman car seemed much more than just a journey, the end of which was merely a place. There was an inescapable conviction of finality in the words, as though this was to be the end of everything.

[3]Uncertainty surrounds the origins of the name. Some say the town received its christening from a Union Pacific railroad conductor, who named it after the jewel he thought he perceived in the nearby mountains. Others insist that the name came from a sheepherder, who called his dog "O-pal". Several ranchers, according to historian Glen Barrett, gave birth to Opal, the names of three that survive history are: Charles F. Robinson, James Davidson, James Stockman. Mae Urbanek, *Wyoming Place Names* (Boulder, Colo., 1967), p. 148. Glen Barrett, *Kemmerer, Wyoming, The Founding of an Independent Coal Town, 1897–1902* (Kemmerer, 1972), p. 3.

Ridiculous, I tried to argue with myself—absurd. I was a young man, really just starting out in life. This was nothing more than a mere adventure. If I'd made a mistake, if I shouldn't like the place, why of course I wouldn't stay. I'd just move on, go back home, go somewhere—anywhere—anywhere I wanted to. But argue as I would, the ugly words clung with a tenacity that was frightening.

Determined to put the unhappy thought out of my mind, I moved across the aisle and looked out of the south window. To my amazement we were skirting a broad valley of meadow land, thousands of acres of it, dotted by scores of haystacks; and hundreds of white-faced cattle were feeding at racks scattered throughout the area. Not far away stood a large ranchhouse surrounded by big trees, and back of it a number of barns and sheds, all, like the house itself, well painted and in excellent condition. Here, I was obliged to admit, was unmistakable evidence of prosperous and comfortable living.

The train was gaining speed. In less than half an hour we were out of the valley, and again there were the barren low hills on either side of the track.

"Kemmerer, next stop!" The porter was picking up my bags. Gloomily staring out the window, I noticed a coal camp sprawled over the hillside to the south and a long string of cars at the tipple for loading. A moment later we passed Diamondville,[4]

---

[4]Though coal veins had been noted, almost thirty years previously, Thomas Sneddon founded Diamondville in

another coal mining town but considerably larger. The engineer closed his throttle. We were coasting into Kemmerer.[5] A large green frame building standing all alone at the bottom of a ravine that led away from the tracks momentarily excited my curiosity. Pulling through a deep cut that hid the town from view, the train came to a stop in front of a small frame depot of the same dirty yellow I had observed at the section houses earlier in the day. Driven by a scarcely perceptible breeze, streaks of light snow, seeming to come from nowhere, moved like living crawling things over the ground.

"Hello buddy. S'pose you're Ralph's friend. So you're goin' to practice law in Kemmerer." Whether the words were spoken in derision or by way of friendly greeting I wasn't at all certain. The speaker, dressed in baggy overalls, smiled pleasantly, spat

1894, when he created the Diamond Coal and Coke Company, a corporation which later became part of the Anaconda Company. Except for the most enthusiastic residents, Diamondville has been considered a suburb of Kemmerer.

[5]Historian Glen Barrett, who has written a most learned account of the early years of Kemmerer and the role of P. J. Quealy, points out that the first building sites in Kemmerer were selected in 1897. Quealy named the town after his fellow investor from New York and Pennsylvania, Mahlon S. Kemmerer. As a community guided by the entrepreneurial enterprise of P. J. Quealy, and as the site of some of the most productive natural resource reserves in Wyoming, Kemmerer has played a major role in the economic growth of Western Wyoming. Glen Barrett, *Kemmerer, Wyoming, The Founding of an Independent Coal Town, 1897–1902* (Kemmerer, 1972), p. 16; Kemmerer *Camera*, March 23, 1921.

a quid of tobacco from his mouth, picked up my bags, and started in the direction of a horse-drawn dray that stood beside the depot platform. Mounted on the driver's seat, dressed like the other in loosely hanging overalls, was a much smaller man. He too was smiling. When I inquired for the best hotel in town he jerked his head to the south and said half apologetically, "Guess that's it buddy." I looked in the direction indicated to see a three-story gray stone building on the corner scarcely more than a block away. "Wanta ride buddy?" "No, thank you, guess I'll walk," I said. The driver called to his partner, "Throw the grips in the wagon buddy, let's get goin'." Everyone seemed to be "Buddy" around here. What an interesting pair, and how pleasantly agreeable! But why should they smile and be pleasant? Why should anyone smile and be pleasant in such surroundings?

Walking up the short incline that led to the street level, I noticed a big sign painted the length of a two-story building that stood on the corner— "Blyth-Fargo-Hoskins-General Merchandise."[6] It

---

[6]A pioneering mercantile firm in Wyoming, Blyth & Fargo Company, was started in 1872 as Blyth, Pixley & Edwards. Three years later Pixley retired from the firm, and in 1884, Edwards left the organization. Six years later, the firm became Blyth & Fargo and Company with headquarters in Evanston, Wyoming and branches in Park City, Pocatello, Kemmerer and Fossill. In 1906, this Evanston emporium, was described as, "fifty feet front by fifty feet deep and contains three storeys and a basement. Starting in the basement you will find it piled full of groceries and other reserved

was the largest structure in sight. What appeared to be the entire business section of the town, composed for the most part of one-story false front frame buildings, was built around a triangular shaped park, across the lower tip of which was a brilliantly lighted place with "Saloon, T. Nishi, Prop." painted across the broad plate glass front. Next to that was the Lyceum Bar, and adjoining that a dry goods store with "Golden Rule, J. C. Penney"[7] painted in bright yellow letters over the entrance.

On the farthest corner of the triangle stood the First National Bank, and a few rods west of it the Kemmerer Savings Bank, with a few smaller structures between, among which was a shabby looking building so small that I wondered to what use it could possibly be put. From the Hoskins corner I could see most of the town, and beyond it, in every direction, low barren brown hills. In every direction but one. Just north of the depot and railroad

stock . . . . On the ground floor are the grocery and hardware departments, and on the east side connected by arches, is their dry goods department . . . . A display of furniture occupies the second floor . . . . Attentive clerks are always in attendance to wait upon customers." Industrial Edition, *The Wyoming Press*, May 5, 1906.

[7] In 1902, Mr. J. C. Penney opened his first dry goods store in Kemmerer, Wyoming. Called the "Golden Rule," this little store was the forerunner of today's J. C. Penney Company, Inc., a multibillion-dollar retail and catalog merchandising concern with operations in Europe as well as throughout the United States.

tracks was a narrow valley, and running through it a small stream which I thought, though now covered with ice, might conceivably be quite lovely in the summertime when perhaps the leaves would come out on the willows and the occasional cottonwoods that grew along its banks. Beyond the valley a great hill lifted its steeply rising barren slopes until its crest was hidden in black threatening clouds.

As I walked the short distance from the Hoskins store to the hotel, I noticed the signs on the windows. There was the post office housed in a shabby storeroom, Harman Strine's barber shop, the Frank Curtis jewelry store, a small notion shop, and two bars, with a vacant lot on the corner. Approaching the hotel, I looked down the street that formed the south side of the triangle. My heart sank when over the door of the little structure that I had thought too small for any possible use, I saw a weatherbeaten sign. It read "Ralph W. Smith, Lawyer."[8] That

[8]Shortly after Rose formed his partnership, Ralph Smith decided to go West. First he migrated to Sacramento in 1915, and then to Los Angeles. There C. Watt Brandon found him enjoying the goodness of life in 1942—a life replete with a thriving law practice, a beautiful home in the Bel Air district of Los Angeles, and an income which permitted Smith to undertake innumerable trips abroad, interspersed with deep sea fishing expeditions off the coast of lower California. Brandon could not resist relating to his hometown readers that Smith handled "a very high-class clientele, having just finished distribution of the estate of Tom Mix, a former film star." Ralph Smith died in August of 1950. Kemmerer *Gazette*, January 2, 1942; August 25, 1950.

PEN SKETCH OF KEMMERER, 1908
by Roy A. Mason, one of Robert R. Rose's close Kemmerer friends

was to be my office. The thought was most terrifying.

A few moments later I found myself staring disconsolately out of my hotel window. The cloud that only a few minutes before hid only the crest of the great hill north of town now blotted it out entirely. A cold heavy rain was falling driven by a strong north wind, and pools of water already stood in the unpaved streets. From my vantage point on the third floor of the hotel the town seemed even smaller and more dismal than before.

The situation seemed utterly intolerable. How could anyone live in such a place! Surely I would find the inhabitants to be very strange people, each with a peculiar bent of mind that had caused him to isolate himself in this little community in the midst of a barren waste. How could my old friend Ralph Smith, fine gentleman and capable lawyer that he was, have settled here and stayed more than three years? It was he who had persuaded me to come to Kemmerer;[9] and from the hour's conversation we had had in my office in Denver a few weeks before I had gained the impression that he loved this little town and the people in it.

It was getting dark now. The dim street lights were burning and the rain had turned to snow. A happy thought struck me. It wasn't too late; the die wasn't yet cast; whatever insane idea had brought

[9]In view of Ralph Smith's abortive practice in Kemmerer, this statement is ironic. Obviously, Mr. Smith was a persuasive attorney!

me to this place there was still time to repent; my home in Denver wasn't yet sold; I would return and within the week be back at my office quite reconciled to wait for the practice that comes sooner or later to all the young lawyers and would surely come to me.

Cheered by the prospect of escape from this intolerable situation, through snow now ankle-deep, I hurried back to the station to send a telegram canceling the order for the shipment of my household goods. It was with a sense of great relief that upon returning to the hotel lobby, I settled myself comfortably in a big leather chair and began reading the Salt Lake paper.

I knew before sending the telegram that Ralph would be looking for me early in the evening but was in no mood to see him or anyone else. Now I wanted him to come. We would have a pleasant visit together. I would steer the conversation around to our law school days, carefully avoiding mention of the plans we had made for my taking over his office, and would say nothing of the telegram. Tomorrow morning I would take the train back to Denver without saying anything to him about it. It would be an embarrassing thing to do— rather a nasty trick; but I would think up some excuse and write him.

Ralph and I had been talking only a few moments when two of his friends arrived. Guessing that I might feel none too cheerful, he had evidently arranged to give me a little entertainment, and, as I afterwards discovered, something of an initiation into life in this western frontier. After chatting a while someone suggested a game of pool.

I was a little surprised at the appearance of the place to which Ralph conducted us, with its floors covered with spotless linoleum, its freshly varnished furniture, well conditioned cues, brilliantly illuminated rich green table coverings, and particularly the attitude of alertness and good humor that seemed to pervade the establishment. My ignorance of the game being obvious, Ralph and his friends apparently decided to have some amusement at my expense. A game was proposed in which the players who downed the one-ball and the nine-ball were to be partners, and, of course, the losers were to pay for the game. Though we played most of the evening, it happened somehow, and I'm sure not without careful planning on the part of the others, that almost invariably it was I who downed not only the one—but the nine-ball as well, so that throughout the evening I was my own partner and, playing against the other three, the loser.

I paid for the evening's entertainment, and each time I paid Ralph and his friends let out a roar of laughter, joined in by the dozen or more bystanders who had stopped playing to share in the fun that was going on at our table. Although I knew my friends were "taking me for a ride"—to employ an expression that came into common use a number of years later—I was determined to be a "good fellow" and entering heartily into the spirit of the occasion enjoyed the evening's diversion quite as much as the others.

About eleven o'clock the pool game broke up in a torrent of laughter and I invited Ralph and his friends to my room at the hotel. Obviously delighted with the fun they had already had at my expense, they began regaling me with fabulous yarns of wild game they had killed, enormous fish they had caught, controversies that had occurred over sheep crossing the cattlemens' "deadline," some of them with fatal consequences to sheep and herder, and, most incredible of all, the prevailing method of 'docking' sheep, a method that none but westerners would either understand or believe, and one that can scarcely be described with any degree of politeness.* Admitting that they had 'jobbed' me at pool, I stoutly refused to believe their fantastic yarns. It was not until some time later that I learned that all they had told me was really true. My initiation complete, the conversation turned to more serious subjects.

I had spent a most agreeable evening with Ralph and my new-found friends, a banker and two lawyers, one of whom has for many years been an out-

---

*This quick and effective operation is performed upon the very young lambs by the weather-beaten sheepherder with the aid of his teeth, instruments for which science has never devised an effective substitute.

standing member of the bar in Los Angeles, and the other an eminent jurist in my state. As they were leaving a little after midnight, Mr. Smith—"E.L."[10] as the others called him—remarked that his family was visiting in the east and said he would be glad to have me occupy a spare room at his house until my wife should arrive. I must have flushed with embarrassment, for tomorrow I would be on my way back to Denver. I felt I ought to tell them so, but decided not to.

When they had gone I sat down and pondered a long time. Certainly I had been entirely mistaken and, as I was now obliged to admit to myself, very foolish, in the low estimate which, without even having seen them, I had placed on the people of this little town, for more spontaneously friendly, more generously hospitable men I had never known. Feeling thoroughly ashamed of myself, and very tired, I went to bed. But it was a long time before I could sleep. I rebuked myself for not having been courageous enough at least to tell Ralph that I had decided to go back home. At last I dozed off and dreamed of low hanging clouds, of jackrabbits and coyotes, and of shabby little children staring at the train moving with incredible swiftness westward through the desert.

[10]A member of the banking community his entire life in Kemmerer, E.L. Smith's wit and wisdom endeared him to the Kemmerer community. From the moment Bob Rose arrived in Kemmerer to the last hour before he left town in 1923, E.L. Smith remained one of his closest friends.

As I finished breakfast the next morning a telegram was laid at my plate. Our household furniture had already been shipped. The die *was* cast! It was a terrible blow. Half dazed, I sat—for how long I have no idea—looking aimlessly out of the dining room window. The snow, which had evidently been falling all night, was now a foot deep. A group of children went by laughing hilariously and shoveling handfulls of fluffy light snow into each other's faces as they passed the window. Little groups of men and women walked briskly by, all apparently as happy and carefree as the school children. It all seemed to me to be very strange.

I was aroused from my reverie by a very pleasant voice. "You like Klemmer?" At the side of the table stood a somewhat rotund Chinaman wearing an immaculately white waiter's coat and apron, his round face wreathed in as friendly a smile as I've ever seen. What reply I made to his inquiring salutation, or whether I made any at all, I don't remember. "Maybe you like sleegar?" Without waiting for an answer he was gone; but scarcely was there time to observe that I was alone in the place when he returned, laid a clear Havana on the table before me, and politely held a match to light it.

For half an hour or so I sat at the table smoking, and thinking. The men with whom I had spent the previous evening, the men and women and children whom I had seen this morning through the dining room window, all seemed to be perfectly happy and contented. The men were as alert, and the women certainly as attractive and well-dressed, as those with whom I had been accustomed to associate. And this pleasant old Chinaman, what a kind fellow he was. I wondered if all the people in Kemmerer were like these. Perhaps I had been entirely wrong—perhaps people who had lived in cities all their lives were to be pitied for their lack of understanding of those who live in little towns such as this.

I noticed two or three waiters preparing the table for the noonday meal. I looked at my watch. It was after eleven—and I had been sitting there since eight-thirty. I looked at the check—the cigar wasn't on it. As I laid the change on the counter to pay for my breakfast I said a very sincere "thank you" to the smiling old Chinaman at the cash register, and went out feeling very much better than I had at any time since leaving Denver scarcely thirty-six hours before. As I started to open the door I heard him say, "Me hope you like Klemmer." Perhaps I would.

I was to learn that there was really no reason at all for the despondency which had at first utterly overwhelmed me. I was to see a grandeur which no words can describe in the Wyoming plains reaching away at sunset to meet the sky. I was to breathe the indescribably stimulating fragrance of sagebrush after an early morning shower. I was to learn that there is no picture to compare with the everchanging beauty painted by the rays of the descending sun aslant a timbered mountain side, shading from somber green to purple and, when the sun has gone down, to deep black. I was to learn that there is almost human courage, hope, determination, and tragedy in the clump of quaking aspens daring to live at the crest of a high hill, bent and twisted and gnarled by the pounding of a west wind that is never still. I was to learn that the rugged men who tend cattle and sheep on Wyoming's hills and plains, till its fields, build their homes along its streams and in its mountain valleys far from the highways and Pullman car windows, dig coal from its depths, drill oil wells a mile deep, and provide food and fuel for hundreds of thousands, do all this because they had the courage to brave hardships and the vision to see the rewards that courage and industry bring out here in this last frontier of America.

But it would take a long time.

The second day after my arrival was Sunday. Awakened by a scraping sound and noisy laughter, I looked out of the window. It was still snowing. A score of men were shoveling snow from the sidewalks, already piled three feet high at the curb. Hotel proprietors, bankers, saloonkeepers, merchants, clerks, lawyers, doctors, gamblers, each busy with a shovel, called banteringly to one another across the triangle. Their merriment and their easy undiscriminating friendliness were hard to understand. I wondered if the snow would ever stop falling, if ever summer would come. I thought again of the tulips and hyacinths blooming in my garden at home.

It was going to be a dreary day. There would, of course, be the Salt Lake and Denver papers, and fortunately I had two or three books in my bag. One of them I had started reading on the train the evening I left home, a fascinating Wyoming novel by William McLeod Raine[11] whom I had known at the Highland Park Presbyterian Church in Denver when I played the organ there during my first year at college. But for Will Raine's book, filled with romance and adventure, my first Sunday in Kemmerer would certainly have been a very lonesome one.

Having just finished the book, I laid it aside and walked to the window to look out upon what seemed to me to be a very somber sight. Though a slight tinge of color on the western horizon indicat-

[11]One of the West's most prolific manufacturers of blood and thunder, William McLeod Raine (1871–1955), came into the world in London, England, and moved with his family to Arkansas in 1881. After graduation from Oberlin College, Raine became a rural school teacher and then a reporter. As a "tubercular," Raine came to Colorado in 1898. Sixty years and eighty books later, Raine could look back on a life possessed by a typewriter and sales of over 19,000,000 copies of his works. In an interview shortly before his death, Raine complained about the modern cowboy, "jiggling about in a jeep," as "not my sort of fellow." But then Raine had seen the old west, or what he thought was the old west, "vanish in front of his eyes." *Time*, 64 (July 19, 1954), pp. 82–84.

ed that the storm had spent its force, I could see nothing suggestive of romance in the deserted streets, the dark clouds that hung like a pall over the town obscuring all but the shadowy outlines of the great hill to the north, the cold light snow drifting from the roofs of the little store buildings onto the sidewalks below. It must have been amid scenes far different from this, I mused, that Will Raine had found the material from which to construct his delightful novel, if indeed the story had not been entirely the product of his own lively imagination.

Suddenly aroused from my gloomy forebodings by a knock at the door, I opened it to find E.L., the bank cashier with whom I had played pool the evening before, his face red with the biting cold, his sparkling coal black eyes and hearty laughter reflecting a state of mind quite different from my own. "Got your bags packed?" Startled by the entirely unexpected question, I wondered if he had divined my unmentioned decision to return to Denver and had come to help carry my luggage to the eastbound train which would be due within a few moments. Without waiting for an answer to his question, E.L. began throwing the few things he found on the dresser into a small bag, and picking up the larger one which remained on the floor where the hotel clerk had placed it upon my arrival, led the way through the hall, down the stairs and out onto the sidewalk. Bewildered by these strange antics, I followed unquestioningly, although I was quite uncertain as to just where we were going.

Waiting at the side door of the hotel were the two men who had met me at the station upon my arrival. The team of horses was not headed toward the depot. E.L. threw my luggage into the back of the dray and we walked the two blocks to his home, at the door of which a half dozen guests greeted me as though I were an old friend. E.L. had evidently arranged a surprise party in my honor. A few moments later we sat down to a veritable feast prepared by a Chinese cook and served by a Chinese waiter. There were no drinks. In all the years we lived in Kemmerer, I remember liquor being served in but one home, and there only moderately and on rare occasions. E.L.'s guests needed no stimulant. They were in a hilarious mood. There was much jesting and laughter, most of it at my expense; and there were more fantastic tales of sage chicken shooting, big game hunting and incredible catches of trout. When I bravely told them to go on and have their fun, but that, of course, I knew no such quantities of fish could be caught, E.L. invited me to join a party a little later in the season and guaranteed to prove to me that what I had heard was not fiction. After dinner there was an evening of bridge; and I retired to a very comfortable bed in E.L.'s guest-room convinced that nowhere in the world were there finer fellows than those with whom I had spent this delightful evening.

Chapter Two

O<small>N MY FIRST MONDAY</small> in Kemmerer Ralph and I consummated the arrangement which we had tentatively made some weeks before the purchase of the little frame structure that had served as his office and the few books and items of furniture which it contained.[12] Ralph evinced some amusement when I expressed doubt concerning the suitability of the tiny building for a law office. It was tiny indeed, and rather shabby inside and out. The exterior, when the structure was built some years before, had been painted white with a pale green on the door and window-sills; but the winter snows and the rains and dust of many summers had given the little house a very sorry appearance.·

Inside it was little better. The walls had been finished in plain one-inch boards and covered with the same pale green paint that decorated the exterior door and window-sills. There were two rooms, each about ten by twelve feet, separated by a thin wall made of the same material as the interior finishing. Against the wall in the front room was a cheap desk, which, with a typewriter on a wobbly little table, a small swivel-chair, and two decidedly inexpensive straight ones for the use of any clients

[12]The office of Robert R. Rose, Attorney, was at either 803 or 805 Pine. Mrs. Jacob Antilla to Gene M. Gressley, November 6, 1976.

who might happen in, completed the office equipment, except for a shabby rug and a small coal heating stove in the corner with a stove-pipe extending through the low ceiling and roof. Though Ralph's office furnishings seemed to me to be decidedly inadequate, I was obliged to admit that they were all the room would hold. The back room appeared to have been used mostly for storage purposes, though on improvised shelves on the east wall were a hundred or so law books, mostly of a nondescript character. On the floor in one corner of the room was a little pile of coal for fuel.

This was the office in which I was going to practice law. It was indeed a most uninviting establishment. It seemed to me that clients, if there should be any, would shun such a place. But Ralph laughed at my misgivings. He had enjoyed a lucrative practice here and assured me that I had nothing to fear. The little building, so far as I could see, had only two advantages. It was well located on the main street between Kemmerer's two banks, and since I now owned it there would be no rent to pay. The next morning, after we had arranged to have my name painted below his on the rusted metal sign that hung over the front door, Ralph left for California. I felt very much alone in what appeared to me to be a most discouraging situation.

Each morning promptly at nine I was at my little office, and except for an hour for lunch, remained until five in the afternoon. The first day there were no clients. A little disappointed, I consoled myself with the thought that there might of course be days when there would be but little business or even none at all, but there would be others when it would be all that could be desired. The second day was the same as the first, and the third the same as the second. And so the fourth, the fifth, and the sixth. I was glad that the next day was Sunday and I could spend it with E.L. in his pleasant home.

Again the following Monday I was at the office at nine. There was a letter from Ralph saying that he had already made a connection with one of the leading law firms in Sacramento, and another from George Winters, my very good friend and former office associate in Denver, asking all about my new location and what sort of office I had, and saying he supposed that clients were already crowding my reception room. If I were in need of an additional stenographer he knew of a young lady who was looking for a position, he said. Neither Ralph nor George knew how terribly those letters hurt. Why should Ralph, I thought bitterly, have emphasized his own good fortune when mine was at such a low ebb? George, of course, didn't know that I had neither a reception room nor a stenographer and not the slightest need of either.

The second, third, and fourth weeks passed, as had the first, without a sign of a client, except that at rare intervals, I earned fifty cents or a dollar by taking an acknowledgment or filling in a chattel mortgage. By the end of the fifth week my feeling was beginning to be one of desperation. Though I had brought books to the office—biographies, fiction and even detective stories—I found reading them impossible. The little room that I called my office had become a prison. Each day the green of its walls became more horrible and the rattling of the tin sign over the door more unendurable as the raw wind blew it back and forth on its rusty hinges. Again and again it occurred to me that I might as well have set up a law office with a sign over the door in the midst of a trackless desert.

Each morning in my box at the post office there was an envelope with "EBR" tastily engraved in the upper left hand corner. Now and then I pondered the monogram, even before reading the letter the envelope contained. Eleanor Bronaugh Rose! It had been less than a year ago that the last word had been added to her name. We had been very happy together in our pleasant little home on Raleigh Street standing on high ground overlooking beautiful Clear Creek Valley, in the outskirts of Denver, with high foothills covered with shrubs and occasional pine trees scarcely ten miles west, and on beyond the long jagged range of mountain peaks capped with eternal snow.

Occasionally I had worried a little impatiently at what seemed to me to be the slow progress I was making in the law office that I had opened only a few months before, but Eleanor had suffered no

misgivings. I was already earning enough to meet
our somewhat modest living expenses and to make
the monthly payments on the home we were buying, and she was quite willing to wait for the larger
measure of success which she was sure would come.

And so we had been very happy. She kept our
little house in perfect order, and there was always
an appetizing dinner waiting when I arrived home
from the office toward evening. After dinner we
would sit together in a swing on the front porch and
watch the sun sink to rest in a couch of flaming red
behind the snow-capped peaks. Soon a million stars
would glitter in the blue overhead, and we would
watch for the headlight of the Moffat train far back
in the mountains a little to the north, at first a mere
speck of light, disappearing every few moments in a
tunnel, then growing brighter and brighter until it
finally emerged triumphantly into the valley below.
Soon the train would pass out of sight on its way to
the Union Station to discharge its passengers eager
to get to homes as pleasant and happy as ours. At
last, when the cool air had streamed down the
mountain slopes and crept up from the valley below, I would take her little hands in mine, the most
beautiful white hands I've ever seen, and we would
go in out of the night.

And now all this we had left behind to come to
this shabby little town with its muddy unpaved
streets and its one-story false-front frame store
buildings, this little town surrounded by a score of

forlorn looking coal camps, each with its tipple,[13] its great creeping dump of black waste, and its commissary, surrounded by a hundred or so half-painted little houses. For a pleasant home overlooking a beautiful valley that went to sleep in the shadow of high mountains around whose snow capped crests the stars played hide-and-seek at night, there would be nothing better than a tiny drab-colored house looking out upon a muddy street and a ramshackle frame laundry building on the other side.

And it was I who had made the choice, not only for myself but for her. To be sure Eleanor had cheerfully assented, but I knew it was only because she thought I wanted to go. She couldn't have known what our new home was going to be like. Now I knew I could never forgive myself. If only she had argued against it, if she had just intimated, though ever so mildly, that she didn't think we should go!

Eleanor's letters, written from the home of her sister in Chicago where she had gone until I should be able to get a house, were at first the only bright spots in the dreary hours that dragged themselves so endlessly throughout all the long days. Filled with affection and cheer, each letter lifted me for a few moments out of my unhappy surroundings. Certainly it would not be long until she would begin

[13] A tipple has been defined as a platform used for emptying mine cars. Albert H. Fay, *A Glossary of the Mining and Mineral Industry* (Washington, D.C., 1920), p. 689.

KEMMERER, APRIL 1918
four years after Robert Rose first saw this street

asking questions; and what answers could I make? She would want to know what sort of office I had. Could I tell her about this stuffy little place with its shoddy furniture, its shabby rug, its faded window shades, and the rusted coal stove in the corner? She would want to know about business. Could I tell her that no client had yet darkened the door of my miserable little office? She would want to know what arrangements I was making for a house and when I would be able to send for her. Could I bring myself to tell her that the only house I had been able to find was a tiny drab brown structure just off the main street?

It wasn't long until I almost feared getting the letters which had meant so much to me at first. Some of them I hesitated even to open. Fortunately there were some things I could write about. I told her of the wonderful people I had come to know, of the Masons, the Whitneys, the Embrees, the Witherspoons, the Wilsons. I told her of E.L.'s kindness, and made much of his hospitality and the pleasant evenings we were spending together in his home. Once I resolved to tell her the whole truth. I wrote until after midnight and then tore up the letter I had written, determined to say nothing until the wheel of fortune had turned, as, I kept trying to assure myself, turn soon it must.

Day by day my meager bank account was getting smaller and smaller. How long would it last? And if I remained here much longer would there be money enough left to enable me to get to some other place where perhaps I could make a living?—or would I have the courage to try? Now and then, unable any longer to endure the solitude of this room, I would go out on the street and walk around the triangle; but certain that everyone I met knew the worries that were surging through my distracted brain, I would hurry back to the office and close the door behind me.

Frequently I would take down some of the text-books that I had used in law school, among them Webb's Pollock on Torts[14] and Williston on Contracts;[15] and reading over again their familiar texts I would find surcease from the worries that constantly beset me. There was scarcely a page or a paragraph some part of which I hadn't underscored as night after night I had pored over the cherished volumes thrilled with the logic and the majesty of the law. And now as I perused those volumes in the all-too-quiet solitude of my little office, I wondered that their contents were so clearly remembered that just by glancing at the pages I could recite much of the text. "A contract is an agreement between two or more competent persons, upon sufficient consideration, to do or not to do a particular thing." I recalled that Professor Bannister[16] had told us again

[14]Frederick Pollock, *The Law of Torts* . . . (London, 1908).

[15]Samuel Williston, *A Selection of Cases on the Law of Contracts* (Boston, 1903), 2 volumes.

[16]A graduate of Leland Stanford, Jr., University in the

and again that that was the very foundation of the law of contracts. I remembered how Dean Manly[17] had insisted on our committing definitions to memory, and how I had written and underscored on the fly leaf of the text book that we used his own definition of a tort—"A tort is the violation of a right that gives rise to an action that is not an action on a contract." A perfect definition I thought when we first discussed it in class, and the more thoroughly I studied it the more certain I was of its perfection.

How I had admired those professors of my law school days, and how I had cherished the ambition someday to reach the position of eminence in the profession to which they had attained. And then the

class of 1893, followed by an L.L.D. from Harvard University in 1896, prepared Lucius Ward Bannister to take his post on the Law School faculty of the University of Denver in 1899. A position from which he retired in 1944. Philip E. Gauthier to Gene M. Gressley, December 2, 1976.

[17]George C. Manly's (1863–1936) tenure at the University of Denver exceeded in length that of his colleague Lucius Ward Bannister. Manly matriculated at the University of Denver in its second class in 1881 in a time ". . . of small beginnings—few teachers, small libraries, little equipment . . ." Upon graduation from the University of Denver, Manly continued his education at the University of Michigan receiving his Bachelor of Laws and Master of Arts degree in 1887. He returned to Denver to practice law until 1892, when he joined the newly organized law school of the University of Denver. Manly rose to the eminence of Dean in 1911. From 1896, with the exception of one short period, he also had the unique position (for a faculty member at any University) of serving on the Board of his first alma mater. Philip E. Gauthier to Gene M. Gressley, December 2, 1976.

utter hopelessness of the situation that I had put myself in would come back to me. Here in this little town there would never be an opportunity to achieve even a moderate degree of success, or, perhaps, even to make a most meager living.

In the retirement of E.L.'s home was the only escape from the dreariness of the miserable little office during those first weeks in Kemmerer. Frequently when he finished his work at the bank a little before five, E.L. would come in and sit down for a few moments chat. I soon began to look forward eagerly to those visits. E.L. could not have failed to know that I was thoroughly discouraged, but never did he presume to mention the subject.

Most of the evenings we spent alone together in his pleasant living room. There were the Denver and Salt Lake papers, the leading magazines and an ample supply of good books with which his shelves were stocked. We played a little cribbage now and then, and occasionally some of his friends would drop in for two hours or so of bridge. Altogether the evenings passed very pleasantly; but usually E.L. retired early, and then, left to myself, the feeling of despondency that had haunted me all day at the office would return. Try as I would I could not escape it. When at last I would go to bed sleep seemed impossible. Night after night I read for hours until, utterly exhausted, I switched out the light and fell asleep.

Chapter Three

LATE ONE SATURDAY AFTERNOON the rector of the Episcopal Church called at E.L.'s house to inquire if I would play the organ at the services the next morning. He said that Bishop Thomas[18] would be there and the organist was ill. Somewhat reluctantly I agreed. He gave me the keys and I went over to try out the instrument.

As I sat down to the organ a rich warm glow from the rays of the setting sun streaming through the stained glass windows filled the little chapel and tinted its east wall a mellow orange. In a few moments I had forgotten the worries of the dreary days and the endless nights as I reveled in the melodies

[18]A dynamic, highly personable and aggressive clergyman, Nathaniel S. Thomas (1867–1937) served as Bishop of the Protestant Episcopal Church of Wyoming from 1909–1927. One of the early discriminating collectors of Western Americana, Bishop Thomas wrote Grace Raymond Hebard, the University of Wyoming historian, in 1924, "I think I shall continue making collections on Wyoming history; some day may place the collection somewhere in Wyoming, probably in Laramie, where the same may be used by Wyoming students, though as to this I have no clear plan." Within two years Bishop Thomas' vision cleared. The sale of the Thomas library occurred at the Anderson Galleries in New York for a total of $11,559. The major purchaser was the late W. R. Coe; and Bishop Thomas' books are now part of the Coe collection of Yale University Library. N. S. Thomas to G. R. Hebard, June 30, 1923, Hebard Collection, Western History Research Center, University of Wyoming, Laramie. Laramie *Republican-Boomerang*, February 8, 1929.

of Mendelssohn and the sublime harmonies of Handel and Wagner, then the beautiful music of the Episcopal service, and finally a few of the grand old hymns that have inspired the hope and sustained the faith of generations. Hours had passed when I arose and felt my way slowly down the aisle of the church and out through the door. There sitting on the steps were Roy Mason and his wife. I hadn't known that I had an audience. The Masons invited me to their pleasant little home across the street where we had coffee and talked for an hour or more.

It had been a marvelous evening. The majestic chords of the Pilgrim's Chorus were running through my mind as I walked the hundred yards or so to E.L.'s house and, lounging in an easy chair in his unlighted living room, lit a cigar. Late as it was, I had no thought of sleep. The organ in the little chapel and the hour with the Masons had changed everything. After a long interval of darkness life was again filled with light and enchantment. It would be only a few days until Eleanor would arrive; the furniture had already been set up in the little house which I had rented a few rods down the street from E.L.'s home; there would be our piano and books; and with our new friends we would be as happy as we had been in our much nicer home in Denver.

But the feeling of ecstasy soon began to fade. Then the haunting misgivings, banished for a time by the stained glass windows, the inspiring tones of the

Courtesy of Mrs. Helen Mason Gernert and Mrs. Roy A. Mason

EPISCOPAL CHURCH IN KEMMERER
where Robert R. Rose played the organ

organ, and the pleasant hour with the Masons, began to return, and stern reality again stared me in the face. Was there any reason to suppose that Eleanor would be less miserable than I had been during these past few weeks? Reared in an atmosphere of refinement, accustomed to every comfort in a large home in the midst of spreading lawn and timbered acres, what happiness, what contentment could I expect her to find in this ugly little town with its shabby frame storefronts and muddy streets more than a thousand miles from family and friends? What right had I—what right had any man—to bring a wife of only a few months to this lonely little place in the wilderness? These were questions I had never dared seriously to ask myself; and now the answers were inescapable. Though I knew she would betray it by no word or act, I was sure her disappointment would be terrible.

The beautiful picture that reverie had painted but a few moments before had now completely vanished, and I imagined myself sitting at my desk in that miserable little office on Pine Street. I struggled to put it out of my mind. I tried to recall the tones of the organ, the pleasant hour I had spent with the Masons, the delight of greeting Eleanor at the station only a few days hence. It was impossible. There were those horrible green walls, the shabby and worn rug, the torn windowshades, the cheap chairs, the rusty little stove over in the corner, and the detestable old dusty law books standing silently and unattractively against the wall in the back room.

Distracted almost beyond endurance, I resolved to settle the question at once. Either I would go back to Denver tomorrow and try to forget this horrible experience, or I would stay in this little town at least until I had demonstrated to myself that I could master my own emotions and achieve success, even though in only a small way, in the practice of my profession.

I slipped quietly out of the house. The snow had melted under the rays of the late spring sun that had been shining for two weeks or more, and in the light of a full moon not far above the eastern horizon I noticed for the first time yellow jonquils in the strip of garden against E.L.'s front fence. Walking briskly in the direction of the town hall on the second floor of which was the District Courtroom,[19] I sat down on the curb across the street and stared resolutely at the unlighted windows in the second story of the gray-stone building on the other side. The street had long been deserted; there was no sound save the low whispering of the spring breeze through the new leaves just beginning to come out on the big trees that surrounded the Quealy home two or three rods away. In the midnight stillness I began my search for a reasonable solution of the

[19]A district courthouse was not erected in Kemmerer until 1925. During the Rose era, the court was convened in the Kemmerer city hall, which dates from 1913. Mrs. Jacob Antilla to Gene M. Gressley, September 17, 1976.

question that would wait no longer to be answered.

I was perfectly free, I argued to myself, to give up the whole thing. There was nothing to prevent my returning to Denver on the very next train. But what then? E.L. and his friends would think my conduct very strange; but whatever they might think would make little difference, for I'd never see them again anyway. I felt a little ashamed that this line of argument should even have occurred to me, but dismissed the feeling and went on. What would my friends at home think? They knew I had come to Wyoming with the intention of staying. Would they also know that I couldn't make a go of it? Perhaps they would be kind enough not to ask questions. What would Ralph think? Well, I didn't know. And Eleanor. She would not complain, whatever the decision might be. But *I* would know that I had failed, that I had failed utterly, failed because I lacked the fortitude to brave the storm of disappointments that all the courageous men who had pioneered this western frontier had met and overcome.

And what was the alternative? Kemmerer, to be sure, was a small town;[20] but many lawyers of whom I had read had risen to fame and fortune in towns even smaller than this. Besides, the size of the town itself wasn't the whole consideration. There were a dozen thriving mining camps within a radius of that many miles; and Lincoln County, with its rich

[20]Kemmerer claimed 843 souls, more or less, in 1910.

farming areas and herds of livestock, extending almost across the entire width of the State, had only
six or seven lawyers. Surely there was room for one
more.

I walked across the street and tried the door at
the foot of the stairway leading to the courtroom. It
was unlocked. Opening it, I ascended the stairs and
stood reverently a few moments directly in front of
the judge's bench in a flood of soft moonlight that
streamed in through the window. There the decision was made. I would not admit defeat. Whatever
the disappointments, and however long they might
last, I would stay in this little town and wait for the
clients who surely would come to me as they had
come to the half-dozen other lawyers, who, I assured myself, were no more capable than I. The
decision once made, it was as though a staggering
burden had fallen from my shoulders. I looked
about the courtroom, its bare walls and crude furniture dimly illumined in the diffused moonlight.
Somehow the place which until tonight seemed so
forbidding had acquired a strange fascination.

Reluctant to leave the room, I opened the gate,
walked outside the rail, and sat down at the end of a
bench near an east window, and there I sat almost
motionless while incidents and experiences from my
earliest childhood in the big farmhouse in South
Dakota[21] would slowly move before me in order-

[21] Eight years of the childhood of Robert Rose were spent
on a farm near Tripp, South Dakota.

TOWN HALL, KEMMERER

On the second floor was the District Courtroom, where Robert R. Rose tried his numerous cases

ly procession. I remembered when I was just tall enough, by getting on tiptoe, to see over the dining room table, the sorrow that engulfed the whole family when Mother clipped the golden curls from my baby brother's round head, and how we all shouted with glee when he took his first steps alone and tumbled laughing onto a blanket that lay on the floor. I remembered the snow that fell for weeks at a time and how Father and the hired man frequently spent hours shoveling an opening to the stable door to get in to feed and water the livestock, and the blizzard that took the lives of a half dozen school children not far away when the teacher made the fatal mistake of letting them start home in the storm.

I remembered how my father had made his way through the blinding blizzard along a wire fence to the railroad track, followed it to the little town of Tripp where he had felt his way along the store fronts to Mr. McLean's drug store, fastened a rope to the building, and when he and the druggist had at last reached the school house a few rods away, they had made the other end of the rope fast to the building, tied my brothers and sisters and the other children together and following the rope, had brought them all safely to the drug store, many with frozen ears, noses and fingertips.

There were the pleasant winter evenings we all spent around the glowing fireplace while Father smoked his pipe and Mother read aloud from books of poetry, adventure and heroic deeds. To finish the evening and make its happiness complete there would be music, Father playing the flute and Mother the guitar, while she sang in her low contralto such songs as "Kathleen Mavourneen" and "My Darling Nellie Gray." It was the sweetest music I've ever heard. And there would usually be two or three hymns before we went to bed, joined in by all the members of the family except Father, who would sit in troubled meditation silently smoking his pipe.

Child that I was, I wondered a little sometimes that Father never joined in the singing of the hymns and that it was always Mother and never he who taught us children our prayers and read a chapter from the New Testament or the Psalms before putting us to bed. I remembered that when, once in a long time, Mother would say in her soft voice, "Papa, don't you want to read a chapter tonight?" He would shake his head just a little, and once I thought I saw a tear roll down his cheek as he did so. I never knew why. It seemed to me that Father and God must have quarrelled about something, and I anxiously hoped they'd make up before long.

Too young to go to school in the little town a mile away, I spent most of my time with Father at his work about the farm—repairing fences, trimming apple trees in the orchard, husking corn, and the like; and, of course, there was the particular delight of following his plow and sinking my bare feet in the soft freshly turned earth. I thought farm work entirely too hard for my father, slender and small of stature as he was, for he toiled with a fury and relentless determination that seemed to me far beyond his strength, never stopping until the task was finished though it might take until late into the night.

Always from my earliest childhood there was a German hired man about the farm and a German woman in the house, so I learned to speak English and German at the same time. Others might come and go, but "Old Criss"—I never heard his last name—stayed on year after year, and much of my time was spent with him as he went about his work telling me of the beautiful things in what he spoke of as the "Old Country."

Shortly after the blizzard that claimed the lives of the children in a nearby school and those of many of our neighbors, I overheard Father and Mother talking now and then about moving to some place where the winters wouldn't be so severe and there would be better school advantages for us children. In the early spring Father received a letter from his brother, a Congregational minister in Denver. A little later he went away and was gone for what seemed to me to be a very long time. The first I remember of his return was when we all were at the supper table. He told us children about a great city he had visited. He called it Denver and said that it was a place where there were streets covered with some sort of hard material so that the horses' feet and the buggy wheels couldn't sink into the mud, and great high buildings made of brick and stone.

Sitting at his immediate right, the place I always occupied at the table until I left home a dozen years later, I questioned him about the size of this fantastic city. Was it twice as big as Tripp? He said it was bigger than that. Three times as big? Yes. Four, five, six times? He said it was larger still. Ten times as big? He said it was bigger even than that. Then I began to cry. My father was making fun of me: I knew there couldn't possibly be a town ten times as big as Tripp.[22]

The next evening after supper Munn Martin and his wife came in and they and Mother and Father were soon engaged in what seemed to me to be a very serious conversation. I heard them say something about two thousand dollars, and a deed, and three hundred and twenty acres of land, and horses and cattle. Mother mentioned a few things she wanted to keep. Beside the bedding, there were her little rocking chair, the large clock that sat on the mantle and rang out the hours in soft musical tones, and a coal oil lamp that Father had bought in Madison, Wisconsin, just before the birth of my oldest

[22]William H. Rose, the father of Robert Rose, forsook the life of an agrarian when he moved to Denver for a career as an insurance salesman. He retired in 1909, and left for Los Angeles, where he died in 1929. *Uinta County Herald*, July 31, 1943; Interview with Judge Robert R. Rose, Jr., October 18, 1976.

brother and had carried on horseback eighty-five miles to the family homestead. It seemed for some reason that I couldn't understand to be a most serious occasion. I noticed that Mother was trying hard not to cry.

Father got out a long sheet of paper, sat down at the table, and wrote for a long time, while the others talked in subdued tones so that their conversation would not disturb him. When he had finished he handed the paper to Mr. Martin, who looked at it a moment and said it was all right. Then Father and Mother signed it and handed it back to Mr. Martin, and Mr. Martin took a package from his inside pocket and handed it to Father. Father unwrapped the package and began counting a lot of little pieces of strange looking paper. When he had finished he said something about two thousand dollars, wrapped up the package again and handed it to Mother. Pretty soon Mr. and Mrs. Martin said it was time to go, and Father and Mother shook hands with them at the door and said goodnight.

Father then called the older children into the room and told them what had happened. The three hundred and twenty acre farm, with all the machinery, all the livestock except seven of the best horses, and all the furniture except the bedding, Mother's little rocking chair and a few other things such as pictures and the big clock and the coal oil lamp, had been sold to neighbor Munn Martin for two thousand dollars, and we were all moving to Denver, that fantastically great city hundreds of miles away. My older brothers and sisters were elated. Father looked very serious. Mother, sitting in her little rocking chair, began to cry.

The next day Father drove to town and returned with a load of lumber, and he and old Criss went to work. Three or four days later there was what looked to me like a little house on top of the running-gear of the lumber wagon. It was only a little longer than the wagonbox but much wider, with the sides built out over the wheels and the roof rounded to shed the sun and rain. Along the inside walls were places to put things.

The morning after the little house was finished, Mother got me out of bed at daybreak. Everyone was carrying things and packing them carefully in the little new house on the lumber wagon wheels which, with Father's best team of horses hitched to it, stood close to the kitchen door. Mother and Father and the older children had already had breakfast, and toast and hot milk were waiting for me on the kitchen table. Mother said to eat fast so we could get started.

As soon as I had finished I ran outside and Father lifted me into the little house. A moment later Mother came out with my baby brother in her arms. Father helped her to a comfortable chair facing toward the rear, climbed into the driver's seat, spoke to the horses, and, followed by two of my older brothers in a light wagon and the other on horseback, we started slowly down the long lane between two rows of poplars, and then turned south onto the country road.

In a few moments we came to the meadow, and the cattle lifted their heads to watch the strange caravan go by. My older sisters and I stood by Mother's chair and we all looked back at the old house whose well-painted east wall glistened in the sun now just above the horizon, the house where all of us children except the two oldest had been born. No one seemed to want to say anything. There stood the big white house and some distance west of it a great red barn with loose hay hanging out of the loft window. A granary, corn bins, and numerous small structures stood between. North of the house was the apple orchard. On one side of the road, half ripened grain waved lazily in the morning breeze. We were now coming to a ravine where the road led out over low country. When I last saw it, Mother was sadly waving her handkerchief in the direction of the big house now disappearing from view and big tears were coursing down her cheeks. Then she dropped her face in her soft white hands and remained motionless for a long time.

It must have been about the third afternoon that we reached the home of Aunt Orpha.[23] It was a hap-

[23]No one of the present Rose generation remembers Aunt Orpha. Her Nebraska home was obviously a way station on the Rose family trek between South Dakota and Colorado. Interviews with Judge Robert R. Rose, Jr., October 18, 1976; Ms. Virginia Rose, November 4, 1976.

py occasion. We children spent the evening playing games with our two cousins and singing—there was always singing—and when we went to bed Father and Mother and Aunt Orpha were still talking. The next morning I remember well. Goodbyes had been said, and we were in the wagons ready to start. Aunt Orpha struck up a hymn and we all sang. The horses moved slowly down the road, but we kept on singing until we had finished the last verse and could no longer hear the voices of Aunt Orpha and cousins Gordon and Nellie.

Of the many interesting things which I am sure must have happened during the long journey through a largely desert country and over roads that in many places were little more than trails, I have only the faintest recollection. Once one of the wagons tipped over on a steep hillside. Another time there was considerable difficulty in fording a swollen creek when the wagon drifted down stream and almost overturned. The long hours on the dusty road sometimes grew tedious, but there was always the cheering campfire at night, and more singing. Mother had brought her guitar and Father his flute, and often it seemed much the same as it had been around the fireplace in the big house on the South Dakota farm.

At last after crawling along for six weeks in a covered wagon over hills and plains, toward the close of a hot August afternoon, we drew up in front of my uncle's home in the outskirts of Denver.

Seven cousins ran out to greet us. That night four-teen tired children slept soundly under my uncle's roof.

Two or three weeks later we moved into a small frame house which Father had bought a few blocks from my uncle's home.[24] Carpenters were soon at work building two large additions. In September we all entered classes in the old Villa Park School,[25] long since demolished to make way for a new and much larger structure. The years dragged slowly, but looking back it seems but a short time until my brother George and I graduated from high school and left the parental roof to fend for ourselves and enter college.

I suppose there are a few people who tremen-dously influence the life of every boy. I was no ex-ception. Rosa Cohan was one of these, although looking back I scarcely know why. Perhaps it was her dignity, her uniform kindness, her impartiality, and her consistent devotion to the serious business

[24]The Rev. George L. Rose and brother Robert married sisters from Muskogee, Oklahoma. Almost the entire minis-try of Rev. Rose and his wife was spent as singing evange-lists. They were frequent visitors to the Rose home, both in Kemmerer and Casper. Virginia Rose and her brother, Judge Robert R. Rose, Jr., recall their uncle and aunt with fondness. Ms. Virginia Rose believes that her uncle George passed away in January of 1971. Interview with Judge Rob-ert R. Rose, Jr., October 18, 1976; Ms. Virginia Rose, No-vember 4, 1976; Kemmerer *Camera*, December 26, 1917; February 13, 1918.

[25]A suburb west of Denver, the Villa Park area can now be located in the 2500 block of West Colfax street.

of teaching. Anyway, for one reason or another all the boys and girls were better behaved and worked harder in her classes than in any of the others. I still remember the kind of dress she wore, the way she combed her curling black hair, and even the peculiar way she trimmed her fingernails.

Another was Elsie Ayers who taught a class of seven- and eight-year-old boys at my uncle's church in the neighborhood. One Sunday morning Miss Ayers announced that she was leaving during that week to study art in Chicago. I cried most of the night.

Elsie's mother meant to me scarcely less. For about two years we spent an hour or more after school two or three days each week playing duets on her little square piano. For some reason or other we played, so far as I can recall, nothing but Mendelssohn and Schubert. Mrs. Ayers was a beautiful old lady, and though her soft hands were somewhat gnarled, she played very acceptably and had an unusual appreciation of the beauty of tone and the poetry of music. Perhaps it was for that reason that we played only Mendelssohn and Schubert.

And then there was Oscar Mayo, the last of three piano teachers under whom I studied, and who, abetted by my father, almost persuaded me to become a professional musician. A very old man when I knew him, Professor Mayo had been a pupil of Richard Wagner, and I learned to play most of his piano arrangements of the Wagner operas. Music was the professor's life—music and hot toddies, one of which his wife Gretchen regularly placed on the Steinway grand piano at the beginning of each lesson. If he gave eight lessons during the day, he had eight toddies; if he gave seven, there were only seven toddies. Of course I had no way of knowing how many he had during the evening.

More lasting, of course, was the influence of my parents. Few boys, I suppose, ever fully appreciate their mothers until it is too late to adequately show their appreciation. My mother's patience and her solicitude for the comfort and happiness of her seven children knew no bounds. She had time for everything. When I was struggling with the drudgery of my first music lessons, she found time to sit with me an hour each day at the piano to keep me interested. She had time to care for her little flower garden, to get seven children ready for school, Sunday School and church, time to have a kettle of hot porridge on the stove when we returned from skating on the creek nearby.

I think my father meant more to me than do most fathers to their sons. We were almost constant companions. I frequently walked down to his office after school to ride home with him in his rubber-tired buggy. He took me with him Saturday mornings for my piano lessons, and then to the Knight Campbell music store[26] where I would play for a half hour or

[26]Founded in 1874, Knight-Campbell Music Company was recalled by Charles W. Brown in "Land Marks of Early

so on one of the gorgeous Steinway grand pianos while he and Mr. Campbell sat listening. I went with him to the Saturday night meetings of the Grand Army Post, where after the secret work was finished I was permitted to go in and listen to the speeches of Col. W. T. S. May and General John B. Kennedy, whom I thought to be the greatest orators in all the world. He taught me to play the drum and took me with him to the national encampment of the Grand Army in Washington. There were many thousands of Civil War veterans in the parade that day, and as the mascot of the Old Soldiers' Fife and Drum Corps which Father had recruited for the trip from Colorado and Wyoming, I received no little attention from the spectators as we marched proudly down Pennsylvania Avenue and past the White House.

The next day, in company with a lot of men who wore the blue uniform, the bronze button, and the black slouch hat with a gold cord around the brim, he took me in an old steamboat down the Potomac to Mount Vernon. I remember how we walked ashore on heavy planks that extended out into the water, how we stood reverently at the open tomb containing the flag-draped caskets of the first President and his wife, the shuffling old negro selling walnuts on the great lawn that swept majestically down to the river's edge, the quiet upstairs room where Martha Washington died, and, most of all,

Denver," *Colorado Magazine*, 26 (January, 1949), p. 15.

the sacredness that seemed to me to pervade everything about the home of the Father of His Country.

Father would frequently take me on Saturday afternoons to the West Side Criminal Court where we would sit for hours listening to the examination of witnesses and arguments to the jury. While all the lawyers appeared to me to be very unusual, some of them seemed to my young mind to be nothing less than supermen. The boldness with which District Attorney Harry Lindsley[27] ripped open his shirt and high wing collar to graphically portray the manner in which an assault had been perpetrated, the assurance with which his assistant argued to the Court and jury with a quid of tobacco in his mouth, walking casually now and then to a conveniently placed cuspidor to deposit an excessive accumulation of tobacco juice; Tom Patterson's[28] masterful

[27] Henry A. Lindsley (1871–?) moved to Denver from Tennessee in 1893. Quick recognition of his legal ability came often. At the age of 28 in 1898, Lindsley was elected District Attorney, a position he held until 1912. He then gave up active politics for private practice. State Historical Society of Colorado, *History of Colorado* (Denver, 1927), pp. 174–176.

[28] Robert L. Perkin described Thomas Patterson (1840–1916) as "a Black Irishman, a Presbyterian," and incidentally, the first successful Democrat in Colorado, who had the unconquerable habit of always being where the excitement was in his forty-year career in politics and journalism. Eighteen months after he first saw Denver in 1872, Patterson was elected city attorney; three months later his brilliance and quiet maneuvering brought him the nomination of Territorial Delegate to Congress. In later years, he followed these early political triumphs by serving in the U. S. House of

cross-examination of the State's expert witness forc-
ing from him the admission that the stains on the
defendant's hat were certainly not from the blood
of the man that had been killed—such things, and
the quiet dignity of Judge Allen,[29] whose straight
snow-white hair hung almost to his shoulders, convinced me that somehow judges and lawyers must
be an entirely separate race of people, quite superi-
or to all others. Each time I visited the West Side
Court I came away with a firm determination that
someday I would belong to that superior race.

So far as I can recall Father never told me to do
or not to do anything. Somehow I knew what was
expected of me and the thought of disappointing
him seldom entered my mind. He had a singular
way of impressing upon me the lessons he thought I
ought to learn. One Saturday afternoon we stopped

Representatives and as U. S. Senator from Colorado. In
1890, Thomas Patterson made his first investment in the
Rocky Mountain News. From then on, the political view of
the *News*, if not inseparable from Tom Patterson's view of
the world, were at least closely allied. Regardless of political, civic, social or economic causes, the *News* could be
counted on for either staunch opposition or enthusiastic endorsement. Robert L. Perkin, *The First Hundred Years*
(New York, 1959), pp. 380–84.

[29]George W. Allen (1845–1919) led an active political life
and legal career from the moment he arrived in Leadville,
Colorado in 1879, as a young lawyer from Pennsylvania.
Elected Judge of the District Court on four different occasions, spanning a twenty-eight year period, Judge Allen's
wit and erudition impressed succeeding generations of Colo-
radoans. Wilbur F. Stone, *History of Colorado*, (Chicago,
1918), III, pp. 59-60.

at Mr. Johnson's grocery store on Larimer Street to buy the family provisions for Sunday. While he was doing his shopping I stealthily took a luscious cherry from a well-filled box and hastily ate it. I thought he wasn't looking. When we were back in the buggy and started homeward, he said, "Rob, whose cherry was that?" When I hesitated, he repeated the question, as quietly but a little more firmly than before, "Rob, whose cherry was that?" I said, "Why, I suppose it was Mr. Johnson's." Pursuing the matter further, to my great embarrassment, he asked, "Did you pay him for it?" I said I hadn't. "And so," he said, "you ate a cherry that didn't belong to you!" That was all that was said. It was enough. I've never forgotten it. I presume he meant that I never should.

The bench in the Courtroom was hard and I had grown tired with my long vigil. Not wishing to stem the tide of long forgotten memories that surged through my exhausted brain, I lay down on the hard bench and was soon sound asleep dreaming of little incidents that occurred in my early boyhood. I dreamed of driving a beautiful team of collie dogs and of their running away and spilling five gallons of buttermilk that was to be delivered to a long list of customers; of my first bicycle purchased with the proceeds of a summer's daily sales of that refreshing drink; of running away from home after school hours and on Saturdays to sell newspapers, and the endless abuses heaped upon me by the other newsboys because they said I wasn't as 'tough' as they, though I made every effort even to excel them in that highly esteemed quality, even going so far as to take a puff at one of their cigarettes and becoming deathly sick. I dreamed that I was flying through space astride the planet Earth as the presidential election returns were coming in, and how the great globe shriveled almost to the size and barrenness of a baseball when the returns were favorable to the Republican candidate and expanded to its normal size and grew green and beautiful when the Democratic candidate was winning.

I dreamed of practicing seven hours a day on the piano the summer before I entered high school hoping to win a four-year scholarship at the Denver University Conservatory of Music.[30] I dreamed of falling night after night into a terrifyingly deep well on the South Dakota farm—and never striking the bottom; and then of riding a train that moved with breath-taking swiftness through space, only now and then returning for a brief interval to the rails, and of groups of ragged little children peering with sad eyes into the car windows.

The rumbling of the milk wagon on the street

[30]The University of Denver Conservatory of Music, founded in 1908, included the professional objectives of "solo" performance, dance, public speaking and a community choral ensemble. Florence Lamont, in 1924, took over the conservatory as part of the Lamont School of Music. Roger Dexter Fee to Gene M. Gressley, November 2, 1976.

under the window startled me out of my dreams. The sun was coming up like a great ball of fire out of the east. I hurried back to E.L.'s house, entered as noiselessly as I could, and went to bed, to awaken just in time to get to the morning service.

The organ prelude finished, the choir in black and white vestments singing one of the old hymns moved slowly up the aisle toward the chancel followed by the rector and the bishop. It was the usual morning prayer service of the Episcopal Church. When time came for the sermon the tall, graying bishop, clothed in the clerical robes which seemed to me to become him so well, announced his text from the first verse of the one hundred twenty-first Psalm: "I will lift up mine eyes unto the hills." Just what the bishop said I have no recollection; but in each sentence there was the faith that sees beyond every disappointment, the courage that surmounts every obstacle. It seemed to me that there was deep reverence in the singing of the recessional as the choir walked slowly out of the chancel and down the aisle; the candles on the altar were extinguished, and the service ended.

Chapter Four

BEFORE ENTERING THE OFFICE the next morning I stopped to look at the little park in the Triangle[31] across the street. The grass had turned green, scores of tiny birds were chirping in the branches of the trees, and a half dozen robins hopped about digging their bills into the moist ground. I lifted my eyes to the hill that rose to great heights from the narrow valley just north of the railroad tracks, the hill that under the ceaselessly drifting snow only a few weeks before had seemed so cruelly cold and desolate. It too was covered with a soft blanket of green, and hundreds of white-faced cattle grazed on its steep, long slopes.

An hour or so later two men entered the office. "I'm Pat Quealy,"[32] one of them announced, "and

[31]Triangle Park remains the most significant feature of present day downtown Kemmerer. Donated by the Short Line Land and Improvement Company in 1899, a small, intriguing museum erected in 1941 occupies the center (roughly speaking) of the Triangle. For many years the level of the park was approximately eighteen inches below ground, making it ideal as the winter social center for ice skating. Good skating does not make for good lawns, and in the thirties the town fathers took advantage of PWA labor and had the Triangle filled in and reseeded. Kemmerer *Gazette*, August 2, 1946.

[32]For thirty-three years, Kemmerer and P. J. Quealy were synonomous entities on the Wyoming scene. An entrepreneurial genius, whose obituaries compared him to James J. Hill, Patrick J. Quealy (1857–1930) would have impressed

this is Mayor Salmon."[33] It was my first meeting
with Kemmerer's most distinguished citizen, though
I had already heard him mentioned a number of
times as the man who had founded the town, constructed a large part of the Oregon Short Line railroad, established the extensive coal mining industry
upon which the prosperity of the community to a
large extent depended, owned a number of cattle

many historians as the West's Charles Schwab. For Quealy's
organizational talents would remind many of the talents displayed by the late President of U.S. Steel and Bethlehem
Steel. A Horatio Alger story-hero, P. J. Quealy began work
in the mines in Missouri, Almy and Carbon, Wyoming before 1875. A decade later, after holding managerial offices in
Washington and a business partnership in Montana, Quealy
organized the Rock Springs Coal Company. Selling his
Rock Springs coal interest in the early 1890's, he spent a
short time as cattle buyer and seller. Then in 1897, Quealy
incorporated the Kemmerer Coal Company. A year later, he
founded Kemmerer, Wyoming. For the rest of his life Quealy's financial acumen and organizational leadership became
evident in a series of Western Wyoming businesses including: The First National Bank of Kemmerer, the Denver
Joint Stock Land Bank, the Board of Trustees of the University of Wyoming, and the Democratic Party of Wyoming.
All of this was, in addition, to his coal company activities
and his ranching enterprises. Green River *Star*, November
21, 1930; Kemmerer *Gazette*, November 21, 1930; Glen Barrett, *The Founding of an Independent Coal Town, 1897-
1902* (Kemmerer, 1972).

[33] As a prominent wool grower, T. Hunter Salmon, in tan-
dem with his brother, owned several ranches in the Kem-
merer-Cokeville region. Salmon presided over the 1919
meeting of the Wyoming Wool Growers Association in
Kemmerer. He also filled the office of Mayor of the town of
Kemmerer on two different occasions. Kemmerer *Camera*,
June 5, 1918.

and sheep ranches, and for almost a quarter of a century had represented Wyoming as a member of the National Democratic Committee. There was something about Mr. Quealy—the piercing thoughtful dark eyes, the large features, the heavy jaw, the well-shaped head, the half-troubled expression on his somewhat florid face changing in an instant to a good-natured smile and instantly back again as though the weight of large affairs was never completely off his mind—something about him that, even at first meeting, made you feel that here was a man very different from most men, a man who always had ruled the minds and wills of others and would continue to do so as long as he lived.

Characteristically he went at once to the purpose that brought him and the mayor to my little office. "We want you to make the Fourth-of-July speech," he announced, dropping his square heavy-boned jaw in a short half-apologetic laugh restrained by the thought that there were other and more important things awaiting his attention, and nervously chewing the long end of an unlighted cigar as with a deft movement of the lips he shifted it quickly from one side of his large mouth to the other.

I thanked the gentlemen for the invitation, extended, I thought, as something of a kindness on the part of Mr. Quealy, and with but little ado, they took their departure. The mayor had taken no part in the conversation other than to acknowledge the introduction.

That afternoon I spent reading biographies of Washington, Lincoln, Jefferson and Jackson from the books I had brought to the office and found impossible to read a few weeks before, but which now so engrossed my attention that I was startled when E.L. came for our usual chat a little before five.

Immediately after dinner I was back at the office eager to get to work. Never in my life had I made a speech, nor had it recently occurred to me that I ever would. This might prove to be a great opportunity; it would give me a chance to become known to the entire community, for the men who called to see me that morning had said that the Independence Day celebration was the big event of the year and that people would come from far and near to participate in the festivities. Equally important, it would give me something to occupy my time.

I wrote until after midnight. The next morning I tore up what I had written and started again. Late in the afternoon I went to the station to meet Eleanor. Waiting for the arrival of the train I wondered what I would say to her after our first greeting. Would she ask how business was going? How many clients I had? I thought not, for she had never made such inquiries in her letters. But the problem of what to say never arose, for she seemed to be in excellent spirits as she alighted from the Pullman and spoke enthusiastically of the beauty of the plush green landscape through which she had

PATRICK J. QUEALY, SR.
founder of Kemmerer
Courtesy of Patrick J. Quealy

passed, the same low hills that had been so brown
and desolate when I had ridden through them only
a few weeks before. A light shower had fallen in
Kemmerer during the late afternoon, but now the
sun was shining, the birds were singing in the trees
and the robins playfully chased each other about as
we walked past the park in the Triangle.

It was a little before sunset when we entered the
little house that was to be our first home in Kemmerer.[34] Standing just inside the door, Eleanor then
hurriedly surveyed the living room with its rough-
finished walls covered with a yellow brown paint
and pine woodwork of the same color. Then she
looked at me and began to laugh delightedly. It was
more like a playhouse than one for people to live
in. The piano against the south wall left space for
only two or three chairs and a little table. Back of
the living room and separated from it only by two
square colonnades made of plain pine lumber, was a
still smaller dining room, and back of that a kitchen
scarcely larger than a good-sized clothes closet.

"Now, I'll show you the bedrooms," I said, and
she followed me into the one opening off the living
room. There she stood looking about for a moment,
and this time we both laughed. In front of the bed,
with scarcely space enough to walk between, was

[34]When Robert Rose first decided to purchase a home in
Kemmerer, he selected 421 Emerald Street; later he moved
his family to 1021 Cedar Avenue. Mrs. Jacob Antilla to
Gene M. Gressley, September 17, 1976.

the dresser, and between the south wall and the foot of the bed was the chiffonier jammed in so close that it was impossible to open up the drawers. "Where's the rest of the furniture?" she asked, and I took her to the door of the tiny back bedroom which I was able to open only far enough to permit her to peek in. There packed closely together and entirely filling the little room, were the pieces of furniture for which space could not be found elsewhere in the house.

We went to the hotel for dinner, and scarcely had we seated ourselves when my Chinese friend came up smiling excitedly. "Oh, Mr. Lose, you bling the missus to Klemmer—that make me happy —you tell me her first name?" "Eleanor," I answered. "Eleanor Lose—nice name—vely lovely little missus—Mr. Lose, you vely lucky." "I think so too, Tom," I said, as he stood by chuckling. Then he extended his hand and they shook hands. Eleanor was as pleased, I thought, as he, though I'm sure it was the first time she had shaken hands with a Chinaman.

Scarcely had we returned to the house when there was a knock at the door. It was E.L. with Blanche, his wife, who had arrived the day before. E.L. was the kind of person that when he entered the door gloom flew out the window. He kept us all in an uproar of laughter until a late hour. When occasionally he would make one of his ever-so-slightly off-color remarks, Blanche would laugh

MRS. ROBERT R. ROSE
taken during her Casper years
Courtesy of Ms. Virginia Rose and Judge Robert R. Rose, Jr.

questioningly and say "Ed?"—but E.L. would go right on as though he hadn't heard her.

The next morning I was back at the office working on my Fourth-of-July speech. For days and days I wrote and rewrote, and I remember that when at last it was finished I thought it contained several rather well-turned phrases with perhaps here and there a touch of eloquence. Of committing the speech to memory I did an excellent job. In the solitude of my little office I recited it so many times that I was sure no word or syllable could ever be forgotten.

At last the great day came. The crowd was gathered in front of the speakers stand in the Triangle. A committee of citizens came to escort me to the stand while the band played stirring music. The crowd cheered as I shook hands with Mayor Salmon who was to introduce me. The music stopped and he arose. My turn was coming next.

To say that I was nervous would be a masterpiece of understatement. Perspiration ran down my face, and I was a tremble from head to foot. I felt confident, however, that if only I could remember the first words I would have no difficulty, and so while the mayor was delivering a rather extravagant introduction I kept saying over and over again to myself the first words of the speech which I had so carefully prepared and so perfectly memorized. At last he finished and pronounced my name. There was a round of applause and then an appalling stillness. I arose, the first words of my speech definitely in mind, and addressed the chairman as the Mayor of the City of—Denver.

A wave of laughter swept over the crowd. Habit had played me a mean trick. Not a single word could I recall; the speech had utterly left me. After stammering and stuttering for what seemed to me a very long time, though I suppose it was no more than the fraction of a minute, I started to talk, and, gradually warming to my subject, seemed to do fairly well. When I had finished I didn't feel altogether ashamed of my first effort in public speaking,[35] particularly, when the band had finished playing the national anthem, the mayor and a number of other citizens warmly, and generously, extended their congratulations. But I was waiting for Eleanor's verdict. When a moment later I found her standing

[35]On the 1914 Fourth of July celebration and oration (which left such an indelible impression on young attorney Robert R. Rose—the vividness of the event was seared in his mind almost four decades later) the *Camera* squandered all of one sentence. "The oration was by Robert R. Rose, and was an eloquent discourse for a few moments on the achievements of one of the greatest nations of the world, taking it by periods, of the discovery by Columbus to the present day." *Camera* editor C. Watt Brandon pictured the entire town of Kemmerer basking in the sunlight of the beautiful day and celebration. "The day broke true and early morning was splendid. The parade of the children from the Lyceum thru (sic) the streets and the Triangle park was led by the Kemmerer band, and close to 300 children were in line to receive free gifts of candy, nuts and fruit and they did enjoy it." Kemmerer *Camera*, July 8, 1914.

alone at the edge of the crowd, she pressed my hand a little tightly and said, "It was a good speech, I'm proud of you." How rapidly everything was changing! E.L. called out from the street a few yards away, "Come on you, we're waiting." There in their cars were the Smiths, the Masons, and the Whitneys; and in a few moments we were on our way up Ham's Fork River for a picnic lunch and a delightful afternoon.

Never to this day have I been able, nor indeed have I tried, to recall a single word of that speech; and never since have I attempted to memorize one, although I have delivered perhaps hundreds of them extemporaneously.

Chapter Five

THE NEXT MORNING something happened, the thing that I felt sure must always happen sooner or later but that I had begun to feel never would happen to me. I had a client. He was waiting at my office door when I arrived, a tall fellow in high-heeled boots, soft shirt open at the neck, and blue jeans so tight as to accentuate the thinness of his well-muscled legs and make him appear taller than he actually was.

I unlocked the door, invited him in and motioned him to a chair. While he was leisurely removing his broad-brimmed hat and laying it on the corner of my desk I had time to observe a strong lean face and well-shaped hands. From his dress and appearance I took him to be a cattle man from the upper country, perhaps Jackson Hole; and so he was. He said he had arrived the morning before and had heard my speech. Whether he thought it good or bad, and whether it had anything to do with his visit to my office, or how he happened to seek me out rather than one of the older lawyers, he didn't say, but began at once explaining the facts of his case, which was one of considerable importance involving property worth several thousand dollars.

I listened intently as he outlined all the details, interrupting now and then with questions designed to give me a clearer understanding of the facts.

When he had finished he asked what I would charge for my services. I knew, of course, that that question would come sooner or later, and while he was talking I had sized up my visitor rather carefully in an effort to determine in my own mind how large a fee—within the limits of fairness, of course—he would be willing to pay. It was a crucial moment. With very little money left in the bank and an abundance of time on my hands, I would, if necessary, have taken the case for whatever he might offer, however small the amount. But he appeared to be a fair-minded person, and I was resolved to get a substantial fee if possible.

Affecting an indifference that was by no means real, I said I thought I could handle the case for about five hundred dollars, although secretly I doubted that there was anyone in Lincoln County that could pay as much or that I should ever collect so large a fee for a single case. But to my amazement he drew a check from his pocket without the slightest hesitancy, and asked me to make it out. Unaccustomed as he was to the use of a pen, his signature was written with none of the nervous scribbling that appeared in the body of the check.

In due time his case came on for trial and I was successful in its defense. Meantime I had learned that my client was one of the prosperous livestock men in the county, worth perhaps a hundred thousand dollars or more. Some months after the trial he told me that he had expected to pay a fee of at least a thousand dollars and would gladly have done so but for the fact that I had asked only half that amount. I didn't make the same mistake again.

The rest of the day I spent hard at work on my first case, taking time out now and then to ponder the situation. It would be difficult to describe the feeling that I experienced. The speech I had made in the park the day before I'm sure had something to do with it, and the visit of the tall man in the tight blue jeans more, particularly the readiness with which he had paid what to me seemed a very large fee.

I recalled his quiet, confident manner, his slow speech, the clearness and brevity with which he had presented his case, and the entire absence of bitterness against his adversary. I remembered that not once while he had been talking had it occurred to me to doubt anything he said. He had told me that as a young man he had come to the Jackson Hole country and had run cattle there ever since. He had endured the hardships and discouragements that are a part of pioneer life, but he complained of none of them. I thought that he must have been a man of courage and resolution to have come to this frontier country; and then it occurred to me that perhaps life in this frontier country, with its hardships and discouragements, its long cold winters, its isolation, and the inevitable necessity of relying entirely upon one's self, may have had something to do with making him a man of courage and resolution.

This man, a person of some consequence, had taken a journey that required three days travel each way to engage my services in a law suit. Until yesterday's Fourth of July speech and my employment today by the man in the tight blue jeans, it hadn't occurred to me that I could possibly be of any importance in this frontier community.

Soon after dinner that evening the doorbell rang. I responded to find the county's most notorious cattle thief, obviously more than half intoxicated. I will call him Sam Watson, although any other name would do as well for he had a half-dozen aliases. He insisted upon my going with him to the office at once. Notwithstanding Eleanor's fears, which, as always, proved to be groundless, I went. Once inside, Sam asked me to lock the door and while I was doing so he pulled down the window shades. He told me that one of his friends had been arrested on a charge of stealing cattle. I had heard something of Watson's exploits, and understood that he was generally suspected of being back of the cattle rustling with which a number of his "friends" had been charged, though none of them had been convicted.

Without wasting time or words he asked me what I would charge to defend the case. Emboldened somewhat by the morning's experience, I said that I would want a retainer fee of three hundred dollars and would render a statement later for the balance. This time it was not a check book but a well-filled wallet from which the three hundred dollars was counted out. The conference was adjourned until the next morning, and I hurried home to relieve Eleanor's fears and to make a clean breast of all that had happened—and all that had not happened—during the more than three months since I had first set foot in Kemmerer.

I had never told her the utter futility of those three months, or that during all this time not a single person, except on very trifling matters, had felt himself in need of my services. And she had never inquired. But today had netted eight hundred dollars in real money, and I could tell the whole story. This I did, with much enthusiasm on the part of us both, and not without tears of hers as she confided that she had known all the time that I hadn't had a client. We talked until long after midnight. She told me how terribly homesick she had been and how she had fought to keep from showing it, how she had watched our steadily dwindling account at the bank and wondered how long it would last. We had never said a word to each other about our discouraging situation, perhaps because we were both too proud to admit the possibility of defeat, perhaps because neither was willing to make the other's load harder to carry. Now we had at last come to the turn in the road. From that day until we left the wonderful town of Kemmerer nine years later,[36] there never was a day when I did not have all the business I could well attend to.

[36] Rose forsook Kemmerer for Casper, Wyoming, in 1923.

But to return for a moment to Watson. Every community, I suppose, has its characters. Kemmerer had a number of them, but none outranked Sam Watson, whose rotund little hulk supported by short fat legs, was a familiar sight as, dressed in tightly fitting pants, high-heeled boots and ten-gallon hat, he moved unsteadily along the sidewalk on Pine Avenue veering slightly to one side and then to the other. Sam came to town for the specific purpose, it had seemed to me, of getting intoxicated, although, whether by design or otherwise, his inebriation seemed always to extend only to the stage of accentuating the ill humor which distinguished him even in his rare moments of sobriety.

While he heartily disliked everyone from President Wilson to the town constable, his feeling toward the Green River Livestock Association,[37] its inspectors, and its highly paid special prosecutors imported from Cheyenne, was one of mixed hatred and contempt. At war with all the world, Watson was frequently to be seen at the hotel corner on warm summer afternoons haranguing a small group of amused listeners in a thin high-pitched voice rich

[37]Many western states had small regional cattle growers associations, primarily to protect their members against rustling and associated depredations. The members of the Green River Valley Cattle and Horse Growers Association read like a Who's Who of the Sublette County cattlemen; included were such family names as the Osterhouts, Fears, and Budds. The Green Valley was organized in Big Piney on July 15, 1907. Wyoming Stock Growers Association collection, Western History Research Center.

with the accent of his native Texas, berating everyone who happened to come to his mind and boast-
ing eloquently that he had stolen more cattle than
any other man in Lincoln County and that the
Livestock Association and its professional "dicks"
had never been able to catch him.

In the Fall of 1919 while in Kemmerer for supplies, Sam was taken to the detention hospital suffering with the flu so prevalent at that time. The
following spring he came to my office and wanted
to sue the town for damages. He said the fall cattle
drive had gone by while he was in the hospital and
that he and his family had been obliged to eat his
own beef all winter, for which he thought the town
should compensate him.

Watson had no need to steal. His ranch spread
out for miles on either side of Green River and a
thousand or more white-faced cattle grazed in his
meadows. He stole for fun. Perhaps it was because
he thought stealing to be a sort of game for which
he had been blessed with a superior talent, perhaps
because he took a certain delight in being able to
outwit the livestock association, which included in
its membership most of the men who had grown
prosperous in the cattle business and was anathema
to a few of the less prosperous to whom an un-
branded calf was still a "slick" and always would be.

Whatever the motive that actuated him, Sam was
an incurable thief. Stealing was his hobby. Never
did he overlook an opportunity; and while his pref-

erence was for cattle, he would steal anything he
could lay his hands on. On a cold autumn night
Jimmie Mythen,[38] the young Episcopal clergyman,
had engine trouble close to Sam's ranch gate. Hail-
ing a passing car he rode on into Big Piney, leaving
his own car by the roadside and in it a suitcase

[38]Former communicants of the Episcopal church of Kemmerer remember the Rev. James Mythen's tenure in Kemmerer as happy, brief and sleepy. Allegedly sent west for
Kemmerer's version of Keeley's cure, John Barleycorn tri-
umphed on many a bright Sunday morning. Commonly, one
of his parishioners had to assume the responsibility of shaking the good pastor awake from his slumbers (in anticipation
of receiving an inspiration message on the Sabbath morn).
The *Camera*, understandably, observed the Episcopal rector's comings and goings with silent decorum. On September 22, 1915, Rev. Mythen celebrated his ordination in the
Episcopal Cathedral in Laramie; the *Camera* told its readers
that the ceremony represented a day of joy for all. "This of
course is something which means a great deal to a minister,
and no doubt many of the church communicants will be
present to celebrate the event with him." Two weeks after
the felicitous Sunday in Laramie, Rev. Mythen stood before
the worshippers in the Kemmerer church for the last time.
The *Camera* conceded that he had been considering depart-
ing his parish for some time, but had just that Sunday decided to leave, "accompanied by his aunt, who has been visiting
with him. They will visit the coast prior to returning to
Baltimore. Rev. Mythen has been in poor health for some
time past, and his leaving has been considered for some time,
but it was not until last week that he decided to give up his
charge here. He spent some time this summer in an eastern
hospital." Presumably, Rev. Mythen decided against going
back to Baltimore, for on October 20th, it was reported that
he was located in Oakland, California, "where he had been
assigned special work by the Bishop of California." Kemmerer *Camera*, September 22, October 6, October 20, 1915.

containing the very elaborate and expensive vestments which a rich aunt had given him. A half hour later Sam came along, half intoxicated as usual. Seeing the car by the side of the road, he instinctively began to explore its contents, and, finding the suitcase, threw it into his buckboard and drove on. During the long winter evenings he amused the freighters who customarily made the Watson ranch an overnight stopping-place by dancing hilariously about clothed in the beautifully ornamented vestments which should have adorned the figure of the young clergyman who served the missions at Kemmerer and Big Piney.

Only once, so far as I ever heard, was Sam caught with stolen loot in his possession. It was a very cold winter day when he had driven his sleigh to the little town of Opal. Most of the day he spent in Bill Salliday's saloon. A number of cowboys, wishing to have a little fun at his expense, placed a five-gallon gasoline can beside his sleigh. At last Sam staggered out of the saloon and spied the can. Looking cautiously about to make sure that no one was watching, he threw it into the sleigh, casually covered it up with a horseblanket, untied his team, and started up the road, as usual, at break-neck speed.

Giving him time to get well on his way, the cowboys mounted their horses and overtook him a few miles north of town. Finding the gasoline can in the back of his sleigh, they charged Sam with stealing it and gave him the choice of submitting to arrest or paying them twenty dollars and taking a long drink of the gasoline. The twenty dollars he was quite willing to pay. That was not enough—the cowboys insisted; and with much grumbling and profanity, Sam lifted the gasoline can to his lips and took a long drink of—water, with which the boys had filled it before they "planted" it at the side of Sam's sleigh. For once Sam Watson had been caught.

Chapter Six

EARLY IN AUGUST E.L. called at the office to say that he was ready to dispel my skepticism concerning the claim he had made during my first evening in Kemmerer that the lakes and streams of Western Wyoming were alive with mountain trout. The party was to include Dr. Stafford,[39] another physician from a remote part of the State whose name I have forgotten, E.L. and myself. Starting early the next morning, Dr. Stafford was to drive us in his shining new Auburn car to Big Piney,[40] a little town seventy miles north, thence west to the Charlie Budd ranch.[41] There we were to get a buckboard and drive back into the mountains to Middle Piney Lake.

We were off at daybreak the next morning, along

[39]C. D. Stafford, M. D. (1877-?), deserted Indiana for Wyoming in 1898. First Dr. Stafford came to Diamondville, then Fort Bridger, and finally in 1905 he arrived at Kemmerer. Mayor of Kemmerer from 1908–1910, Stafford also was recognized by his fellow physicians when he became President of the Wyoming State Board of Medical Examiners in 1911. I. S. Bartlett, *History of Wyoming*, (Chicago, 1918), III, p. 342.

[40]Created by D. B. Budd in 1888, Big Piney achieved a degree of local fame as the site for the Big Piney Fiesta, replete with barbeque, barn dance and rodeo. In recent years, the development of the natural gas and oil reserves by Belco Petroleum Company has brought additional wealth to an area noted for its huge and successful ranching industry.

[41]For Charles Budd see notes 66 and 68.

the river bottom to the Frontier camp,[42] under
Number One Mine tipple, climbing over miles of
dugway hillside road, past the Matthews shearing
corrals, at last rounding the west end of the great
hill north of Kemmerer.

Far to the north stretched a high plane carpeted
with soft purple-green sagebrush. A great black
cloud hung like a vast curtain against the east broken by patches of flaming red where the rays from
the rising sun were beginning to burn through. A
light shower had fallen during the early morning
and the air was laden with the clean tangy scent of
sage. Now and then a brood of half-grown sage
chickens scurried from the road scarcely in time to
escape the wheels of Dr. Stafford's car. White faced
cattle dotted the landscape as far as the eye could
see, and a couple of cowboys swung easily in their
saddles as they trotted lazily along a half mile from
the road.

Turning north on the soft dirt country road resil-
ient from the light rain that had given the countryside an air of exhilerating morning freshness, within
an hour or so I observed a fringe of trees stretching
away until it disappeared in a mountain canyon far
to the west. A few moments later we came to the
valley of the Fontenelle River, and as we crossed
the rattling board bridge, scores of frightened trout
scurried upstream through the clear water. From

[42] A small community, immediately north of Kemmerer,
originally supported by the Frontier mine opened in 1897.

the fields on either side of the road came the sweet scent of new-mown hay.

A few miles farther north was the valley of La Barge Creek with another fringe of trees reaching far to the west, and more fields of new-mown hay, and then another stretch of sagebrush with white faced cattle everywhere and young calves scampering about.

A little before noon the road turned sharply to the east down a short steep hill and cut through a narrow defile to the floor of a wide valley, through the center of which, less than half a mile away, flowed the rippling waters of Green River. A log house surrounded by a carefully kept flower garden stood by the side of the road. Here we were to have lunch.

A few rods to the west a perpendicular rock wall about thirty feet in height, as even and smooth as though it had been built by skilled workmen, extended some distance on either side of the road. Perhaps ages past it had formed the west bank of a much larger river. As E.L. and the doctors went inside I sauntered over toward the wall, and when close enough discovered hundreds of names carved in the soft sandstone, some of them almost illegible from the driving storms of more than half a century.[43]

[43]In a manner reminiscent of many a weary traveller on the Oregon Trail, Rose had stumbled on to Names Hill. Emigrants passing this way had started carving their names and

Along this way long ago must have come some great migration. Perhaps night after night on the very ground where I stood, groups of weary travelers had made camp within a circle formed by covered wagons placed end to end as a barrier against marauding Indians. I could almost catch the appetizing scent of bacon and coffee as the women prepared supper, and see the faces of the men sitting around the campfire lit up by its flickering flames against the blackness beyond, and grotesque giant shadows moving fitfully against the wall of rock behind them. Who were these people? And where were they going? Why had they left home and friends to suffer the hardships of an endless trek through a pathless wilderness far from the frontiers of civilization? What had become of them? Perhaps they had made their way to the Pacific slope to build a new civilization. Here on Nature's Monument a generation of adventurers had carved their names to make future generations wonder.

"Interesting, isn't it?" Startled from my reverie, I turned to see an old gentleman in freshly laundered soft shirt and coveralls, his short neck supporting a massive round bald head that glistened in the noonday sun, his almost youthful face set off by a pair of laughing blue eyes. "They all came by this way," he

initials in the soft limestone as early as 1822. One of the most recognized of names which was legible for generations was "James Bridger—1844." *Wyoming Guidebook*, (New York, 1941), p. 371.

went on in a soft pleasant voice, "in covered wagons, ox-carts, on horseback and on foot, those whose names you see carved in the rock and thousands more. Up the North Platte, along the Sweetwater, past Independence Rock, over South Pass, down Green River. And they camped here under the rock. Then on West over the Sublette Trail, some to Utah, some over the Great Desert and the High Sierras to the gold fields of California, others down the Snake and the Columbia to Puget Sound. Courageous souls they were, fighting off savage Indians, fording rivers, enduring the blistering sands of the desert and the numbing cold and deep snow of the mountains."

The old gentleman led the way to a spot a few rods south of the road. "This is where we buried our dead," he said, a faint note of sadness in his voice. Scattered rather promiscuously all over the ground were a half dozen stone slabs that had once marked the graves of tired travelers who could go no farther.

Just above us were more names carved in the wall of sandstone, but less distinct than those I had already seen, the names of scouts, traders, and trappers of a still earlier generation, the first white men to explore the region. A little apart from the others and more deeply engraved was the familiar name of Jim Bridger, and beneath it the figures 1844.

"Shall we walk down toward the river?" As though not expecting an answer, the old gentleman started off, and I followed. When we had fought our way a short distance through a jungle of dwarf willows we came to a small patch of ground that had obviously been kept cleared of underbrush. There half-buried in the sand, lay two or three old rusted wagon tires and half-burned pieces of a wagon tongue and whiffle-trees.

"This," he said bitterly, pointing at the charred remnants, "happened just before we came along. The damned savages massacred the whole family— men, women, and children. We buried them over there under the rock." Silently the old gentleman led the way back to the log house and the flower garden by the side of the road.

Just before going in for lunch he chuckled a bit and went on to the sequel of his story: "And here I am at eighty-five, me and the missus, back at old Names Hill feeding and lodging a new generation of travelers. Interesting, isn't it?" I followed him into the house too bewildered by what I had seen and heard even to express my appreciation.

An hour later we were on our way. But I could not get the old gentleman out of mind—or the endless procession that had camped under the rock wall and gone on over the old Sublette Trail toward the land of the setting sun—or Names Hill—or Jim Bridger and 1844.

When the famous pathfinder chiseled his name on the sandstone, savage Indians killed their game along Green River and the plains above it where now white faced cattle grew sleek and fat on the rich short grass in a stretch of land that at different times had been claimed by England, France and Spain, and in Bridger's time was a part of Mexico. Before finding its way into Wyoming, it would be embraced within the Mormon State of Deseret, and the territories of Oregon, Dakota and Idaho.

Eighteen forty-four to nineteen fourteen. It was only a little more than three-quarters of a century. But what a wealth of history had been written in that short span! In eighteen forty-four the eloquence of Clay, Calhoun and Webster reverberated through the old Senate Chamber in the northeast corner of the yet unfinished capitol in Washington; the great City of Chicago was nothing more than a booming town on the swampy shore of Lake Michigan at the outer edge of civilization; the first telegraph message had not yet ticked out and over that thirty miles of copper wire stretched from Washington to Baltimore; nor had anyone yet dreamed of the incandescent light, the telephone, the internal combustion engine, or of building a transcontinental railroad or flying like a bird through the air; slavery had yet two and a half decades to live before it would be washed out in the blood of thousands of brave men; Abraham Lincoln had scarcely been heard of; most of the western half of the continent was an uncharted wilderness; the great tide of immigration had scarcely begun to engulf the fertile plains west of the Mississippi; the Mormon invasion of Salt Lake Valley, the gold rush to California and the race for possession of the great Oregon territory were still in the future.

I wondered why these great migrations had occurred, why men had torn themselves and their families from comfortable surroundings in the East to move in constantly swelling streams ever westward. Perhaps to escape the restraining conventions of established communities, perhaps to plow new soil, to discover new wealth, to seek new adventure. But was it only that and nothing more? Or in pushing the Indians from the reservations guaranteed them by treaties signed in Washington, in swarming into Salt Lake Valley, California, and the vast Oregon country well before our Government had acquired these vast areas, were they but instruments of a destiny that had set half a continent apart as the proving ground of freedom and democracy?

"There's the Spur Ranch—the 'Rocking Chair' outfit."[44] It was E.L. who brought me back to the present. To the right of the road was a great expanse of hay meadow sloping gently toward the river, just beyond the east bank of which a sheer wall of rock rose to a height of a hundred feet or more. Atop the wall was a huge spur pointing westward over the river, and underneath it, dwarfed by its immensity, hovered a cluster of ranch houses, barns and corrals. Immediately east of the dusty road we

[44]Rocking Chair and Spur brands abound in the West. Rose referred to the John Metcalf ranch.

were traveling, millions of huge raindrops fell from fluffy white clouds overhead, each glistening like a diamond in the sun. Washed clean by the falling rain the rock wall on the other side of the river turned into great bars of purple, pink, green and yellow as though in some upheaval it had imprisoned a gigantic rainbow that only the rain and the sun could release briefly from captivity.

After an overnight stop at Charlie Budd's ranch we arrived early the next morning at Middle Piney Lake. It was the first time I had seen anything of Wyoming mountain scenery, and Middle Piney, I thought, was the most beautiful lake imaginable. From the north and the south banks heavily timbered mountains rose to magnificent heights, while west of the lake where it was fed by the waters of Middle Piney Creek, a beautiful meadow stretched far back into the mountains. Through a low hill that formed a natural dam along the east end of the lake the water had cut a narrow channel so even that it appeared to have been made with a steamshovel and dragline. Through this channel Middle Piney Creek, almost entirely hidden from sight by down timber floating on its surface, moved leisurely a short distance and then went tumbling and boiling over the rocks to the valley below.

Just above the outlet were the trout E.L. and his friends had told me about. Thousands upon thousands of them. Great big fellows lying lazily close to the sandy bottom of the lake in eight or ten feet of marvelously clear water. One of the compensations for living in this far-away country, I had often thought, would be the opportunities it would afford to indulge in my favorite sport of trout fishing. This was my chance—and what a chance! Without losing any time I got out my tackle and made my first cast. I had taken no pains in the selection of a fly. Any fly would do. Some, at least, of the thousands of trout would strike at anything. But they didn't strike. I tried another fly, and another and another, but with the same result. I caught a grasshopper, put it on the hook with a lead sinker to weight it to the bottom, and slowly dragged it right over the snouts of the big fellows lying almost on the sand at the bottom of the water, but they only stirred a little to brush the bait aside.

Having moved a short distance along the shore, I glanced back to notice that E.L. and the doctors seemed to be having no better luck than I, and that they had given up fishing and were lying in the sun on the hillside. Laying my tackle on the ground I decided to explore the north shoreline toward the west end of the lake. After making my way for more than an hour, through the dense forest that extended down to the huge boulders which lined the water's edge, I came to a clearing low on the mountainside overlooking the meadow at the west end of the lake. There, oblivious of my presence or entirely indifferent to it, were scores of deer and elk browsing in the tall grass along the creek banks not more than a hundred yards away, and a little farther upstream a great bull moose was feeding upon the tender shoots at the tops of the dwarf willows. For hours I sat in the shade of a huge pine tree watching these handsome wild animals, the first I had ever seen except in the zoo in Denver's City Park.

Quite content that I had not caught any fish, I arose to retrace my steps, for it was now mid-afternoon and by the time I could get back my companions would be ready to start home if indeed they hadn't been ready for hours. As I did so I inadvertently stepped on a dry twig and turned to see the startled deer and elk bounding gracefully into the timber on the other side of the creek. But the big bull moose only shook his great wide horns, watched me for a moment, and continued eating the tender shoots at the tops of the willows.

From a high point on the mountain side I could see the east end of the lake, but no sign of E.L. and the doctors. Could it be possible that, tired of waiting, they had started back to the Budd ranch leaving me to walk? The sun had gone behind a cloud, and it was almost like night in the dense timber. I was beginning to feel the terror that comes when one first realizes that he is far away in the high mountains and alone.

I quickened my step. I started to run. Two or three times I tripped over fallen timber and fell bruising my hands on the rocks. Once the sharp broken limb of a tree made a painful cut on the side of my face. Back to the west I heard the ominous groaning of the pines in the wind. Closer it came and louder. Angry waves lashed the huge boulders on the shore just below me. There was a roar of thunder, and looking behind me I saw great purple-black clouds driving toward me with terrifying speed. It was getting cold. Lightning cracked all around. Then the clouds opened and water poured out of them. Instantly a torrent was plunging down a deep cut in the steep mountainside just ahead and another just behind me. Taking shelter under a great pine tree on the high ground between the waters, I waited.

Soon the fury of the storm began to abate. The black clouds and the cannonading moved swiftly eastward toward the valley below. Squirrels chattered and birds sang in the trees. The sun bathed the forest in a flood of light and painted a brilliant rainbow so close that it seemed I could almost reach out and take hold of it.

Hurrying on, I approached the place where I had left E.L. and the doctors earlier in the day. No one was in sight. Certain they had gone, I determined to get over the canyon trail and out onto the road leading to the Budd ranch as soon as possible. When closer to the lake outlet, a strange and wonderfully reassuring sight met my eyes. E.L. and the doctors had not gone. There they were on their knees on the logs in the channel forming the outlet of the lake peering down into the water, each with the butt end of a fishing pole in his hand with a copper wire fastened onto the other end. Every minute or so they would jerk a big trout out of the water caught in a wire noose around the gills, and throw him onto the bank. There, to my amazement, were hundreds of trout, great fine ones of the kind Ralph and E.L. had told me about; but they had not been caught in the way I had expected.

It took only a few minutes to put the fish in hundred-pound sugar sacks. We fastened the well filled sacks each to the middle of a small pine pole, and, forming a line, each with the end of a pole on his shoulder, made our way over the rough trail a mile or so to where we had left the buckboard early in the morning.

We were all soaked to the skin, and now it was snowing and I was shivering with the cold. Fortunately I had brought with me an extra suit of heavy underwear and a rough towel. In the shelter of a big pine tree, as hastily as I could, I removed my wet clothing, rubbed myself vigorously with the towel, put on dry clothes, and we were on our way to the Budd ranch where we spent the night, and by mid-afternoon the next day were back in Kemmerer. For several days our friends had all the trout they could eat, though none of us offered any explanation as to how such tremendous quantities had been caught.

Chapter Seven

A FEW DAYS after returning from Middle Piney Lake, I had occasion to visit Star Valley,[45] separated from the valley of the Green River by a narrow range of mountains. A letter from James Kiser, a lawyer in that section of the county, of whom, however, I had never heard, said he had a client, Dan Cole by name, who had been charged with stealing a calf and wished me to assist in his defense.[46] The man was a poor farmer, he said, and unable to pay a fee of more than fifty dollars, a check for half of which sum was enclosed with the letter.

Twenty-five dollars was a very small fee since not less than three days would be required to make the round trip, assuming that the trial would consume only one. But there were other considerations. I wanted to extend my acquaintance throughout the county as soon as possible, and particularly did I

[45] A beautiful, Alpine-like valley in Western Wyoming, Star Valley was settled by Mormons in the 1870's. It is approximately fifty miles long and four to seven miles wide; intensive agriculture on an irrigation base has produced a flourishing dairy industry, which has resulted, according to the renown culinary artist, James Beard, in one of the two finest Swiss cheeses in America.

[46] Cole and Kiser have left little in the way of historical tracks, for several inquiries in the Star Valley area have failed to reveal any biographical information. Rose may have been using pseudonyms.

wish to see Star Valley, a rich farming community inhabited, as I had been told, almost entirely by Mormons.

The next morning I boarded the westbound mail train, and within an hour we were speeding through an irrigated valley with great fields of native hay waving in the early morning breeze, in the center of which was the little town of Cokeville,[47] which, the conductor had told me, shipped more wool and lambs than any other point on the Oregon Short Line Railroad. A half hour later, having passed through miles and miles of sagebrush land, we were in another valley of irrigated fields and a short distance farther on the train came to a stop at Montpelier,[48] Idaho, where I had been told I was to take a stage to Afton.[49]

The stage, a somewhat delapidated vehicle driv-

[47] Established by Tifford Kutz, Cokeville received early fame as a major shipping point for sheep; and also as the center of a flourishing cattle industry. At one time, Cokeville, on a per capita basis, had the reputation of being one of the wealthiest communities in the U. S. *Wyoming Guidebook* (New York, 1941), p. 250.

[48] Although the first settlers arrived in 1864, Montpelier underwent several name changes until receiving a visit from Brigham Young, who promptly settled the unsettled nomenclature by naming the community after the capital in his native state.

[49] The distributing and mercantile center of Star Valley, Afton came into existence in 1896, upon the completion of a survey by Mormon immigrants. Clarence D. Jayne, *Star Valley and Its Communities* (Laramie, 1952). (A volume offering a survey matching its title.)

en by a tall, slender man of advanced years, was waiting at the hotel. I climbed into a seat next to the driver, thinking that from there I would get a better view of the country through which we were to pass and that he could give me some information about this section of the country and the people who inhabited it.

What reading I had done had not been conducive to a favorable opinion of the disciples of Joseph Smith and Brigham Young. On the other hand the Mormons whom I had come to know in Kemmerer seemed not at all unlike other people. In fact some of them occupied prominent places in the business life of the community and most of them demeaned themselves in such a manner as to command universal respect. But there was the question of polygamy, a word which I had always supposed to be practically synonymous with the word Mormonism, although, to be sure, I had seen no evidence of it in Kemmerer. I wanted to know. The stage driver might be able to tell me.

A few miles west the gravelly road continually crossed and recrossed a little stream whose clear waters, singing happily as they went, hurried from their source in springs high on the timbered mountain-sides to the wide valley below. Patches of aspen trees grew on the low green hills on either side of the road, their myriads of little leaves quaking nervously in the scarcely perceptible breeze. Soon we were beginning to climb the last steep slope toward the top of the ridge. The horses leaned heavily into their collars; the little stream fell noisily over the boulders that stood in its path; and the forest of pine trees half moaned, half sighed in the rising wind. Far to the East, lazily drowsing in the warm sun, lay another range of mountains under a forest cover of deep purple. Star Valley must lie on this side.

We had covered half the journey and nothing had been said by either of us. If I were to learn anything about Mormonism and the Mormons it was time to get started. "Have you lived here long?" I casually asked the driver by way of starting a conversation. "Yes, a long time—came here as a young man with the first settlers." "Tell me about it," I said frankly.

"Well, Star Valley's a nice place," he began. "It's not much like it was forty years ago—nothing then but sagebrush as far as you could see. The 'star of valleys'. That's what it was called by the scouts sent out by the Church long ago to find a location for a new colony. And that's how it got its name. There was only a few of us—a dozen families or so. Pioneers we were, just like all the others that have made this great western country." He spoke with an earnestness that suggested the courage, the venturesomeness, the hardihood that have marked every pioneer from Daniel Boone to the driver of the Afton stage. "There was hardships, of course, just as there have always been in a new country. Not much to eat—a little cornmeal, a little sugar, a little flour, a little salt, a little sowbelly. That's about all. But there was plenty of wild game in the fall and sage chickens in the summer, and swarms of trout in Salt River.

"There was lots of work to do and not much to do it with. Had to have houses to live in, but there was lots of timber and it didn't take long to put the logs together. Them first little cabins wasn't much to look at, but they kept out the rain in summer and the snow and cold in winter. Yes, the first two or three winters was pretty bad—deep snow and awfully cold. My oldest brother and two other young fellows was killed in a snowslide up here on the mountain—just over there"—he pointed to a canyon a short distance away—"getting out logs to build a cabin for a new family that had just come into the valley. And there was lots of sickness those first two winters. A little bad without a doctor closer than Montpelier, and no chance to get through the snow on the mountains. But the women folks could be pretty good nurses when they had to, and most of us pulled through.

"Well, that was a long time ago. As time went on we got our houses and barns built—got a little land cleared of sagebrush—made dams along Salt River to run the water onto the land—got a school started, and built a meeting house. Then new families came in, and the settlement began to grow. Now there's stores, flour mills, post offices, irrigated farms, creameries all over the valley; there's a nice high school in Afton, and a tabernacle—and we send our boys and girls to college. Why, we've got a regular inland empire in here."

After hesitating thoughtfully for a moment he went on: "Let me tell you something, young man. We Mormons believe in six things: We believe in religion—that's why we give a tenth of everything we earn to the Church; we believe in education; we believe in wholesome amusement; we believe in work; we believe in thrift;—and we believe in helping each other." The old man spoke with an earnest eloquence born of deep conviction. I had not hoped to learn so much of Star Valley and the Mormon people from the driver of a stage.

There was one question that I wanted to ask him, but somehow didn't feel that this was just the right time. Perhaps I would bring it up later. What about polygamy?

A half hour later he spoke again. "At this turn in the road you get your first view of Star Valley." I looked to the right—and there it was five hundred feet below, the Arcadia of the west. Salt River came down from the hills to the south and growing wider and wider from the streams that flowed into it from the mountains on either side, continued through the center of the valley some twenty-five miles until it disappeared in the narrows at the north end. There were waving fields of hay and half-ripened grain everywhere, with sleek horses and thoroughbred dairy cows feeding in the meadows. Shadows from the mountains from which we were descending blanketed most of the valley; but waving fields of grain on the steep slopes of the hills to the east reached up to bathe in the mellow glow of the setting sun.

As we reached the level country the horses pricked up their ears and went into a brisk trot—they were within a few miles of home. We were passing a little cluster of houses. "This is Smoot," the driver said. At one corner of the road's intersection was a store with "Postoffice" painted over the door, at another the "meetinghouse," another a schoolhouse, and across from it an amusement hall. There it was, the typical Mormon community—religion, education, amusement.

Down the road a little farther I noticed an unusually well-kept farm with better-than-average fences and buildings. A man irrigating a patch of potatoes called out cheerfully as we passed, and the driver waved his greetings. "My oldest son," he said. "The other two are in business in Salt Lake." Pride in his offspring was unmistakable. "See that log shack back of the house? That's where I brought my bride thirty-five years ago. That's where our sons were born. Mary's gone now and soon I'll join her; but we'll live on and on in our sons and our son's sons." Again there was that deep earnestness that had marked his earlier speech.

We turned north along a row of poplars such as

distinguishes almost every Mormon settlement in the West. "Do you know Dan Cole?" I asked. "Brother Cole? Well, yes." "What sort of man is he?" "Can't say that he's exactly what he ought to be. That's his place there," pointing to a fine farm with freshly painted buildings standing a quarter of a mile back from the road, "the best farm in this end of the valley." I thought of what Kiser had said about his client being a poor farmer unable to pay a decent fee. As though thinking that he might have done "Brother" Cole an injustice, the driver went on. "Oh, he's not altogether bad—has a wonderful family." He didn't seem disposed to discuss my client, and I saw no reason to pursue the subject any further.

I noticed some distance from the road two or three groups of little log houses, three in each group, standing a few rods apart and each exactly like the others. They suggested the question I'd hesitated to ask the old man some time before. Pointing to one of these, I casually remarked that it seemed curious to see three identical houses so close together. "Relic of the old days before the Manifesto of 1890," he said, "one man—three wives—three families—three houses. Polygamy may have been alright years ago. I've always doubted it, though I'm the son of a plural marriage myself." "That's true, I suppose, of most Mormons," I suggested. "Well, not exactly—how much do you know of the Mormon people?" There was a sugges-

tion of resentment in the way he put the question.
"Very little," I confessed—"the only Mormon I
ever knew before coming to Wyoming a short time
ago was a boy that was in my class when I was about
twelve." I was thinking of young George Bourne
and two other boys whose father was a missionary
to the Mormons, how they used to pick on George
because of his religion, and how I befriended him,
partly because I was sorry for him, and partly because I admired him for stoutly standing up for his
church.

"Most people believe all Mormons are polyga-
mists," the old man went on. "They're wrong. Even
before the Manifesto of 1890,[50] 95% of the men had
only one wife. A man couldn't enter into a second
marriage without the first wife's written consent and
without satisfying the church authorities that he was
able to provide for a second family. Most of our
people were poor, with the result that it was usually
only the high church officials and those who were
fairly prosperous who had more than one wife. The
Church has, of course, strictly forbidden polygamy
since the manifesto." I wondered at the time whether this were really true, though in later years the old

[50] A passing reference to the Edmunds-Tucker federal law
of 1890 prohibiting plural marriages. The vast literature on
the Church of the Jesus Christ of Latter Day Saints, both
positive and negative, eclipses in amount, if not insight,
most topics in Western History. A brief, although not always totally satisfying review, may be found in Thomas F.
Dea, *The Mormons* (Chicago, 1957).

man's statements were verified on excellent authority and proved to be true.

"I understand that most of the people in Star Valley are Mormons," I observed inquiringly. "All except Brother Cole and perhaps a dozen others," was the stage driver's answer. "In fact our church is growing faster in proportion to its membership than any other Christian denomination." "*Christian?*" I asked with some surprise. "Oh, yes," he said, the Mormon Church is as orthodox as any other. We believe everything the other churches believe, but we go further—we believe that the Book of Mormon is a divinely inspired history of the people in the Western Hemisphere just as certain books in our Old Testament contain the inspired history of the Jews."

He seemed more than willing to talk about the subject, but we were nearing the end of our journey. "Well, that's Afton," he said. A half mile down the road was a little town of perhaps three or four hundred people. A block east of the main street was an imposing brick structure resembling a church but not exactly like any I had ever seen. It must be the tabernacle. The old man said it was.

He pulled up in front of the Allerd Hotel,[51] a flimsy ramshackle two-story frame building that

[51]Constructed in 1908, the Allerd Hotel "grew" eventually to fifty-six bedrooms. Mr. and Mrs. Nelson C. Allerd presided over the premises for some fifty years. Mrs. Hortense Hanson to Gene M. Gressley, September 17, 1976.

looked as though it had been thrown together in a hurry, and though it had apparently been standing there many years, there seemed never to have been time enough to finish it. The structure was only about half painted and there was a wide strip of tarpaper across the front that no one had taken the pains to cover with siding.

Inside a large swarthy man with a huge bristling mustache that seemed continually to jump nervously upward on one side as though in a frantic effort to meet an equally massive eyebrow, was serving dinner to a half-dozen traveling men in a large room that served as a dining room and lobby. In the parlor adjoining someone was playing a Beethoven sonata. I glanced in to see a beautiful dark-haired young woman seated at a grand piano. A tall raw-boned man with black curly hair and mustache, pulling hard at a bad-smelling pipe, stepped up close to where I was standing and listened a moment to the music. "Nelson Allerd's oldest gal," he said finally with a note of pride in his voice. Again he listened for a brief interval. "Saw you looking at the big fellow waiting table." He was still pulling hopefully at the smelly pipe in an apparent effort to bring the dead ashes back to life, then emptied them on the floor. "He's the gal's old man—owns the place here—another one of those goddam Mormons—Valley's full of 'em." With the last sentence his voice rose to an angry crescendo. Quickly recovering his composure he turned to me with a grin that exposed a row of dirty gold teeth. "Spose you're the young lawyer from Kemmerer. My name's Cole. Dan Cole," he added, extending his calloused hand.

Together my client and I ascended a flight of squeaking stairs to the room to which I had been assigned by another of the Allerd girls. There were four or five of them I afterward learned, all as attractive, or nearly so, as the one I had heard playing the Beethoven sonata.

" 'Fraid you wasn't goin' to git here," Cole began, lighting his pipe. "The goddam Mormons seem to think I've been stealing their damned calves—always accusing me of somethin." He was grinning exuberantly and seemed immensely pleased with the situation. "Jim Kiser send you the money?" I replied that he had sent me twenty-five dollars and said he'd pay my expenses when I arrived. "He said you were a poor farmer and couldn't pay any more," I said questioningly. Cole exploded. "Me a poor farmer—couldn't pay—twenty-five dollars— he's just another goddam Mormon crook! Me a poor farmer—why, everyone knows I've got the best farm in Star Valley—poor farmer—the ——— ————— Mormon ———!" He counted out two hundred and fifty dollars and handed it to me.

My client was too busy castigating the Mormons to talk about the case, and left in a few moments saying he'd see me in the morning. But before going he took one parting shot. "The goddam Mormon justice of the peace'll decide the case against me, of course, but we'll take it to the District Court. I'll show these damned Mormons they can't push me around." Despite his evident hatred for his Mormon neighbors and the fact that he had a felony charge hanging over his head, he was in high spirits.

In one brief afternoon I had heard two widely divergent estimates of the people of Star Valley, but my client suffered badly by comparison with the stage driver.

I went downstairs for a late dinner. Someone was playing the piano in the parlor. While I was eating a number of young fellows came in, and soon the Allerd girls and their friends were gathered around the piano singing, and they were still singing when two hours later I retired for the night.

The next morning Cole and I walked down the main street toward the amusement hall where the trial was to be held. There seemed to be more people on the sidewalk than the size of the town warranted, many of them farmers in their working clothes. But, strangely it seemed to me, no one appeared to manifest the least unfriendliness toward my client. Those who knew him spoke pleasantly, most of them addressing him as "Brother" Cole, and, to my greater surprise, he returned their salutations with almost equal good nature though with a somewhat contemptuously cynical smile.

A middle-aged farmer was seated behind a table as we entered the court room. He was evidently the justice of the peace. The wooden benches arranged facing him were well filled with spectators, and scores of others were coming in. It was not often that a hearing on a felony charge occurred in Star Valley, and this one, particularly because of the defendant's prominence and the difficulties in which he was frequently involved, was enough to excite general public interest, although I noticed no hostility toward the accused. Neither did the judge at any stage of the trial manifest the least disposition to favor the prosecution. On the contrary, he seemed obviously inclined to give the defendant the benefit of every doubt.

The evidence, of course, was conflicting, Cole and his witnesses flatly denying most of the State's testimony. There seemed to me to be sufficient evidence to hold my client for trial to the District Court. I was therefore very much surprised when at the close of the arguments late in the afternoon the justice announced that in his opinion there was not sufficient evidence to hold "Brother Cole" for trial and ordered that he be discharged. Even more surprising was the round of applause that greeted his decision. My client was obviously disappointed. The "damned Mormon" justice of the peace had deprived him of his chance to fight the case out in the District Court.

But there were other cases. In fact Dan Cole proved to be one of my most valuable clients. I could depend on him for at least one case in each term of court for the next two or three years, all of them growing out of his animosity toward his Mormon neighbors and his determination to annoy and tantalize them in every way possible. There was a wide variety of cases. He was accused of interfering with irrigation ditches, tearing down fences, putting his brand on other men's cattle, driving his livestock into his neighbors' pastures, to say nothing of such common offenses as assault and battery and disturbance of the peace. He seemed obsessed with the idea of making life as miserable as possible for the "damned Mormons."

On one occasion he was charged with shooting a pet beaver belonging to one of his neighbors, and I was employed to defend him in Justice Court at Afton. Upon my arrival at the Allerd Hotel he seemed to be more delighted with himself than usual and hurried me upstairs to the room which he had reserved for me, saying that he didn't want to take the chance of being overheard. "I've got a joke on the damned Mormons this time," he said, "and it's a good one. If it works there won't be no trial." Always prepared for almost anything from this strange client, I suggested that he let me in on the secret.

"Well, it's like this," he began. "My neighbor had a pet beaver. A regular nuisance—kept coming over and gnawing the bark off of my trees. Someone shot the little cuss—they seem to think it was me." He hesitated a moment, a sly grin on his face. "Anyway the fellow came over and found the hide hanging in a tree in my back yard. Then he went and had me arrested. But I fooled 'em. That beaver hide ain't there anymore—it's buried up on the mountain where they'll never find it. There's a beaver hide hanging in that tree alright, but it ain't the one this damned Mormon neighbor of mine saw there. It's one I caught in a trap and it ain't got no bullet holes in it." "Ain't got no bullet holes" was spoken with deliberate emphasis. Seeing that I was about to interrupt and anticipating the question I intended to ask, with a triumphant flourish he pulled from his pocket and handed me a permit signed by the State game warden authorizing him to trap beaver on a creek that ran through his place. "That's all clear enough," I suggested, "but where's the joke? How are you going to avoid a trial?" "Just leave it to me," he said, his face flushed with excitement.

A little later the county attorney arrived at the hotel, and Cole began putting his plan into effect. "These damned Mormons are just crazy," he was telling the prosecutor. "Sure someone probably shot their goddam beaver; sure they saw a beaver hanging in my tree; but what of it?—It was my own beaver—caught it in a trap." And he handed the county attorney the permit signed by the game warden. "Tell you what I'll do, Jack. I'll take you out to my place—you examine the hide yourself. If you can find a bullet hole in the hide, I'll plead guilty and pay the fine. If you don't find a bullet hole in the hide, you dismiss the case." The county attorney went out to look at the hide and, naturally, found no bullet holes. He came back to Afton, dismissed the case and started for Kemmerer.

Cole and I went to my room, where he cheerfully paid my fee. He said he'd had me come to Afton to be there just in case his trick didn't work. This trick he'd played on his Mormon neighbor he regarded as his crowning achievement. His exultant laughter could have been heard in the middle of the next block. In high glee he reminded me that, with all the charges that had been preferred against him, and all the controversies he'd been involved in, he'd never been convicted and he'd never lost a civil case—a fact I had occasion to know as well as he, since I had defended him in all of them.

Dan Cole died many years ago. Some years before his death, moved perhaps by the example of his noble wife, perhaps by the general kindly attitude of his Mormon neighbors to whom he never ceased to be "Brother" Cole, he re-entered the Mormon Church in which he had been reared and from which he had separated in his young manhood. Dan Cole was never altogether bad—no one is. He was only a man who, in some respects, never grew up.

Chapter Eight

LOOKING OVER the Kemmerer *Camera* one evening my attention was attracted by this striking headline: "Paroled Convict Charged with Stealing Rocking Chair Horses." The story that followed, most of which had been told me a short time before by a Rock Springs lawyer, was a fascinating one.

Bascom Skaggs,[52] the son of a prominent clergy-

[52]Exhibiting the mixture of the bravado of a "Butch" Cassidy and a Tom Horn, Bascom Skaggs's life consists of the stuff out of which legends are created, or at least a grade "B" movie made. Incredible as it seems, the name of Bascom Skaggs does not even conjure up a ghostly figure in the memories of Wyomingites. The earliest reference we have to Skaggs's illustrious career is an undated, unidentified clipping in the Hebard Collection of the Western History Research Center. According to the author of this item, Bob McAuley, Skaggs was a man of "weak intellect and seemed incapable of considering the inevitable consequences that were certain to result from his acts." Obviously, Robert Rose knew a different Bascom Skaggs!

The Kemmerer *Camera* followed the episodic adventures of Skaggs in three breathless articles. On September 2, 1914, the *Camera* told of Skaggs being arrested for stealing nine head of horses from the Rocking Chair ranch. The reporter reminded his readers that the same Skaggs was out of the Rawlins penitentiary for having " a few years ago" murdered a man in the Lander, Wyoming, country over an argument centering on sheep. Sentenced to a term of twenty-five to thirty years, Skaggs had recently been paroled. Justice R. Lee Craig arraigned him on the charge of horse stealing in September of 1914 and returned Skaggs to Rawlins.

After escaping his guard in Rawlins, Skaggs was followed south to Bitter Creek, but literally, going in one cabin door

man, upon his graduation with honors a few years earlier from one of the leading universities in the East, had come to Wyoming for a vacation. Fascinated with ranch life he had decided to remain in the West and secured a job as a cowhand at the Spur Ranch, usually known as the Rocking Chair outfit because of the design of the brand used on its livestock. Already an excellent horseman, he soon became expert in the use of the lariat and branding iron and a favorite at the local rodeos where he took first money in bronco busting, bulldogging and calf roping. A tall, handsome fellow, there was about him an air of quiet assurance that won him the confidence of the owner of the Spur and a position of leadership among the men who rode the range.

Skaggs had not been long in the neighborhood when there began to be rumors of cattle rustling. A few were reported missing from one outfit and a few from another. Someone claimed to have noticed that each time a bunch of cattle disappeared from the range, Skaggs would also disappear for a few days. Suspicion grew from week to week as new

and out the other, Skaggs easily evaded his pursuers. Two years went by before Kemmerer heard anything of "gentleman" Bascom. When information was heard, it arrived via Sheriff Rick McMinn. While in El Paso, McMinn understood that Skaggs was riding with Villa. Whether Skaggs ever met up with Cassidy in South America, (presuming Cassidy went to South America) remains a mystery—not even the subject of a Western ballad. Kemmerer *Camera*, September 2, October 7, 14, 1914; March 29, 1916.

reports of missing livestock came in; and Deputy Sheriff Rick McMinn,[53] a quiet, unassuming and fearless officer, was assigned at the request of the Livestock Association to investigate the rustling. Although it was never determined with any degree of certainty that Skaggs had anything to do with the disappearance of the cattle, he was made very definitely to feel that he was under suspicion and that his departure from the Green River Valley would not be regarded as a calamity in the vicinity.

It was from his experience at the Spur Ranch, I think, that Skaggs acquired the deep contempt for the law and the bitter hatred of its officers that led to later difficulties; but whether he was justly accused or whether he was the unfortunate victim of unfounded suspicion, whether in fact there was any cattle rustling at all during his stay at the Spur Ranch, I have never been entirely certain. Anyway Skaggs left the Rocking Chair outfit and went to work at the Kelly ranch a few miles east in Sweet-

[53] A respected peace officer who found himself constantly in the thick of things, Sheriff J. R. McMinn died in June of 1918 of pneumonia "complicated by rheumatism." The publisher of the *Camera* and confidante of the deceased sheriff, Bob Rose, wrote, "The very large number, who attended the funeral and joined in the procession spoke volumes for the deep devotion in which the Sheriff McMinn was held by his fellow citizens. As a man, he was kind of heart; as a friend, he was true at any cost; and as an officer, he was fearless, energetic and faithful. Rick McMinn filled a place in the life of Lincoln County which can never be filled by anyone else and endeared himself to his fellow citizens." Kemmerer *Camera*, June 5, 12, 1918.

water County. If in fact inclined to a disregard of legal restraints, he could scarcely have fallen into worse company, for Kelly enjoyed a somewhat unsavory reputation and was said to have two or three notches on his gun.

One day Skaggs rode into Green River City, entered the Sheriff's office and exhibiting a vicious cut over the left eye, announced that he had been brutally assaulted by a man on the Kelly ranch and had been obliged to kill him. Apparently confident that he would be exonerated, he told the sheriff that he supposed he should be charged with homicide and given a trial. And he was, although the result was quite different from what he had expected. After more than twenty-four hours' deliberation the jury brought in a verdict of murder in the first degree and Skaggs was sentenced to life imprisonment in the penitentiary at Rawlins. The jury didn't believe his self-defense story. Notwithstanding the jury's verdict, there were many who thought that it was Kelly and not Skaggs who was guilty of the homicide. So general was this feeling that a petition signed by several of the leading citizens of Sweetwater County was presented to the Governor asking for the exercise of executive clemency; and in less than two years Skaggs was given a parole, which was effective, of course, only during good behavior.

It was a short time later that he was arrested charged with stealing the Rocking Chair horses. The evidence against him, according to the *Camera* account, was strong. An eye-witness by the name of Jackson had signed a statement accusing him of the crime, and Skaggs was arrested when he rode into Kemmerer the next day.

What a case, I thought, as I laid the paper aside. In this cattle country nothing—not even a murder trial—could excite public interest as did a case involving the stealing of livestock. When Skaggs came to trial, half the stockmen of Green River Valley would be in the courtroom. Suppose I should be employed to defend! That, of course, wasn't likely. I was a new lawyer in the community and in all probability Skaggs had never heard of me. And then I was a Democrat, and the sheriff was a Republican and strongly disposed to favor his political friends. Skaggs would probably ask him to recommend a lawyer, and he certainly would not be inclined to recommend me. No, nothing would come of it so far as I was concerned—but it couldn't do any harm to think about it and even to do a little wishing. Well, it would be a great case anyway. Dismissing the subject from my mind, I then picked up the paper and began reading the other local happenings.

I had some difficulty in concealing my exuberance when early the next morning Sheriff Hansen called to say that Skaggs wanted me to see him at the County jail. As we walked together down the street he casually remarked that his prisoner's parole had been revoked and that Deputy Warden

Billie Mills[54] had already arrived to return him to the penitentiary at Rawlins. The information was very much of a disappointment—in that event there would, of course, be no trial. We descended the stair in front of "Scoot" Embree's furniture store to the basement underneath. The sheriff unlocked the door and we went in. It was the first time I had occasion to visit the jail. In the center of the stuffy ill-smelling room, lighted only by two or three half windows in the east wall, was a row of iron cells. The sheriff pointed to the farthest one and then withdrew.

Skaggs, dressed in cowboy boots, trousers and soft shirt, stood at the front of his cell gripping the bars in his well-shapen upraised hands. Even in such an unfavorable situation his appearance was striking. Slender, more than six feet tall, with coal black wavy hair, and sharp gray eyes looking out from under heavy black eyebrows, the left one marred by an ugly scar, I thought him unusually handsome.

[54]At "about forty" years of age, Billie Mills came to a tragic end. He held the office of deputy sheriff under sheriffs Hansen, McMinn and Bell. Two years before his death, Mills worked in the Big Piney Drug Store; then followed a short tenure on the Henry Budd ranch. An insanity hearing was held in Kemmerer in December, 1920, at which one local physician, Dr. Goldberg, pronounced Mills condition as "probably incurable." Accordingly, he was committed to the state mental hospital at Evanston, Wyoming, where he died ten days after the Kemmerer proceedings. Kemmerer *Camera*, December 22, 29, 1920.

Our conference was brief. He assured me that if I could obtain an extension of his parole a sufficient time to permit a preliminary hearing before the justice of the peace, Jackson, the State's witness, would not testify against him. So completely impressed was I with his gentlemanly manner and apparent sincerity that it did not occur to me until after I had seen him for the last time a month later that he hadn't even denied stealing the horses. I went out determined to do everything possible for this man in whose innocence, for some strange reason, I had full confidence.

The first thing to do, if possible, was to induce the governor to extend Skaggs' parole and order the filing of a criminal complaint. How could it be done? I did not know Governor Carey;[55] and what

[55]The patriarch of a distinguished political and socially active family dynasty in Wyoming, Joseph M. Carey (1845–1925) was appointed U. S. attorney for the Wyoming territory in 1869. The Carey name soon became intertwined with a host of economic and political activities in the Cowboy state. During the forty years after Carey first stepped off the Union Pacific in Cheyenne, he successively held the offices of: Mayor of Cheyenne (1881–1895); Territorial Delegate to the U. S. House of Representatives (1885–1890); U. S. Senator (1890–1895); Governor of Wyoming (1910–1915). As promoter of irrigation and reclamation, his name was given to the Carey Act. This federal legislation, passed in 1894, offered to each qualifying state up to one million acres of arid domain provided that the state would reclaim the land and populate it with settlers on small acreage. In addition, the Carey influence was found in a host of businesses including: The J. M. Carey Livestock Company, Cheyenne real estate, banking and the Wheatland Develop-

reason was there to suppose that he would give any
consideration at all to my request on behalf of a
convicted murderer who, by the sworn statement of
an eye-witness, had violated his parole by stealing
horses? Knowing no better procedure, I decided to
call the governor on the long distance telephone. I
told him that I was a lawyer who had but recently
come to Kemmerer, that I had interviewed Skaggs
and was convinced that his innocence would be established if he were accorded a trial. To my great
surprise the Governor said that some time before he
had carefully reviewed the evidence in the murder
trial, that he himself doubted Skaggs' guilt and was
more than willing that he should have a chance to
clear himself in court of the charge of stealing the
Rocking Chair horses. He said he would immediately wire the Deputy Warden to return to Rawlins
leaving Skaggs in the custody of the Lincoln County sheriff. By his generous act Governor Carey won
my complete admiration, which remained undimin-
ished when I became acquainted with him a year or
so later.

Leaning heavily on his cane, old Judge Carnahan,[56] who had been badly crippled in a coal mine

---

ment Company. A brilliant history of this period can be
found in Lewis L. Gould, *Wyoming: A Political History,
1868–1896.* (New Haven, 1968.)

[56]Though present day Kemmererites produced a vague
look of recognition, little is known about the Judge. The
Camera announced to the public that Carnahan had lost
eighty-seven pounds due to a recent illness. March 7, 1917.

disaster years before, limped clumsily into the little Pine Avenue office that served as his courtroom. The place was already filled with spectators about equally divided between cowhands anxious to see Skaggs discharged and members of the Livestock Association equally anxious to see him held for trial in the District Court, although I suppose few of either group had any actual knowledge of the facts of the case or much concern on that score.

The atmosphere in the courtroom was tense as Carnahan, who had served several terms as Justice of the Peace and had acquired a disagreeably autocratic attitude, brought his gavel down on the little table before him, commanded silence, and announced that he was ready to conduct the preliminary hearing in the case of the State of Wyoming vs. Bascom Skaggs. The heated conversation that had been going on among the standing spectators came to a complete halt as Ivan Jones,[57] the prosecuting attorney, arose to make his opening statement to the assembled crowd.

The State's case would be brief, Mr. Jones said. There would be only one witness, but his testimony, the prosecutor thought, would be sufficient to establish the prisoner's guilt beyond any ques-

[57]The prospect of a natural resource bonanza consistently possessed the attention of Attorney Ivan Jones. In March of 1918, Jones, with high anticipation and long foresight, was the guiding light behind the organization of the Little Colorado Desert Oil Shale Company. Kemmerer *Camera*, April 3, 1918.

tion. The State would prove that the witness Jackson, a cowpuncher employed by one of the cattle outfits in the vicinity, had chanced to meet Skaggs on the range in the southwestern corner of the County. Jackson would testify that Skaggs was driving a small herd of Rocking Chair horses, that he and Skaggs rode along together for a half hour or so, and in the course of the conversation Skaggs manifested a bitter enmity toward the owner of the Spur outfit, and, after pledging Jackson to secrecy, told him that he had stolen the Spur horses and was driving them into northeast Utah where he had already arranged for their sale. Jackson would testify further, the prosecutor said, that he knew positively that the horses were the property of the Spur Ranch.

There was a shuffling of feet as Mr. Jones concluded. Not knowing what else to do, I announced that I would reserve my statement until the conclusion of the State's case; and Jackson was called to the witness stand. Judge Carnahan's gavel abruptly terminated the angry whispering that swept the courtroom as the State's witness elbowed his way out of the crowd and took the oath. I noticed that the nervous little man winced as he caught Skaggs' eye and appeared very uneasy.

The examination was brief, as the prosecuting attorney had promised. After a few preliminary questions Mr. Jones asked the witness if he had seen Skaggs on the range in the southwestern corner of

the county a few days before. Jackson said he had.
Jones asked what Skaggs was doing. The witness
said he was driving a small bunch of horses. Jones
asked if he had had a conversation with Skaggs.
Jackson said he had *not* talked with the defendant.
The prosecutor was noticeably surprised. The witness was increasingly nervous. Now and then he
looked at Skaggs sitting only a few feet away, and I
observed that the prisoner's keen gray eyes were
fastened upon the witness. A little disconcerted by
now, Jones asked uncertainly, as though he feared
an unfavorable answer, "Whose horses were they?"
And somewhat hesitatingly, as Jackson's eyes appre-
hensively met Skaggs', came the answer "They were
Skaggs' horses."

Immediately the little room was in a turmoil.
The judge pounded his desk for order and threatened to clear the courtroom. There was angry suspicion in his voice as he turned to Jackson and said
sharply, "The witness is excused." The prosecutor
was completely stunned. So was I. I looked at
Skaggs sitting unmoved in a chair beside me, the
only unexcited person in the room. The State's witness had proven to be a witness for the defense. I
remembered that Skaggs had told me that Jackson
would not testify against him. I was pretty sure that
there was some mysterious reason for the strange
turn his testimony had taken, but couldn't imagine
what it was.

When the hub-bub had subsided I moved for a

dismissal. The prosecutor asked for a short recess, and he and Rick McMinn withdrew to a corner of the room for an excited conference. Jones came to the judge's desk and opened the statute book. I thought I knew what was coming. When Judge Carnahan again rapped with his gavel the prosecuting attorney, in a voice trembling with emotion, told the court that he had been completely surprised by Jackson's testimony, which he said was exactly contrary to what the witness had told him before the trial, and asked that the case be continued for thirty days in order that special deputy McMinn could make a thorough investigation. The request was unhesitatingly granted. I had gloomy forebodings of what the stock detective's investigation might disclose.

"I'll be confined in this place for some time I presume," Skaggs said when I visited him at the jail the morning after the hearing. "Wonder if you could let me have something to read—Shakespeare, Byron, Emerson, perhaps some of your old text books in higher mathematics." It was with books such as these that Skaggs occupied his time during his stay in the county jail. I often spent an hour or so visiting with my client in the dingy basement under the furniture store. No subject was outside his field of information, and he conducted himself with a dignity and courtesy such as one might expect to find in the drawing room of a cultured home.

On only two occasions did Skaggs make a display of temper during his incarceration. Undersheriff Joe Godmundsen[58] usually brought the prisoners' meals. I had often noticed a sinister look in Godmundsen's eyes whenever Skaggs' name was said in his presence. There was evidently a very deep-seated hatred between the two men, and the officer, I observed, treated his prisoner with uniform and studied arrogance when he came to the jail. One evening Skaggs said to me in his usual mild tone, "I wonder if you would do me a little favor—wish you would ask Sheriff Hansen to send Charlie Salmon with my meals hereafter." And then with measured emphasis he went on, "If Godmundsen comes down here again I'll break his neck, I'll tie his long thin body in a knot, and throw his vile carcass out the window." From the flash in his eye and the set of his jaw I felt that he meant what he said. After that Deputy Salmon brought the prisoner's meals, and "Godie" stayed away from the jail until Skaggs had gone.

One evening I heard that Rick McMinn had returned. The next morning the prosecuting attorney told me that McMinn had interviewed almost everyone who had known Skaggs since his coming to Wyoming, that he had taken sworn statements from a half dozen men who had seen Skaggs with the Rocking Chair horses, that the deputy had submit-

[58] Joe Godmundsen served as deputy sheriff during the exciting days of the Kemmerer "crime" wave of 1915.

ted the affidavits to Governor Carey in Cheyenne, that the governor had issued a second order revoking my client's parole, and that Deputy Warden Billie Mills had arrived early in the morning and would return Skaggs to Rawlins on the evening train.

I went to the jail and outlined the situation just as Jones had told it to me. When I entered Skaggs was sitting on a bench outside his cell playing solitaire. Slowly he picked up the cards and held them in his right hand. As I proceeded with the story his jaw tightened and there was a frightfully sinister look in his eyes. When I had finished he pinched the cards in such a manner as to scatter them all over the place, and even now speaking in a quiet voice, but every word charged with bitter hatred and cool determination, he said, "They want to make a crook of me, and God-damn them, I'll be a good one." Then slowly he picked up the cards and resumed his game of solitaire as though nothing had happened. I felt sure he would keep his promise.

In a moment he laid the cards aside, slowly rolled a cigarette, lit it, and went on, quietly but a little sorrowfully. "I hoped they'd give me a square deal; but they didn't. Certainly I'm not what I ought to be—I've made my mistakes—I was carried away with the glamour of life here in the West—and I've been very foolish. When a man makes one mistake does he have to pay for it the rest of his life? Maybe he does. Maybe it's right that he should. I don't know." He sat quietly a few moments with his head in his hands as if in deep meditation. Then, with bitterness in his words, he continued, "The biggest mistake I ever made was to stay in this vile hole like a caged beast. I could have walked out any time. There's been a pair of horses cached down in the willows ever since I've been here. If I'd've known how this was going to come out—if I'd've known they weren't going to give me a chance—I'd be so far away right now that all the Goddamn dicks in the country couldn't get me."

In a moment, his composure completely restored, he remarked calmly, "I appreciate what you've tried to do for me, and I'm sorry I haven't yet been able to pay the fee we agreed upon." He asked me if I was usually at home during the evening. Thinking it a strange question, I said I was unless I should happen to be out of town. He inquired whether in my absence my wife would be frightened if there should be a knock at the back door. To this even stranger question, I said I thought not.

He appeared to be studying a moment, and as if talking to himself he said half aloud, "No, it shouldn't take more than a week." Then, turning to me he continued: "I'll be back. I'll steal McMinn's horses, take them to Utah and sell them. At ten o'clock a week from tonight there'll be a knock at your back door. I'll be there to pay the money I owe you." I started to argue against his plan, but he turned the subject.

A little before six that evening I went to the station to say good-bye to this man for whom I had grown to have a deep affection. He was sitting handcuffed on a bench in the waiting room surrounded by a half dozen officers, including Billie Mills, Sheriff Hansen, deputies Godmundsen and Salmon, Town Marshall Dan Harrity, and perhaps one or two others. "Mr. Mills," Skaggs was saying as I entered, "do you intend to keep these handcuffs on me when we get on the train?" "Yes, and by—," was the reply, "I'm going to put an Oregon boot[59] on your leg and chain you to the seat." "I wish you wouldn't do that," Skaggs said in his never failing soft voice. "If you treat me like a gentleman, I'll give you no trouble. If you don't, you'd better take all these officers with you. You'll need them."

The next morning it was rumored that Skaggs had escaped. Nate Jennings, who had known Skaggs years before at the Spur ranch and had been a devoted friend ever since, told me how it happened that Jackson didn't testify against Skaggs at the hearing in Judge Carnahan's court. Jennings had met Jackson when he arrived on the three o'clock train that morning and had taken him through the areaway to a window a few feet from Skaggs' cell.

[59] An Oregon boot has been depicted as a device analogous to a ball and chain, but presumably less cumbersome (occasionally a heavy steel band locked around the ankle). Legend would have it that the appellation derived from having been devised in Oregon. Mitford M. Mathews, ed., *A Dictionary of Americanisms* (Chicago, 1951), II, p. 1166.

What Skaggs said to Jackson had evidently made him feel that it wouldn't be entirely safe for him to give any testimony damaging to the defense.

The Salt Lake Tribune which reached Kemmerer the next day contained an account of Skaggs' escape. Deputy Warden Mills, a short fat fellow, had made the mistake of attempting to walk his prisoner from the station to the penitentiary when the train reached Rawlins at one o'clock in the morning. As the two passed an alley three blocks from the station Skaggs had given Mills a shove and while the officer was picking himself up, had made his escape down the alley. Several bullets from Mills' revolver had failed to reach their mark. It was surmised that a horse was ready nearby. Posses, the Tribune said, were already scouring the countryside in the vicinity of Rawlins.

A few days later I found an unusual envelope in my box at the post office with a postmark I had never heard of but which I learned to be from an office in the desert country some distance south of Rock Springs. The envelope was addressed:

> Sr. Roberto Rosen
> Kemer, Wiomin.

When I reached the office I opened the envelope with a good deal of interest, wondering who it could be that had addressed me as "Sr." instead of "Mr.", and had incorrectly spelled not only my name but the name of the town and that of the State as well. Probably a Spaniard or a Mexican person, I thought.

The letter itself was even more baffling, and although I haven't seen it for almost thirty-five years, I think I can set it down practically word for word:

> Amigo Roberto—i rite yu bout deevorse, the last nite i se yu mi wife she shuto te me meny times but she no hit me. Yu tela mi mama I feela prety good. Yu keep it my sadel and bridel
>
> Archuleta Sanchez

I was completely puzzled. No client had consulted me about a divorce, nor did I know anything about anybody's saddle and bridle. I was certain that no Mexican or Spaniard had called at the office; and what did the fellow mean about having been shot at by his wife, and wanting me to tell his mother? And who was his mother anyway? And, moreover, who was he?

I laid the letter aside and took it home with me in the evening. Eleanor was as thoroughly puzzled as I. After a while she looked up from the magazine she was reading with the ejaculation, "Why, that letter's from Skaggs." Of course it was. Why hadn't I thought of it? He wanted me to get word to his mother that he hadn't been hit by the bullets from Billie Mills' revolver, and he wanted me to have the saddle and bridle that he had left at the livery stable just before his arrest. The rest of it—the reference to "deevorse," the poor scribbling, the bad spelling, and the foreign touch—was pure deception, and effective too, for when before opening it I foolishly showed the envelope to postmaster McNamara, he said he had never heard of the office whose postmark it bore and had to consult his directory before he could locate it.

A month or so later I met Matt McCourt,[60] the Sweetwater County sheriff, at the Union Pacific station at Green River. He told me that two or three days after the escape he had organized a posse and had gone south from Rock Springs thinking Skaggs might be heading through the desert for the mountains in northern Colorado. About ten o'clock in the forenoon the posse had reached a sheep camp and the herder had told him that a man answering Skaggs' description had stayed there overnight and by the time the sheriff could get there would probably be having dinner at a ranch house several miles farther on. McCourt said that when the posse reached the place they saw a horse tied at the kitchen door and surrounded the house. Skaggs, he went on, evidently hearing or seeing them, ran out of the door, jumped on his horse and started shooting. Though many shots were exchanged, no one was

[60]Matt McCourt discovered Sweetwater county, Wyoming, in 1893. Initially, he sought employment in the coal mines; and in 1907 he began his career in law enforcement. First a member of the Rock Springs police force, then from 1908–1917, McCourt was elected Sheriff of Sweetwater County. In the latter year, he joined the Union Pacific railroad as Special Agent, a position he held until his retirement in 1946. The Green River *Star*, March 22, 1946; Rock Spring *Miner*, March 23, 1946. Courtesy of Michael Snyder.

hit. Skaggs soon outdistanced the posse, and the last McCourt saw of him he was riding at breakneck speed through the brakes and ravines far to the south heading for Colorado.

Months later there was another letter in my box at the post office, this time properly addressed and in an excellent hand. It was postmarked somewhere in Mexico, where Skaggs said he was operating a machine gun in General Villa's army. He told of his escape from the custody of Deputy Warden Billie Mills, how he had finally been able to file off the handcuffs, how he had eluded Sheriff McCourt's posse and riding at night, sleeping in hidden places through the daytime, had traveled through the mountains of Colorado and by unfrequented roads through New Mexico and Texas to Mexico.

So far as I know that letter was the last anyone has received from Bascom Skaggs, the most adventuresome and the most lovable criminal, if indeed he was a criminal, I have ever known.

Chapter Nine

IF THERE WAS ANYTHING to be gained by entertaining regrets about things that have long since happened, I might easily be persuaded to wish I had never heard of the Dry Piney Oil Field,[61] although I

[61] The Dry Piney Oil Field was located fifty miles north of Kemmerer and twenty miles south of Big Piney. The petroleum potential of the area was first noted by the Western explorer, F. W. Lander in 1859. In 1907, the U. S. Geological Survey mapped the region, and issued a *Bulletin* (no. 543) describing the field. However, by 1920, only five wells had been drilled.

In a promotional extravaganza publication in 1921, Rose's friend and "educator," Charles Lackey heaped scorn on previous activity and activators in the Dry Piney field. The favorable syntax, used by Mr. Lackey, appeared again and again in mineral pie-in-the-sky literature of the West. Quoting this promoter, "Many, fairly accurate reports have been made on this field by much more competent writers than your humble servant, but the majority of them have embraced a region, the magnitude of which is so vast that legitimate operators, who are familiar with oil fields turn away in disgust and their usual comment is—bunk!"

"There is no desire on the part of the writer to discredit anything that is fair and legitimate, but we do think it is high time for the public to know, who is who and what is what and where . . . ."

At this stage of the game current opinion took a trend to the other extreme, college bred geologists of renowned reputations and profound knowledge flooded local newspapers with titles such as: Colonel, Doctor, Professor, Captain, Sir, etc.

Charles Lackey, "Facts Concerning the Dry Piney Oil Field and confusion of the same area with surrounding areas, A Geological Report." (n.p., 1921).

would doubtless have found some other equally effective way of dissipating my modest surplus of time and money. Moreover, I would have missed the intoxicating delight of anticipating numberless pleasant ways of making use of untold riches, and, what is no less important, I would have missed knowing a pair of interesting characters of the sort one meets only once in a lifetime.

Kemmerer refused to get excited about the discovery of oil at La Barge.[62] We just knew that it couldn't amount to anything. To begin with this was livestock country, and that fabulous riches in the form of liquid gold should lie underground where unsuspecting cattle lazily grazed upon the surface seemed somehow to be inherently improbable. We knew that the almost unbelievable production of oil in the Salt Creek Field[63] was making the

[62]In the nineteen twenties, optimists referred to Kemmerer as Wyoming's Tulsa. Obviously, Robert Rose had plenty of company in his enamourment with the petroleum possibilities of Western Wyoming.

[63]Located forty miles north of Casper, Wyoming, the Salt Creek oil field is one of the legendary oil fields of the world. In an area roughly defined as 22,000 acres, Salt Creek by 1970 had produced over 400,000,000 barrels of light oil. The first so-called well (in reality a seep or sump) was drilled in 1881. Three years later this same well had been deepened to 350 feet, with accumulated daily output of 350 barrels. The Salt Creek boom really got under way in 1908; and in the next ten years this wild, barren land, attracted entrepreneurs, promoters, zealots, engineers and wildcatters. Some of the more substantial, with the names of—Verner Z. Reed, Henry Blackmer, H. E. Stock, William M. Fitzhugh, Oliver Shoup, Cy Iba—have been permanently engraved in

fortunate few tremendously wealthy; but Salt Creek was more than three hundred miles from La Barge. We knew also that for a number of years there had been a few wells fifty miles south of Kemmerer in Uinta County,[64] but the best of these had never produced more than about ten barrels daily and everyone who had tried to operate them had gone broke. Anyway, only a few shallow wells had been drilled at La Barge; and the geologists said that the small quantities of oil that had been found there came from stray sands, that there was a big fault at the

Wyoming's history. Harold D. Roberts, *Salt Creek, Wyoming: The Story of a Great Oil Field* (Denver, 1956); Gene M. Gressley, "The French, Belgians, and Dutch Come to Salt Creek," The *Business History Review*, (Winter, 1970) 44, pp. 498–519.

[64]In referring to the Spring Valley field, Rose was recognizing one of the earliest oil discoveries in the state of Wyoming. Jim Bridger is said to have collected petroleum from nearby oil seeps to "grease" the wagon axles of emigrants passing by Fort Bridger in the 1850's. A. C. Veatch of the U. S. Geological Survey characterized the geological structure of the field in *Bulletin* 285 of the U. S. Geological Survey in 1905. Typically, the Spring Valley field has been discovered again and again, with boom after boom. An Amoco discovery in southwestern Wyoming, in 1976, created such excitement that this "play" has been compared to the Alaskan discoveries—erroneously it might be added. "Oil Industry in Spring Valley Field," *Wyoming Industrial Journal* (July, 1902), p. 43; *Wyoming Industrial Journal* (April, 1903), p. 255; W. R. Calvert, "Report on Part of the Spring Valley Field, Uinta County," and "Report on the Geology and Oil Possibilities of the Barnsley-Spaulding Block," by Bertrand deGraff, both manuscript reports located in the Petroleum History and Research Center, University of Wyoming.

edge of the mountains just to the west, and that there was no closure.

None of us knew anything about stray sands, or faults, or closures. We didn't even know that oil occurred in sands or what an oil sand was.

But one day someone said he had heard an oil-man from Salt Creek say something about the possibility that there might be a "mother pool" to the north of the La Barge field. By the next day, everyone was talking about the mother pool and wondering what and where it might be.

The words seemed mysteriously convincing, particularly when an elderly gentleman with a benign countenance and streaks of long hair combed across the top of a bald head registered one afternoon at the Kemmerer Hotel, dressed in high laced boots, khaki pants and leather jacket. He said he was a geologist from Salt Lake City and talked glibly about anticlines, synclines, escarpments, faults, oil sands, closures, and other things the rest of us didn't know anything about. He'd been up to Dry Piney, he said, about ten miles north of La Barge and felt confident that Thomas Mackey[65] had discovered the mother pool.

That proved to be my undoing, although, listening eagerly to the geologist's learned dissertations, I felt an ardent wish that I might have known Mr.

[65]Thomas Mackey was Rose's pseudonym for Thomas Lackey. Although few even recall Lackey today, he left an indelible impression on Rose's mentality and pocketbook.

Mackey and have been on friendly terms with him, realizing, of course, that, with the "mother pool" so firmly in his grasp, he would need the services of an energetic and enterprising lawyer. Later I became pretty well acquainted with him, and found the acquaintanceship to be a rather expensive luxury.

The Salt Lake geologist said that Lemuel Bird[66] and Donald McIntosh[67] were providing Mr. Mackey with funds for exploratory drilling. With these gentlemen I had a slight acquaintance already. Mr. McIntosh, who lived outside the little town of Big Piney, was cashier of the State Bank which he had organized at that place two or three years before, and was of course a person of some consequence in the Green River Valley. Bird was a much more important individual, being the owner of two or three large cattle ranches in the vicinity, and the sponsor of the new town of Marbleton[68] where he had recently erected a log hotel, a general store of the same material, a frame bank building and a saloon, all which, except the saloon, he operated himself and with but little assistance.

No one except Lem Bird could see any possible

[66]Lemuel Bird was Rose's pseudonym for Charles Budd, the founder of Marbleton. The Budd family, from the 1870's, have played a tremendous role in the livestock industry of Wyoming.

[67]Donald McIntosh, another Rose *nom de plume*; he may have been Lackey's son-in-law.

[68]Marbleton had its being in the dreams of Charles P. Budd. Begun in 1912, its storied life was but brief, and soon Budd moved back to Big Piney.

excuse for the existence of the town of Marbleton or any of the enterprises which its sponsor had brought into existence, except perhaps the considerable number of less prosperous ranchmen and itinerant cowhands who found the credit denied them at the bank, bars and mercantile establishments in Big Piney cheerfully extended, if not actually urged upon them, in Marbleton.

But to the conservative businessmen of the old town, Lemuel Bird was nothing more than just a bullheaded outlaw. Big Piney was an up-and-coming town. Why the hell did Lem Bird want to go and try to start another town only a mile across the creek? Everyone in Big Piney was quite certain it was just Lem's damned bullheadedness and that his new town would never succeed anyway.

And everyone was right on both counts, at least the latter. For a time Marbleton hummed with activity. On Saturday nights the saloon was crowded with cowpokes from all over the valley, buying round after round of drinks, usually "on the cuff;" and patronage at Jim Black's saloon next door to his Big Piney Hotel suffered a sharp decline. Cattlemen of the less prosperous sort found no difficulty in borrowing at the Marbleton Bank whatever amounts they might need to carry their outfits through the winter; and if cashier Joe Daly hesitated to make a substantial loan on a second mortgage, all the borrower needed to do was to go across the road and get Lemuel Bird's endorsement on his note.

With that endorsement the loan was never denied, for Mr. Bird was not only president of the bank but its board of directors as well, and withal a most obliging person. He seemed to take no little satisfaction from the fact that the Big Piney Bank's loan account was gradually growing smaller and smaller, while attaching little or no importance to the obvious fact that most of the loans his own bank was making were those that the rival bank had refused.

At the Marbleton general store the situation was very much the same. The place was crowded most of the time, especially in the evenings; and the patrons usually went away with their vehicles loaded down with flour, sugar, bacon, clothing, and canned goods of all sorts. Seldom did anyone pay cash, and as it ultimately turned out, many of the customers never paid at all. To court disaster the more effectively, Mr. Bird did his own bookkeeping as well as waiting on the trade; and many of the customers, all of whom were free to wait on themselves, frequently forgot to check in their purchases with the storekeeper, whom they naturally regarded as a very fine sort of fellow, while the storekeeper, on his part, frequently forgot to enter purchases on the books.

Bird's world was a small one, extending no farther than his general store, his log hotel next door, his nice-looking bank across the street, and his two or three ranches a short distance from town, one of which he soon found it necessary to sell in order to provide funds with which to bolster his sagging bank and put merchandise on his shelves to sell on credit to his appreciative customers. But in this little world he was king, a modest king to be sure with none of the trappings of royalty, small of stature, reserved though confident, friendly but inclined to be somewhat patronizing, and with a manner of dress but little better than that of his loyal subjects, in whose integrity and ultimate success he cherished unbounded faith—but none the less a king, and a most beneficent one.

The saloon, as I recall it, was the first of what might be called the Bird enterprise to fold up, and the bank came next. A tragic incident contributed to both failures, though neither was really a failure since the depositors of the bank were ultimately paid in full, and so far as I know, so were the breweries and distilleries that supplied merchandise to the saloon. Anyway, just as these two institutions had been linked closely together throughout their brief careers—the bank freely lending money to the saloon so that the latter could freely extend credit to its thirsty patrons—they both discontinued business about simultaneously and for the same reason.

Old Bill Ransom[69] had for many years been a thrifty and moderately successful ranchman a few miles out of town, but when Marbleton began its somewhat abortive boom the bright lights in the store windows seemed much more alluring than the

[69]While Big Piney residents have pleasant recollections of "Old Bill" Ransom, little remains of a biography.

coal oil lamp with its badly smoked chimney that rested on his kitchen table. The old man soon acquired the habit of coming to town every Saturday afternoon, doing a little shopping at the general store, having supper at the hotel next door, and then attending the dance to which Lem Bird treated the countryside each weekend as a part of his general good will program, a feature far less costly, by the way, than the generous lending of the bank or the equally generous credit policy of the store.

On one of his earliest visits to the hotel Ransom caught sight of the rather broadly built middle-aged woman who presided in the kitchen and served the products of her culinary art to the Bird family and the two or three paying guests, though, like the store customers, few of them actually paid. It was love at first sight; and three or four weeks later old Bill, whose badly crippled leg and advanced years made it difficult to feed and brand cattle, got a job swamping out the saloon and tending bar during the early hours of the day before the rush came. A few weeks later he took the combination cook and waitress to Kemmerer where they were married by the local justice of the peace.

That night they took lodging in Bill's room off the hall that ran back of the saloon, expecting the next morning to go on out to Ransom's ranch to settle down to a quiet and comfortable, if uneventful, old age. But it was a long time before they got there, and not until the tardy bridegroom had served a three-year term in the penitentiary at Rawlins.

It all came about in this wise. There was bitter enmity between the swamper and Slim Creedon, a migrant cowpoke who was inclined to be something of a troublemaker in the valley and very much of a prankster. Creedon had induced cashier Daly, always ready for a little fun after banking hours, to join him in charivariing the newlyweds; and together they ran down the hall about midnight to the door of the bridal chamber, Creedon loudly demanding entrance and attempting to break down the door. This was old Bill's chance to settle his score with Creedon, for well he knew that the law would justify him in going to any extreme that might seem necessary in defending his "castle" against an invader. Suddenly aroused, no doubt from a deep sleep, he seized his revolver lying on the table at the head of the bridal couch, and fired through the door. Unfortunately the bank cashier had just relieved Slim at the task of pushing the door in, and it was Daly, not Creedon, who caught the full force of the bullet from the aged bridegroom's revolver.

The Marbleton bank, of course, closed until after the funeral, which occurred two days later, as did also the saloon; and after the funeral there seemed no very good reason to reopen either. A little later the hotel followed suit for the sufficient reasons that there was neither cook nor waitress and the hostelry's most consistent patron was likely to be absent for some time. Gradually the shelves at the general store gave the appearance of being less adequately stocked with merchandise, and most of its customers resumed paying cash at the Piney Mercantile Company and Frank Birney's store in the old established town across the creek.

The buildings that once housed Lemuel Bird's hotel and general store still stand, as do the half dozen or more log dwellings that Mr. Bird had built for his retainers; but the neat frame structures where money once flowed freely to eager borrowers and hard liquor was once freely poured out to thirsty cowpokes have been moved away. Long ago Lem Bird's cattle went to Ez Truman by voluntary foreclosure, though generous Ez permitted Mr. Bird to retain one of his ranches—and his stock in the Dry Piney Oil Company, in which, though it had long since lost all pecuniary value it may have once had, its owner cherished it with a warm sentimental interest.

As I have already said, when I learned from the Salt Lake City geologist that Thomas Mackey had discovered the "mother pool" some ten miles north of the La Barge field, I experienced a deep desire somehow to become better acquainted with the future oil magnate. The desire itself could have done no particular harm, for it would doubtless have soon passed away. It was its gratification that proved to be costly to an extent quite inconsistent with my limited earning capacity.

One pleasant afternoon three men entered my law office on the second floor of a new brick building[70] that had been constructed next door to the Kemmerer Savings Bank. They were an odd looking trio. One, a short plainly dressed fellow with small slanting blue eyes, a short upper lip, and a somewhat patronizing smile, was Lemuel Bird. Next to him stood a somewhat taller man with a conspicuously high brow, a large round head, long straight black hair, inordinately long arms with a thin bony hand dangling at the end of each, and ears no less conspicuous than Jimmie Durante's proboscis. This was Thomas Mackey. Third was Donald McIntosh, a tall raw-boned ruddy-faced Scotchman whose almost constant smile revealed a mouthful of rusty-hued gold teeth.

I confess to no disappointment upon learning that they and the Dry Piney oil field were already experiencing difficulties that required the services of a lawyer. McIntosh, who appeared to have been selected as spokesman for the trio, related the circumstances that had brought them to my office, omitting none of the details.

Old man Ford[71] had for a number of years held a permit from the Government to dig coal upon a

[70]Although only two doors from his former office, some residents of Kemmerer have insisted that the only office attorney Rose ever had was that "little wooden building."

[71]Conceivably Rose has reference to the Lackey-Durnford title contest spread over the first page of the Kemmerer *Camera* for December 15, 1920.

quarter-section of land in the vicinity of Dry Piney Creek. Although the product was of inferior quality, he and his son Dan had been able occasionally to sell a wagon load in the nearby town of Big Piney and had thus kept his permit in very good standing.

When Mackey discovered what he believed to be an oil structure he found the Ford coal mine to be in the very heart of it. Nevertheless, undaunted, he staked the quarter-section, posted and recorded his location notices, set up his rig and began drilling. When Ford appeared upon the scene a few days later for a load of coal, Mackey invited him to his cabin for a conference. A verbal contract was readily entered into by which each agreed to respect the other's rights. Ford was to continue to dig coal, Mackey was to drill for oil, and in consideration for Ford's agreement to abstain from contesting Mackey's oil location, Mackey was to give Ford a royalty of two percent of any oil that he might produce and young Dan was to have a job at the well. Both men expressed themselves as being thoroughly satisfied with the arrangement. McIntosh was to reduce the agreement to writing and Mackey and Ford were to sign it.

Young Ford reported at the well early the next morning for work. With Mackey handling the drilling line, Red Journet sharpening bits, Dan Ford running the engine and McIntosh serving as general utility man, the work progressed rapidly. Midafternoon a few weeks later there was a tremendous roar deep down in the earth. Instantly, with a deafening sound, a pillar of oil and gas shot out of the hole and over the top of the derrick. Light green oil covered the ground for several rods in every direction. As soon as they could fight their way through the spray Mackey and Red, with the aid of a big wrench, turned the shut-off valve and, except for a small amount of gas leaking through the valve, all was again quiet.

"Eureka" shouted McIntosh. "Don't know what you mean by that," was Mackey's quiet rejoinder, "but this looks like an oil well to me." He pulled a half-full whiskey bottle from his pocket, emptied its contents on the ground, filled it with oil that had been caught in a can standing near the well, and held it up to the sun. "That's the finest grade of oil I've ever seen come out of the ground. You can run your car on that stuff, Mac. Won't need to buy any more gasoline." Then, as he started to walk away, he added, "Well, boys, let's get cleaned up. You're all coming up to my cabin for supper."

That night there was a lively celebration at Mackey's cabin, and a feast such as had seldom, if ever, been spread at an oil camp. The conversation, of course, was all about the discovery of oil. Mackey noticed that young Dan, a little sullen, was not participating in the conversation. The optimism of McIntosh knew no bounds. "We're millionaires right now, Tom." "Yes?" Mackey responded indifferently. "Of course we are Tom. We've got over six thousand acres. That means hundreds of oil wells just like this one." "Oh, is this an oil well?" There was a note of skepticism in Mackey's voice. "We won't know much about it until we make at least a 24-hour test, and I've seen a lot of oil wells turn to water. Anyway, Mac, one swallow don't make a spring, you know." "Aw, you're crazy, Tom." Mac, refusing to be discouraged, turned to Journet. "Red, what do you say? You've drilled a lot of wildcats." "Well, I don't know Mac." Red had also noticed young Ford's silence. "Can't tell anything about it 'til it's tested." Mac still refused to be discouraged. "Whatever you fellows may think about it, I say this thing's worth millions."

Although it was yet early, young Dan Ford said he guessed he'd go to bed, got up from the table, and walked out of the door. "What's the matter with that guy?" Mackey asked, as though thinking aloud. "Must have something in his craw." Mac, obviously puzzled, said *he* hadn't noticed anything out of the way. Mackey stepped outside. A moment later he called to Mac to "come on out." "Well, Mac, you see Dan didn't go to bed." Mackey's quiet manner evinced no surprise. In the bright moonlight they saw young Dan, well past the bunkhouse, walking rapidly in the direction of Big Piney. Silently they looked down the road until he was out of sight.

The two men sat down on a rig timber that lay in

front of the cabin. Mackey took a cigarette out of his pocket, held it in his left hand, and with the fingers of his right began nervously removing the tobacco, bit by bit, until there was nothing left of it. It seemed to Mac that the operation took a long time. He'd seen Tom do the same thing before when something was bothering him. He wished he'd say something.

Mac at last broke the silence. "I didn't get around to put that agreement with old man Ford in writing." Mackey took another cigarette from his pocket and began tearing it to pieces. After a long pause, Mac went on, "Gad, I wish I hadn't talked so damned much—wasn't smart enough to understand why you were so pessimistic." At last Mackey spoke. There was no bitterness in his voice. "Forget it, Mac—let's turn in."

Neither of the men slept that night. Mac spent the night worrying. Why hadn't he put that contract in writing? Mackey spent the night figuring things out. If the Fords should institute a contest, the issue would be whether the land was more valuable for coal or for oil. He would put the well on production as soon as possible, and await whatever action the Fords might take.

One morning a week later Mackey was adjusting some equipment at the top of the derrick when he saw young Dan Ford driving a stake at a quarter-section corner at the top of a hill only a short distance away. As soon as the stake had been driven firmly into the ground he fastened to it a small piece of cardboard.

Mackey called to McIntosh, who was working at some papers inside the cabin, and the two men made their way rapidly up the hillside. "What does this mean, Dan?" Mackey asked grimly. "It means that I've bought this quarter-section from the Government, and you'd better get off." Young Dan seemed confident of his position. "I don't believe you Dan," Mackey responded. "This piece of land's worth a million dollars. I'll fight you for it. If you can whip me it's yours. If you can't it's mine. What do you say?" "I say you're a damned fool, Tom. I'm twenty years younger than you and thirty pounds heavier. If you want to take the beating of your life it's alright with me." Mackey showed no sign of fright.

Both agreed that McIntosh should referee the bout. Mac marked off the regulation squared circle, and called the men to the center of the ring. "This will be the strangest prizefight anyone's ever heard of—ten miles from nowhere, a few prairie dogs for spectators, and a million dollar piece of land for a side bet. If you fellows mean to stake that land on a fistic encounter, shake hands on it, retire to your corners, and come out fighting. I'll hold the watch." McIntosh had been something of a boxer in his youth. Moreover, he had had occasion to observe Mackey's skill in the use of his fists and had little doubt concerning the outcome of the match.

Young Dan came out of his corner swinging as though he expected to make short work of it. But, with an agility that the younger man was not expecting, Mackey stepped inside his blows or ducked them. As the first round was about to end, Mackey ducked a vicious swing and, stepping inside, landed a hard blow to young Dan's chin. The referee called time. Young Dan looked confused. Only one blow had landed, and it wasn't he who had landed it.

As the men came to the center of the ring for the second round young Dan threw a straight right at Mackey's head, but Mackey stepped back quickly and the blow did but little damage. Then, forgetting his earlier experience, the young man began swinging. Mackey again stepped inside and landed a stiff right to young Dan's chin and then another and another. Dan went to the ground, and the referee began counting. At the count of four young Dan got to his feet and, now thoroughly enraged, rushed at his opponent. Mackey was caught off guard. They grappled, and as they did so, moved closer and closer to the edge of the hill. Finally they stumbled and, wrapped in each other's belligerent embrace, rolled two hundred feet to the bottom of the steep hill, where the battle was resumed. By now young Dan had completely lost control of himself and again started swinging at his opponent. Mackey, awaiting his chance, then stepped inside and, with all his remaining strength started to rain rights and lefts to the point of his opponent's chin.

Young Dan went down for the complete count. Nothing further would probably have come of the incident but for the fact that the count proved to be an unusually long one. McIntosh and Mackey carried young Dan into a nearby cabin and doused him thoroughly with cold water. When this procedure failed to revive him, they loaded the unconscious pugilist into a car and hurried him to the doctor's office in Big Piney. Returning a few moments later with Lemuel Bird and finding that the physician had been unable to resuscitate his patient, the three oil men decided that it might be advisable to consult a lawyer.

Scarcely had the narrative of the incident been finished when the sheriff entered with a warrant for Mackey's arrest. I could see that my visitors were likely to prove to be valuable clients; and my ownership of a substantial interest in the newly discovered oil field did not seem to be a completely remote possibility. Later in the same day came the reassuring news that Mackey's young adversary had regained consciousness and seemed to have entirely recovered from the effects of his unhappy experience. Assault and battery was the charge lodged against the winner of the encounter, a moderate fine was cheerfully paid, and Mackey's reputation for efficiency in the use of his fists was so enhanced that no one thereafter attempted to jump his oil claims. In the contest which came on for hearing a few months later the United States Land Office upheld

Mackey's contention that the land in controversy was more valuable for oil than for coal and recognized the validity of his locations. No appeal was taken from the decision.

A few days later the trio visited my office again. They wanted to form a corporation. The capital stock was to be only one hundred thousand shares, par value one dollar each, all which was to be issued in equal parts to my three clients, except one hundred shares which was to go to each of five individuals who had obligingly permitted their names to be used as locators, and except a thousand shares which I was to receive for my services. It was understood, of course, that the newly organized company would require all my time and that the dividends that I would receive would make the ordinary practice of law both unnecessary, and, in view of my anticipated opulence, quite superfluous. Title to the oil claims, was, of course, to be transferred to the company in consideration for the issuance of the stock. It occurred to me to suggest that at least one-half the stock ought to be retained in the treasury for development purposes; but a sufficient answer to my suggestion was that arrangements had been made to lease the field to a big operator from the coast who would fully develop the property. I was to prepare the lease for execution of the deal the following day.

When the "big operator" came in promptly at the appointed hour, he appeared to me to be noth-

ing more than a very small promoter without any
intention of actually drilling and without the means
with which even to purchase the necessary equipment. But my clients appeared thoroughly satisfied
with the assurances he had given them; and their
faith in his good intentions remained unshaken
even when, after the lease had been executed and
delivered, he asked for a small loan, explaining that
he had carelessly left his checkbook at home. Un-
grudgingly, Mr. Bird counted out the currency. The
loan, of course, was never repaid. Upon investigation the man proved to be a fraud; and a little later
I was employed to sue for the cancellation of the
lease. Months passed before the litigation was terminated. In the meantime no progress was made
toward tapping the "mother pool" and I resumed
the quite necessary pursuit of earning a living in the
general practice of law.

Not much later the Bird enterprises in the new
town of Marbleton began their rapid decline, and
Mr. Bird found it inconvenient to advance further
funds, which at first he had poured lavishly into
Dry Pine drilling operations. Donald McIntosh,
who meantime had resigned his office at the bank to
serve as Mackey's toolpusher and runner of errands
and had sold his little ranch to provide his share of
the necessary operating expenses, died. The whole
responsibility of carrying on seemed to devolve
upon Mr. Mackey, to whom in utter desperation the
other directors now gave a lease covering a large

part of the field. Mackey, though without funds, had unbounded confidence in the structure, and in this he was supported by the Salt Lake geologist. The cup of confidence of these two gentlemen was full to the brim and running over; and I may as well confess that my own cup was nearly full; for had I not seen oil shoot from a shallow hole clear over the top of the derrick? And had I not driven my car more than two hundred miles with nothing in the tank but crude oil from this same hole? Somewhat disturbing, however, was the fact that a little later something happened to the discovery well that seriously interfered with the flow of oil and in fact, at least temporarily, stopped it altogether. Mackey, as always, had a ready explanation. Paraffin from the extremely high-grade oil had clogged the casing; all that was needed was to clean the hole out. Meantime the well would produce enough gas for fuel for the camp and further drilling.

Admitting that the situation in the discovery well might prove a little discouraging to prospective investors, Mackey and the geologist were nevertheless certain that they could raise all the capital that might be required to drill at least one well to the deep sands. After that, of course, not only would the operation pay for itself, but huge dividends would pour into the coffers of the few fortunate stockholders. But unfortunately the geologist's friends in Salt Lake City manifested no interest in the proposition. In fact, they admitted that they had invested in the despised La Barge field, a few miles to the south, which now, to our utter surprise, if not secret disappointment, was producing bountifully from newly tapped deep sands. Mackey and the geologist met with no greater success in Los Angeles, San Francisco, or Seattle, and, their funds entirely exhausted, finally returned to Kemmerer convinced that the emissaries of one or more, perhaps all, of the major oil companies had injected poison into the minds of prospective investors in order that, after we had come to the end of our rope, they might go in and have the great "mother pool" all to themselves. To my untrained mind the idea seemed at least somewhat plausible.

Now reduced to the necessity of working for a living, the Salt Lake geologist got a job with one of the companies operating at La Barge, and we were thus deprived of his counsel and prestige. McIntosh was dead. Bird, struggling valiantly to keep his Marbleton enterprises going, had served notice that he could lend no further financial assistance. And on top of all that, the major oil companies had frustrated Mackey's efforts to enlist new capital. Mackey and I were all alone. But the "mother pool" must be tapped. We would not be robbed of our valuable property by the major oil companies, one or all of them. It had become a matter of principle.

I had two or three thousand dollars in the bank which I had saved from a none-too-lucrative law practice. Mackey was an oil well driller of years of

experience in Texas and Mexico, and as he assured
me "By gad," he could "make hole" himself with
only the help of a young ranch lad whose father had
a small amount of stock in the company and who
would charge but little for his time. There was an
old Star drilling rig already at the well, and a Ford
engine. The discovery well would produce an
abundance of gas for fuel. The whole operation
would cost no more than about two hundred fifty
dollars a month, including necessary repairs, and
we'd very soon have enough oil to defray expenses
anyway.

That's the way I got started on the road to ruin.
Perhaps the word "ruin" is an exaggeration. But it
certainly was the road to endless annoyances along
which my scanty funds were strewn with reckless
abandon.

Occasionally in the intervening years I have en-
deavored to explain to myself why a man whose
very profession requires the careful weighing of
both sides of every question and the selection of the
course supported by a preponderance of the evidence, should in his own affairs follow a course dic-
tated by neither reason nor logic, a course for
which, if he were to ponder upon it at all, he could
find not a single plausible excuse. To pretend, as I
have already done, that it was a matter of principle
would be sheer hypocrisy. With some degree of
justification it might be said to have been a determination to carry on an undertaking once entered

upon. With perfect frankness, it should be admitted that it was pure foolishness, and nothing more, nothing less.

When we entered upon our ill-fated adventure, summer was well nigh spent and the "winter of our discontent" would soon be upon us, a winter which at an elevation of eight thousand feet would cover the ground with three to five feet of snow, piled even deeper at the cabins where the fleecy substance would be interrupted in its endless journey before a wind which, at that altitude, blew with a consistent velocity, the like of which I have known nowhere else, even in wind-swept Wyoming.

During those months I made some disconcerting discoveries concerning my partner's methods of carrying on his operations—or perhaps I should better say picking them up and laying them down again under circumstances which, so far as I could see, afforded no excuse for either. Before the snow would fall in stifling quantities there would yet be a month, possibly six weeks. In that time the work on a new well should be at least well started; and the discovery well should be cleaned out and in production.

But when, a month or so after I had delivered my first check, I went to the field filled with lively anticipation, I found that very little had been accomplished. Always convincing, Mackey explained that there had been a "fishing" job to do, the hole had caved in below the casing, the lad whom he had engaged as a helper had been ill, and other unforeseeable conditions too numerous to mention had arisen to impede progress. However, he was now just ready to resume drilling. I remained until the next day to see the drilling line begin pounding away, handed my associate another check, and a little disappointed, but still hopeful, returned to Kemmerer.

A few days later Mackey drove up in front of my office in a brand new Cadillac car, purchased no doubt on credit. Though the thought seemed an unworthy one, I couldn't help wondering whether possibly my last check had been used as a down payment.

As I have said, Mr. Mackey was unfailingly convincing. Manifestly it was necessary now and then to travel some distance to purchase replacements for broken parts; clearly enough a car was indispensible; and when you are buying an automobile you might as well buy a good one. Right now he was on his way to Casper to get a drill stem. It was about ten days later when he stopped at my office enroute to the field. Just what delayed him so long in Casper I've now forgotten; but time was passing, and winter in that section of the state usually arrives disgustingly on time.

Shortly thereafter snow fell in Kemmerer. There was a much heavier fall at Big Piney where the thermometer went to ten degrees below zero. I knew, of course, that at the field winter had arrived for a long sojourn and assumed that work would have to be shut down until late in the spring. There was some comfort in the thought that the interim would afford relief from the financial strain which had already begun to be a little irksome.

Other than a request for funds I heard nothing from Mr. Mackey until almost two months later, when one desperately cold afternoon a few days before Christmas, he walked into the office clad in heavy overshoes, padded pants, sheepskin coat, and fur cap and mittens. He had driven into town in a bobsled with a lumber wagon box on the runners. Mackey thrived on disaster. As I had partially learned and was to learn more thoroughly as time went on, it was his habit to discontinue work in the summertime in order to attend to fancied business matters from San Francisco to Philadelphia, and to toil fiendishly when the thermometer registered from ten to twenty degrees below zero; the cabin where he and his helper lived was a scarely noticeable high spot in the snow, and no one less courageous than he would even think of attempting to drill an oil well.

Since last I had seen him he had abandoned our almost completed well—another practice which I later found to be characteristic of his methods—and had moved the rig to what he thought to be a likelier location. And he seemed to be right, for at a depth of only five hundred feet he had encountered a substantial flow of oil, though in volume far too insignificant to indicate the tapping of the much-sought-for "mother pool," a term, by the way, which we had begun to discard as a little sophomoric, particularly since the wells at La Barge were now yielding still more bountifully and the proven area had been greatly expanded with no indication that the limit had been reached.

Dry Piney, we were compelled to admit, lagged far behind La Barge. Still we now had two holes in the ground, one of which, though shallow, at least yielded oil, even if in small volume. The situation seemed sufficiently encouraging to impel me to hand my collaborator another check, and, having reported that he now had two men working at the field instead of only one, against my urgent advice he started back to Dry Piney in a heavy snow storm.

When next I saw him late the following spring, I learned how the journey had been accomplished and of the vicissitudes encountered along the way. At the end of the third day out of Kemmerer he had reached a point where the trail took off for Dry Piney, and the following morning had started to negotiate the remaining twelve miles with no companion other than Pup, his huge police dog. By the time they had traveled three-quarters of the distance night was upon them, the temperature had fallen to a point not within the recollection of even the oldest inhabitant, and the snow, driven by a howling west wind, blinded man and beast. They were off the trail. The horses knew it and refused then to face the blinding blizzard. Mackey decided to attempt the rest of the journey on foot. Soon he began to feel a drowsiness that no amount of willpower could withstand. Staggering blindly along, completely exhausted, he stumbled to the edge of a dry wash and fell in three feet of fresh loose snow. The last he remembered, Pup was tugging insistently at his coat sleeve while the tired man was languidly telling the big dog to go on away and let him sleep.

About midnight the men at the camp were aroused by the furious barking of a dog. When they opened the door Pup started running down the hill, then back to the cabin, then down the hill again, and all the time barking excitedly. Hurriedly saddling a pair of horses, they followed him. Half an hour later the dog suddenly stopped, and began pawing frantically in the snow. Placing the half-frozen man in the sled, which was found only a hundred feet away, with Pup lying close against his master as if to keep him warm, the long pull to the camp was begun. Mackey had his own foolhardiness to thank for almost losing his life and his faithful dog to thank for saving it.

During the rest of the winter there was but little work done at the field, and the next summer Mackey again had business from San Francisco to Philadelphia. However, he was back at the field in the fall a little earlier than usual, and before I knew anything about it, had moved the Star drilling rig to a new location. By the time winter set in he was ready to drill. Late in January there was a fire at the camp that made the adjacent hills stand out in bold relief and lit up the valley to the east. Two or three feet of snow made the roads around Big Piney impassable, and the fire would be out before anyone could reach the camp anyway. But it didn't go out. On the contrary the flames rose higher and higher. Soon the residents down in the valley noticed that it was just one single flame, a pillar of fire rising a hundred feet or more toward the sky. For a month or more it burned. The fuel upon which it fed seemed inexhaustible.

Mackey was in my office a few days after the fire had been extinguished. In the new hole he was drilling the bit had suddenly released a tremendous flow of gas which had instantly ignited. His hands were badly burned, and, of course, our only drilling rig had been completely destroyed. This seemed to me to be the end.

But I didn't yet know Mackey. My companion in misfortune now turned promoter. Within little more than a week he returned from a trip to Los Angeles with a ten thousand dollar drawing account. He had sold a forty-acre lease and contracted to drill a well to a depth of a thousand feet. A new Star drilling rig was to be furnished which, of course, was to remain the property of the man who was providing the money.

Early the following September Mackey sent word

that the well was about to be brought in. I arrived at the field a little before noon the following day to find him splicing the bailing line, standing astride the spool upon which the line was wound. I noticed that there was a slack in the line as it came out of the hole, perhaps fifteen feet or so, and that this was tied to a derrick post with what appeared to me to be a very badly worn piece of rope. Sitting in a half reclining position against the wall of the "doghouse" that surrounded the well, I was soon half asleep. Suddenly aroused by a strange jarring sound, I noticed that the slack was gone and the line hung quivering in the well.

"Bob, better come over here." Mackey was speaking in an ordinary conversational voice without the slightest tremor of excitement. Running quickly around the bullwheel, I saw what had happened. The line had caught his right leg just below the knee, his leg was crushed almost to the thinness of a piece of heavy cloth, and his right foot thrown up almost to his face.

No one could have failed to observe that I was frantic. Mackey turned and looked steadily down at me a few seconds. Then, still in a quiet tone, but in a way he had of spacing his words for emphasis, "Well, keep your shirt on." For a moment he toyed with the toe of his shoe. "Bob, the boys are down over the hill—better tell them to come over and get me out of this."

Soon we had him lying on a bed in the cabin; and

he was giving instructions as casually as though he were laying out the work for the day. "Red, put a bedspring and mattress in the truck—and string a tarp over the top—let's get going. Bob, go to Big Piney and get old Doc Bush—meet us on the road—make it snappy—and say, bring along two or three quarts of bourbon."

It was two in the morning when we arrived at the Kemmerer hospital. He had consumed two quarts of bourbon on the way. His tongue loosened by the intoxication, he talked incessantly. It was all about Texas—the historic battle of San Jacinto, in which he said his grandfather and three great uncles had been killed—the Alamo—Sam Houston and his historic three-hour speech trying vainly to dissuade the Texas legislature from joining the seceding states—the wildcat drilling he had done for the Standard of New Jersey somewhere in the Lone Star State—something about a shooting affair, and a sheriff's posse. But not a word concerning the agony he must have been suffering, or even the faintest expression of pain.

I saw Mackey, of course, frequently during the long months he was in the hospital. About a year after the accident he limped into my office leaning heavily on a cane. "Well, Bob, I'm getting alright again—pretty near as good as new—'bout ready to get to makin' hole." I didn't show much enthusiasm. Certainly this very badly crippled man wasn't serious.

He laid a supply company catalogue on my desk and pointed to a picture of a water well rig. "That's all we need," he said. "Guaranteed to go a thousand feet—only costs five hundred." I was unable to stifle a smile. His face flushed as, a little resentfully, he went on, "By gad I can make hole as well as I ever did." "You're a great guy," was my sincere response. And I wrote out a check for five hundred dollars and handed it to him.

A few weeks later I drove out to the field to see how he was getting along. He had driven one hole down to a depth of two hundred feet, abandoned it, and started another at a new location. Mackey was running the line while his wife puttered with a sputtering Ford engine in an effort to keep it going in order to supply power to the drilling machine.

One afternoon shortly before the end of World War II, I met Mackey in the lobby of a Casper hotel. His wife was in the hospital with an incurable malady. We had chatted only a few moments when he handed me a note he had received the day before from his daughter in San Francisco, and with it a telegram. "The War Department regrets to inform you,"[72] the usual message that has brought grief to thousands of homes.

Then he handed me a copy of the wire he had sent her. It was brief—"Girl, keep your chin up." Scarcely had I read it when a Western Union mes-

[72]The reference pertained to "Mackey's" son-in-law's death in the Second World War.

senger entered the lobby and handed Mackey a telegram. As he read it tears coursed down his wrin-
kled weather-beaten face. Then he straightened his
stooped shoulders a little, and an expression of exultant pride came over his face as he handed me the
message. It was as brief as the other. "Remember,
Dad, I'm Texas too," it said. As I handed it back he
turned and limped slowly toward the elevator.

To know Mackey was indeed costly. But it was
worth every cent it cost.

Chapter Ten

EVERY LAWYER in the course of years of practice has many unusual cases, all of them interesting at least to members of the legal profession. There are those charged with intense human interest, such, for example, as a case tried in the District Court in Kemmerer in 1918 in which a wealthy Philadelphian sought custody of a small grandchild upon the ground that the child's mother was financially unable to adequately provide for it, and in which a jury required but little time to decide that a mother's love was more important to the child than the governess and nurse which the rich grandparent offered to provide.

Involved in most cases are questions of law, sometimes intricate, sometimes confusing, and these alone are sufficient to command the interest of the lawyer. Frequently a vigorous cross-examination of a witness in an effort to obtain a truthful statement of facts is most stimulating. Many cases are interesting because of the unusual character and attitudes of litigants and witnesses, others because they are just plain funny.

An unusual case was one tried in the District Court in Kemmerer in the spring of 1918, unusual because of the character of the case itself and because of the manner in which it was disposed of. Parley Kent, a Star Valley farmer, was charged with stealing a house. Mr. H. S. Ridgley[73] of Cheyenne, one of the outstanding lawyers of the State, was retained by the county as special prosecutor to assist in this and a number of other criminal cases.

Shortly after I was employed for the defense, Kent told me how the situation came about. A few years before he had borrowed one thousand dollars from a local bank and was to give a mortgage on his eighty-acre farm to secure the loan. Before doing so he consulted a lawyer to whom he explained that he planned building a nice five-room frame house on the land. What he wanted to know was whether, in the event he was unable to repay the loan and the mortgage should be foreclosed, he would have the right to remove the house to another farm which he owned a mile or so away. The young lawyer, doubtless without giving the matter serious thought, ad-

---

[73]Beard's *History of Wyoming* identified H. S. Ridgley (1874–1937) as having "a state-wide legal practice, he being best known for his work in criminal law. . . ." After graduation from the University of Nebraska, Ridgley entered practice at North Platte, Nebraska. In 1903, five years after Ridgley had first hung up his shingle at North Platte, he was lured to Cody, Wyoming, by his North Platte neighbor William F. Cody. When Basin, Wyoming, was first founded, Ridgley decided that opportunities were better in this Big Horn Basin community and moved there in 1906. President Taft named him U. S. District Attorney at Cheyenne in 1911. With the exception of two years in California, Ridgley lived and practiced the rest of his life in Cheyenne. Rose encountered him as the unsuccessful opponent of John B. Kendrick in the 1914 gubernatorial election, and as a recalcitrant investor in the Cretaceous Oil Company.

vised him that he would. The advice was wrong, of course, because a building once constructed on a substantial foundation becomes, in legal contemplation, a part of the real estate itself and, as such, a part of the security for the loan.

As Kent feared, when the note became due he was unable to pay it; and, exercising what he believed to be his right, with the aid of a number of his good neighbors, jacked up the house, put rollers under it, and with an eight-horse team, hauled it off the place and down the road to the place it was to be set up. The bank had him arrested, and he was up for trial charged with stealing the house.

From the facts as they were related to me by my client I could see little chance for him to escape conviction, although certainly he was guilty of no intentional wrong since he had done only what he thought he had a right to do. But there was the old maxim that "Ignorance of the law is no excuse." There is always the chance, of course, that the lawyer on the other side may make some fatal mistake in the presentation of his case; and it occurred to me that in this unusual case the prosecutor might possibly overlook proving the essential fact that the severance of the building from its foundation and its removal from the property were not one continuous act. In that event the offense would be only trespass, not grand larceny, the offense with which Kent was charged.

A few days later the case was called for trial; and

after the jury was impaneled and sworn, Mr. Ridgley began his opening statement in which, under Wyoming practice he was required to explain to the Court and jury what evidence he expected to introduce in order to establish the prosecution's case.

Mr. Ridgley said that the State would prove that the house stood about an eighth of a mile from the road, that on the day mentioned in the Information certain witnesses living across the road from Kent's place saw him with a number of other men sever the house from its foundation, put rollers under it, hitch eight horses to the load, and start hauling it away. He said the operation took all the afternoon, and when darkness fell the house was about six or seven rods inside Kent's fence, still slowly moving toward his gate. What happened after dark, Mr. Ridgley said, of course the witnesses could not see, but early the next morning they saw the house about a quarter of a mile down the road. That, he concluded, would be the State's case.

He had omitted to mention the very thing necessary to make a case of larceny—he had not indicated that the State had any evidence that severing the building from its foundation and removing it from Kent's land were not one continous operation. I moved that the case be dismissed on the prosecuting attorney's opening statement.

"Have you stated to the jury all the evidence that you will be able to present, Mr. Ridgley?" Judge Craig asked. "Yes, I think so," was the prosecutor's reply. "Are you sure you have no additional evidence?" The Judge, very properly, was giving Mr. Ridgley an opportunity, if he could, to supply the missing evidence. "No", said the prosecutor with an air of assurance, "that is the State's case, and I think it is quite sufficient."

"The case is dismissed," said the Judge. "Since larceny is stealing and carrying or taking away of *personal property.* A building standing on a permanent foundation is *real estate*; it is a part of the land itself. If it is severed from the land and taken or carried away and the severance and the removal constitute *one continuous uninterrupted act*, it is only trespass, it is not larceny. This defendant is charged with *larceny*; he is *not* charged with *trespass.* Mr. Kent is discharged."

Knowing now that he had no right to remove the house, Kent moved it back and put it on the original foundation; the bank extended the loan an additional three-year period; Kent's crops during the next three years were good; he paid off the loan; and the house still stands where it was originally constructed.

This is the only case, so far as my observation goes, in which a person was tried on the charge of stealing a house, and the only one disposed of on the opening statement of the prosecuting attorney.

Chapter Eleven

"SLICK"[74] AND "BUM LAMB" are words that so far as I know you will not find in any standard dictionary with definitions that have any significance in the livestock country of the West; but the words have a very definite meaning to every cowman and to every flockmaster. It sometimes, though rarely, happens that a cow will go on with the herd leaving her calf behind before it is branded. That calf then is a "slick," and, at least in the early days, any cowboy who might find a slick on the open range was at liberty to put his outfit's brand on it. Some of the cowhands, of course, had their own brands, and not unnaturally there was the temptation for every rider to use his own brand rather than that of the outfit for which he was working. To some of them there seemed to be little difference between rescuing an abandoned calf from prowling coyotes on the open range and slyly picking one from another outfit's herd, throwing it over the saddle, and riding miles away before putting the rider's iron on it.

And so it happened that after a few years a cowhand who had actually bought and paid for not more than a few cattle—just enough to furnish an

---

[74]"Slick Ears" or "mavericks" were synonomous terms for roundup strays. For the usage of these slang expressions see, Mitford Mathews, *A Dictionary of Americanisms* (Chicago, 1951), II, p. 1366.

excuse for the ownership of a recorded brand—
would find himself to be the owner of a sizeable
herd and engaged in the livestock business on a substantial scale. Tradition has it that rivalry for the
hand of one of the few unmarried women in Western Wyoming in the early days resulted in her coming into the ownership of one of the largest cattle
outfits in that section of the State when cowpunch-
ers employed by other outfits engaged—until she
finally married one of them—in a good-natured
contest to see which one could put her brand on the
largest number of slicks.

It sometimes happens also that a ewe will disown
her lamb and that in trailing a band from the lamb-
ing ground to the winter range,[75] frequently past
one of the numerous coal mining camps in the vicinity of Kemmerer, a few of the lambs will be left
behind. These are "bum lambs." So it happened
that around the homes of a few of the miners in the
vicinity of Kemmerer, you would notice two or
three dozen sheep—"bum lambs" grown up. By the
summer of 1914 the cattlemen and flockmasters had
become pretty well organized and were waging relentless warfare against branding slicks and "rescuing" bum lambs.

One afternoon I looked up from my desk to see
in the doorway a woman of unusual proportions, so

[75]Winter range refers to an area where livestock were driv-
en by ranchers to winter—presumably a more protected region than the summer range.

large in fact that had the opening been a little smaller she would scarcely have been able to get through it. Without so much as nodding she seated herself in a chair opposite mine. Immediately after her a slight, intelligent-looking man entered and seated himself in the only other chair the office afforded, followed by a half-dozen men, whom I took to be coal miners.

The first man to enter started immediately to explain the matter that had brought a large delegation to my office. The men, he said, were Finlanders employed in the mines at Cumberland,[76] a small camp sixteen miles south of Kemmerer. Two of them, Hakaala and Mustonen, had been arrested and were to be tried the next day before Justice of the Peace Carnahan on a charge of stealing two bum lambs. The large woman kept the boarding house where Hakaala and Mustonen lived. Neither she nor any of the men, he said, could speak a word of English, and he therefore had come along to serve as interpreter. The other men were there as witnesses.

The interpreter, whose name I have forgotten, said that the men, including Hakaala and Mustonen,

---

[76]Founded in 1900, Cumberland had a brief moment of regional glory in the 1920's, when its band of brass and reed players, under the tutelage of bandmaster, V. B. Bovero, attracted applause wherever it played. With the coming of the thirties depression, Cumberland folded up and joined the ranks of Wyoming's ghost towns. Mary Lou Pence and Lola M. Homsher, *The Ghost Towns of Wyoming* (New York, 1956), pp. 204–205.

had been present at a wedding in the large woman's boarding house on the very night they were supposed to have stolen the lambs, that the festivities had lasted until daylight, and that they and the woman would all swear under oath that neither of the men had been out of the house from early in the evening until they went to the mine the next morning. They could not, therefore, have stolen the lambs.

As the interpreter proceeded with the narrative, the large woman interrupted now and again, and he was quick to convey to me the corrections that she had apparently made in his statement of the case. Two or three times Hakaala and Mustonen ventured to break in briefly, but each time the stern woman turned on them as though they had spoken out of turn, and I judged from their attitude and hers, although of course, I could not understand anything they said, that she had told them to keep still and mind their own business. It was evident that the woman was in command. A few times I directed questions to the accused men, but each time they were answered through the interpreter by the large woman, who sat stolidly throughout the conference apparently unable to understand a word I said. Her evident interest in the case and her unwillingness to let the others, even the men accused of the crime, have anything to say, excited a little suspicion on my part; but the situation was satisfactorily explained by the interpreter who said that all my visitors had but recently immigrated from Finland and that the boarding house woman, being a person of superior intelligence, was recognized as a leader among them.

The case was called for trial the next morning in Judge Carnahan's court. The old gentleman seemed a little more irascible than usual; and remembering the Skaggs trial only a short time before, I feared that he might not be inclined to look upon my clients with complete judicial impartiality. However, I took comfort in the fact that this case, unlike the other, was to be tried by a jury.

The State made a strong case. Mustonen and Hakaala, according to witnesses for the prosecution, rather than having recently arrived from the old country, had worked in the Cumberland mines for years. One of them had filed on a homestead not far away where he had a bunch of several hundred sheep, many of them with the tips of their ears cut off so as to destroy the owners' earmark. The two men had been under suspicion for a long time and were being closely watched by Deputy Sheriff Angus McDougall.[77] On the night in question the officer had actually seen them bring the lambs to a shed back of Hakaala's house where they had cut off the tips of the ears and clipped the wool so as to

[77]Today Angus McDougall comes to the memories of former Kemmerer citizens as a "hulk" of a man who was a sometime bartender and gambler. Interview with Mrs. Helen Mason Gernert and Mrs. Roy Mason, November 4, 1976.

obliterate the owner's paint brand. As soon as the
job was finished, McDougall had arrested the men
and taken the lambs into his possession. The Deputy's testimony, in its various phases, was corroborat-
ed by the herder, and the mine foreman, a number
of homesteaders, and other disinterested witnesses.
It was evident that either the State's witnesses were
falsifying their testimony, which did not seem to me
to be likely, or that I had not been told the truth
about the case.

The large woman was the first witness for the
defense. I explained to the Judge that I understood
that neither she nor the defendants nor any of their
witnesses were able to understand or speak English
and that an interpreter would be necessary. Carnahan seemed a little doubtful and asked the Deputy
Sheriff what he knew about it. McDougall said that
while he didn't know all the witnesses he knew that
some of them spoke perfect English. The Judge
looked at me inquiringly and not too kindly. I explained that all I knew was what the interpreter had
told me, but that I would be glad to try examining
them without his assistance.

I began by asking the woman to state her name.
With an expression of wonderment on her face she
looked first at me and then at the jury and the
Judge, and began talking explosively to the interpreter, who said to the Judge, "She says she doesn't
understand." The second question brought the
same result, and Judge Carnahan told the interpret-

er and directed me to proceed, to the obvious disgust of the deputy sheriff.

We got along fairly well for a while, the answers of the witness being given briefly in Finnish and repeated by the interpreter as briefly in English. But as the examination proceeded, each question provoked a long dialogue between the two, notwithstanding the direction given by the Judge that the questions and answers were to be translated as nearly as possible in the exact language used by counsel and the witness. At last I asked a question that admitted of no answer other than a simple "yes" or "no." It seemed to me that the interpreter used three times the necessary words in repeating the question to the witness, and she, without contenting herself with the single monosyllable that would have completely answered it, argued vigorously with the interpreter for as much as a minute. When she had finished he said to the court and jury, "She says no."

Deputy McDougall was on his feet instantly. "Why, Judge, I've talked with that woman almost every day for years past. She can speak English as well as I can." McDougall was in a rage. The Judge and jury seemed to think he was telling the truth. So did I. The woman was obdurate, continuing to act the part of one completely bewildered by what was going on around her.

The testimony, all given through the interpreter, dragged on for an hour or so; and the jury lost no time in finding my clients guilty of petit larceny. Judge Carnahan imposed a fine of one hundred dollars upon each in addition to the costs. I gave notice of appeal and told the interpreter to bring his friends to my office the next morning.

Promptly at the appointed hour they all filed in, led by the big woman who seated herself in the chair she had occupied on her first visit without so much as a smile or nod of recognition. I started talking to her in English, but she only made a gesture with her hands intended to convey the idea that she didn't understand. Little doubting from what I had seen in the courtroom that I had not been told the truth concerning either the lambs or my witness' understanding of the English language, I turned to the interpreter and quite firmly instructed him to tell his friends that the evidence against Hakaala and Mustonen was very strong, that the costs with the fines imposed already amounted to almost three hundred dollars in addition to the one hundred they had paid me, that the costs in the District Court on appeal would probably be an additional hundred dollars beside the fee that I would charge, which would be —.

I got no further. "Oh hell," said the fat woman in perfect, though inelegant English, "we've had enough. I'll go up to old Carnahan's office and pay the fine. Damn that Angus McDougall." So saying, she stalked out of the office followed by the interpreter, the defendants and their witnesses before I could recover from my bewilderment sufficiently to tell them what I thought of them. The two "bum lambs" cost Hakaala and Mustonen about two hundred dollars each.

Chapter Twelve

For a long time the American people had realized the evils of intemperance. Early in the present century they began thinking they should do something about it. Wartime prohibition seemed to point the way, and the states began adopting constitutional amendments to that effect. It looked like old John Barleycorn was finally and inevitably on his way out.

Idaho was one of the first states to outlaw liquor. We in Wyoming, a little less progressive perhaps, or perhaps a little less inclined to fall in with every popular movement, held off for a while, long enough at least to give the liquor dealers in the western part of the state an opportunity to reap a rich harvest from the thirsty residents of our neighboring state.

The Kemmerer dealers gave substantial evidence of increased prosperity, but since they sold only on the cash-and-carry plan, the question of the legality of their transactions never arose. Cokeville, however, was forty-five miles west of Kemmerer and only a few miles from the border. It was the Cokeville Liquor Company, therefore, that profited most from the wave of prosperity that Idaho prohibition swept over the state line, particularly since that concern had long been known as a wholesaler and could sell at prices slightly lower than those quoted

in Kemmerer.[78] And while the Cokeville firm usually sold only for cash, it was not entirely adverse to
extending credit to customers of known integrity
and ample means.

One of these was Stanley Merrill,[79] whose thousands of sheep grazed a vast area of rangeland in
eastern Idaho. Merrill's ranch home was one of the
show places in his section of the country and his
wool clip one of the largest on the Oregon Short
Line; his lambs brought top prices on the Omaha
market; and his personal integrity had never been
questioned. So when he dropped in at the Cokeville
Liquor Company's establishment one pleasant day
in the fall of 1918 to place an order for a little over

[78]On a fateful day in May of 1922, The Denver *Post* bally-
hooed, "The Day of the bootlegger will end in Cokeville
within a few days, when the recently elected women's ad-
ministration will take on the government of this heretofore
notoriously 'western' town. Mrs. Ethel Stoner was elected
Mayor, and Mrs. Retta Roberts and Mrs. Goldie Noblitt
councilwomen on a 'law enforcement' platform, and they
propose to see to it that illicit dealing in liquor cease in this
community. They were elected in a contest against two male
tickets, each reputed to be 'wet'. For those quivering in their
boots over the prospect of a W. C. T. U.-run community,
Mrs. Stoner, Mayor-elect campaigned on the promise, "It
will not be our policy if elected to enact any stringent or
'blue laws,' believing that we already have good and sufficient laws for the present, but we will endeavor to enforce
the laws that we have." Denver *Post*, May 21, 1922.

[79]Stanley Merrill may have been sobriquet. At least no
biographical information has come to light in Wyoming or
Idaho on a Stanley Merrill.

Ms. Judith Austin to Gene M. Gressley, December 1, 1976.

four thousand dollars worth of liquor and said he
would mail a check as soon as he sold his lamb
crop, Mr. Smith, the president of the firm, was most
happy, as he pleasantly told Mr. Merrill, to accommodate him. "Just send us the check whenever it's
convenient," gushed Mr. Smith. "You understand,
of course," he added so there could be no uncer-
tainty on the point, "that you'll have to assume the
responsibility of getting the liquor over the state
line."

Mr. Merrill understood that perfectly he said,
Idaho being a dry state. He ventured the guess that
prohibition might last a long time, and seemed happy in the thought that, as he put it, his supply of
liquor would last a long time too. With a cordial
handshake and a pleasant good-bye to Mr. Smith,
he went out, got in his car and drove away.

That was the last the Cokeville Liquor Company
heard of Mr. Merrill for a long time, except for the
letter to be mentioned a little later, the letter which
resulted in the safe delivery of four thousand dollars worth of liquor at Mr. Merrill's Idaho ranch,
and also put the local prosecuting attorney in an
extremely humiliating situation. Weeks passed, and
months, and though a statement was forwarded on
the first of each month, followed as time went on by
polite letters saying that if Mr. Merrill had gotten
returns on his lamb sale, which the writer assumed
to be the case, a remittance for the liquor would be
appreciated. But there were no replies. Mr. Smith

finally decided to drive out and see Mr. Merrill
about the matter, but the latter, evidently thinking
that the account could not be collected because Idaho was dry, treated the whole matter as something
of a joke on Mr. Smith and his company. It was then
that Mr. Smith came to my office in Kemmerer and
brought with him a letter written months before by
Mr. Merrill.

The suit had to be filed in Idaho, of course, because it was impossible to serve summons on Merrill in Wyoming; and a few months later the case
came on for trial in a little town in the neighboring
state. Merrill had a formidable array of legal talent.
Chief counsel for the defense was Mr. Stevens[80] of
Pocatello, a lawyer of the highest repute. Mr. Stevens seemed confident of winning his case, as of
course he had a right to be since Merrill had doubtless told him that my client had delivered the liquor
in Idaho, a fact which, if true, would have made the
transaction illegal and unenforceable. Another con-

---

[80] According to *An Illustrated History of the State of Idaho*
(Chicago, 1899), James M. Stevens, a member of the firm of
Detrich, Chalmers & Stevens of Blackfoot, had the singular
distinction of being a native of Idaho, having been born in
Oneida County in 1873. Educated at Leland Stanford, Jr.
University, Judge Stevens' biographer, in prose typical of
mug books, assured his readers that Stevens, ". . . has a
wide reputation for honorable methods and substantial success. He is an honest advocate, respects himself and the
court, and does credit to any cause with which he identifies
himself." pp. 387–88. Ms. Judith Austin to Gene M. Gressley, December 1, 1976.

spicuous member of Merrill's staff was the local prosecuting attorney. Judge Baum,[81] of Pocatello, presided.

The defendant made a good witness. The case seemed quite simple. He admitted buying the liquor and that it had not been paid for, but he said that the Cokeville Liquor Company had hired a Star Valley farmer to deliver the merchandise to his ranch, all in accordance, as he explained, with his understanding with Smith at the time the purchase was made.

"Take the witness," Mr. Stevens said with an unmistakable air of confidence. My cross-examination was brief. Casually taking a letter from my coat pocket I showed it to the witness and asked him if the signature and handwriting were his. He said they were. Then I told the court that I desired to read only the part of the letter relating to do with the point at issue. Judge Baum said to proceed. But a vigorous protest came from the prosecuting attorney. "Oh read it all," he blustered, "we don't want you to withhold anything from the jury." I said

[81] Judge Ora Baum departed this world at age 83 on December 6, 1970. Born in Kansas, he became a citizen of Idaho in 1910. From 1919–1929, he was Judge of the Fifth Judicial District in Idaho. After his judgeship, he practiced law with the firm of Baum and Peterson the rest of his life. Ms. Judith Austin of the Idaho Historical Society wrote, "Judge Baum was, I am told, a gentleman of sagacity, who much enjoyed talking (and indeed arguing) politics with all comers." Idaho *Statesman*, December 8, 1970. Ms. Judith Austin to Gene M. Gressley, December 1, 1976.

that I would certainly try to oblige him if I could.

This was the letter in the handwriting of the defendant, one of many interesting documents that I have in my files:

> Cokeville Liquor Company
> Cokeville, Wyoming
>
> Gentlemen:
> I have had some little difficulty in making arrangements for delivery of the liquor which I purchased from you recently, particularly in securing protection against hijacking which, as you know, is quite prevalent. The necessary arrangements have now been made. I have hired Jens Jensen to haul the liquor from your store in Cokeville to my ranch. He will call at your place for the liquor day after tomorrow about noon and will drive to his farm in Star Valley. After dark he will drive through Tincup Canyon to my ranch.
> I had a meeting last night with the sheriff and prosecuting attorney, and they agreed—for a consideration of course—to have a couple of deputies meet Jensen at the state line and accompany him to my ranch. They guaranteed to see that the liquor would be delivered to me safely.

The Judge and jury went into an uproar. The prosecuting attorney dropped his head on the table in front of him. As soon as quiet had been restored Mr. Stevens earnestly explained to the court that he had known nothing of the letter and relied entirely on the statement of the case made to him by his client, which he now realized to be entirely false. He asked for a ten-minute recess, which the Judge readily granted, adding that he entertained no doubt whatever concerning Mr. Stevens' integrity in the matter.

Before Judge Baum reconvened court, I had in my pocket a certified check for the amount of my client's bill, with interest and costs expended.

There may be a moral or two in this incident, but it is my purpose only to record the facts.

Chapter Thirteen

IT HAS BEEN SAID that man is a thieving animal.
History supports the indictment, and the records
of our criminal courts supply convincing evidence.
It was more than four thousand years ago that
"Thou shalt not steal" was thundered from Mount
Sinai, and lawyers and legislatures ever since have
been elaborating on the terse commandment in an
effort to keep pace with the intricate methods men
have devised to violate it. From time immemorial
men have stolen from each other their livestock,
their money, their lands, their wives, their king-
doms, and even their good names—the last a kind of
thievery which Shakespeare thought the worst of all
because it adds nothing to the riches of the thief
and makes his victim, as the Bard of Avon put it,
"poor indeed."

In modern times there are men who go in for
thieving on a grand scale while others steal only
little things; some who follow thieving as a vocation
while others indulge their pilfering propensities
only occasionally; some who bring to the business
of thieving a keen intellect while others steal with
clumsy stupidity.

Cal Horn,[82] from day to day, lived just outside
the law. Not that his infractions were of daily occur-
rence, nor that he actually violated the criminal

[82] Presumably Cal Horn was yet another Rose pseudonym.

code oftener than perhaps two or three times a year, but that he was constantly looking for the opportunity to offend under circumstances affording the least danger of detection.

Nor did his journeys outside the law even give promise of any substantial gain. His imagination ran to small things. An expert workman able always to secure employment at good wages, it never seemed to occur to him that had he foresworn his criminal pursuits and devoted himself entirely to his trade he would have been far ahead at the end of the year, even without taking into account the expense of a trial now and then following an occasional detection that was bound, under the inexorable law of averages, to occur. These considerations never seemed to enter Cal's mind; and so he went on from day to day planning how he could "beat the law" in some trifling little way or other.

Once he was charged with stealing a bridle from a neighbor, another time a saddle, and later five drums of "drip" gasoline. He wouldn't have been tried for larceny of the saddle, old and almost worn out as it was and worth not more than three or four dollars, but for the fact that he was seriously suspected of stealing a steer at the same time, though the sheriff had been able to find no evidence sufficient to warrant a prosecution on this more serious charge.

But he was tried on the saddle case. In quest of evidence, two deputy sheriffs took him by surprise one day in the dead of winter when they appeared unexpectedly at his little shack on a dry farm a short distance from town. Fortunately for Cal, his wife was able to delay opening the door long enough to give him an opportunity to drop the saddle through a trap door in the floor and throw a rag rug over it. Though the officers thoroughly searched the house, it didn't occur to either of them to move the rug. Although the saddle was never found, the county attorney decided to proceed with the prosecution anyway depending on what circumstantial evidence he had available. This, however, did not prove to be substantial, and the jury brought in a verdict of acquittal.

After the trial Horn told me how he had concealed the saddle. He said that it wasn't the saddle, however, that caused him the most worry. "The officers," he explained, "approached the house from the southeast and entered at the west door. Thus they got a view of the west, the south and the east walls. If they'd taken a look at the north side of the house, they'd have seen there hanging on the wall in plain sight a hindquarter of the beef they suspected me of stealing. It was a pretty close shave."

Another time it looked pretty dark for Cal when the officers, finding him with five drums of "drip" gasoline in his truck, charged him with grand larceny. He admitted to me that he had taken the gas out of the drips in the pipelines at the La Barge Oil Field a few nights before; and since he was arrested before he got to the main road, he suspected that the deputies had seen the whole operation. Horn thought his time had come. "Might as well plead guilty and take the rap," he remarked dejectedly. "Have it coming to me anyway, I guess." He seemed certain that the consequences of his many misdeeds had at last caught up with him. We decided to go ahead with the trial, however, and see what would happen. Cal would, of course, avail himself of his constitutional right to refrain from testifying.

It was as he had suspected. The two deputies testified that they had seen him driving toward the oil field just before dark with five gasoline drums in the back of his truck. They had followed him and from a convenient distance watched him turn the valves, catch the gasoline from the drips, and pour it into the drums. Then they had made the arrest and were holding the gasoline as evidence. There was no proof yet of its *value*—and to constitute grand larceny the value must be shown to be at least *twenty-five dollars*.

The superintendent of the oil company took the stand for the state to testify that the pipeline and the gasoline were the property of his company. "Just what is drip gasoline, Mr. Jones, and how does it differ from the ordinary product?" the prosecutor asked. And the witness answered, "Well, there's more or less gasoline in the natural gas, which it's necessary to extract. This is done by catching the gasoline in traps, or drips, attached to the gas line.

Hence the name 'drip gasoline.'[83] It's very much lighter than the ordinary commercial product, too light to be used in internal combustion engines." I thought I saw a ray of hope in this answer, and the light became very much brighter as the examination proceeded. "Now Mr. Jones, what is the *market value* of these five drums of drip gasoline?" was the next question, and the answer probably saved my client from a term in the state penitentiary. "Drip gasoline?"—Mr. Jones was speaking with some hesitancy—"Well, *drip gasoline really hasn't any market value at all.*"

The prosecution had failed because there was no evidence of the value of the stolen gasoline, and the judge promptly dismissed the case. "Gosh, that was a tight squeeze," Cal said with a deep sigh of relief. "How was I to know the darned stuff wasn't any good?"

---

[83]The pirating of drip gasoline from pipelines, usually under the cover of the dark of the moon, became common sport in oil camps in the Rockies and elsewhere. A frequent, but totally unsubstantiated claim, among residents today of Midwest, Wyoming, is that in the age of drip gasoline, some law abiding citizens even purchased gasoline—on occasion.

Chapter Fourteen

OLD BILL SALLIDAY[84] kept a saloon at Opal, a little town on the railroad eighteen miles east of Kemmerer. Back of the saloon were a half dozen old log cabins. Stockmen stopping overnight with a herd of cattle for the Omaha market and cowpokes celebrating for a day or two after the fall round-up wanted only a place to sleep, and no one was disgruntled or ever heard to complain of the meager

[84]Robert Rose could not have been more accurate in his characterization of Old Bill (otherwise, but seldom, known as W. H.) Salliday. The other select residents of Opal never doubted for a moment that Opal and Salliday were one. As mayor, as rancher, as bar owner, old Bill ran Opal—the way he liked. One of the many anecdotes about Mayor Salliday occurred during the flu epidemic of 1919, when he announced to one and all, walking down the streets of Kemmerer, that business couldn't be better in Opal—since the flu quarantine in Kemmerer was driving all the folks from the northern part of the country to do their trading in Opal. "Old Bill" never worried about his popularity in Kemmerer.

As to the case of the "rolled" soldier, the *Camera* outlined the events in graphic detail. First, the event attracted so much attention that it had to be moved from the office of Justice of the Peace to the District Court. Then the crammed courtroom heard the witnesses tell of hearing, on the night of March 8th, the screams of Heber L. Young, a recent patron of Salliday's bar and just home from the wars. Salliday dashed to the rescue to find the mugged soldier, *sans* purse. From that point on the story bends with the witnesses you believe, but the jury left little doubt that the accused robber, a Mr. Lehman, received numerous bruises and cuts from assailant Salliday. Kemmerer *Camera*, January 1, April 16, 1919.

accommodations that Salliday provided them.

Old Bill had been a cowpoke himself in his younger days, but a serious spine injury received when he was thrown from a wild horse had forced him to abandon the range and necessitated his wearing a brace ever afterward. Over the years the pain began to show in the lines of his face, his thick straight black hair turned white, his gait became slower and more guarded, and his limp more noticeable; but the sparkle of his clear blue eyes and his kindly manner remained unchanged.

Salliday was not just an ordinary saloon keeper. There were no swinging doors in his place, no white apron, none of the trappings that usually characterize such an establishment. Stockmen after they had finished trading at the "Opal Merc.", as everyone called the general store with merchandise of all sorts jammed haphazard in a large frame building a few rods away, usually dropped in at Bill's place for a chat and a slug of liquor. Old Bill knew all the news of the vicinity—what price Jim Chrisman got for his wool, how many sheep the Salmon Brothers outfit lost in the recent snowstorm, all about the latest well in the La Barge oil field, and the three drillers who were drowned when their car failed to make the turn at the Muddy Creek bridge and pinned them under four feet of water.

When a bunch of cowpokes rode into Opal to relax after weeks on the range there were whiskey and cards, and they could drink and gamble as long as they wished; but Old Bill wouldn't tolerate any of what he called "rough stuff." When his patrons became the least disorderly, he would take a hand himself. Not infrequently his patrons imbibed too freely, and they were assisted to one of the half-dozen rooms upstairs that Salliday called the "hotel" to sleep off their jags—if there were too many of them, some could sleep in the old log shacks back of the saloon—Old Bill never failed to take care of his customers, whatever their condition.

Everyone in the Green River Valley was Salliday's friend, and quite naturally he prospered with the passing of the years. When I first knew him, Old Bill had his saloon and "hotel" paid for, owned a substantial interest in the Opal Mercantile Company and two or three of the half-dozen houses in town, and had a comfortable balance on deposit at the Kemmerer Savings Bank and Liberty bonds in his safe deposit box.

In 1919 the boys were coming home from France, drifting into their old communities to take up life where they had left off when the call came to fight the Huns. One day Ted Smith alighted from the morning train clad in his uniform with sergeant's stripes on the sleeve. Old Bill greeted him with a warm handclasp and a hearty "Damned glad to see you back, Ted," just as he had greeted a score of other punchers on their way home to the cow country. Ted was back to his old stomping ground! Here were the same old card tables, the same old straight chairs, the same old bar—and Bill Salliday. "Good Old Bill," he said warmly, as with his hand on his friend's shoulder he stepped up to the bar for a drink. Tom O'Neill[85] would arrive in the morning to take him back to his old job at the Cottonwood ranch. With the feel of the saddle under him, the smell of scorching calf-flesh under the red hot branding iron, and the breath of sage in his nostrils, all the horrors of trench warfare, zero hour and the rattle of machine gun fire would soon be forgotten.

Until tomorrow there would be whiskey, and plenty of it. Ted soon had enough so that a rough looking fellow hanging around the saloon, though obviously a stranger to the cow country, seemed to him like an old pal, and Ted went on buying the drinks. Old Bill noticed that the stranger usually took gingerale, while Ted gulped straight whiskeys as though he could never get enough. Salliday didn't like the stranger or the way he was acting and tried to tell Ted so; but by this time the sergeant was in no mood to be bothered with advice even from an old friend. Early in the evening Old Bill

[85]One of Wyoming's most successful ranchers, Thomas D. O'Neill (1867–1954), migrated to Wyoming from Ohio in 1891. He ranched near Cheyenne for nearly twenty years, leaving the capitol city for Sublette county in 1909. He soon developed his Cottonwood ranch into one of the most profitable operations in Wyoming. T. D. O'Neill biographical file, Western History Research Center, University of Wyoming.

lugged Tom O'Neill's soldier-cowpuncher off to one of the cabins in the rear of the saloon and put him to bed. An hour or so later the stranger, still thoroughly in control of himself, bid Salliday a casual goodnight, saying he guessed he'd turn in for the night, and sauntered out the front door.

In a little while there was a great commotion outside. Old Bill rushed to the back door. "What's the matter?" he called to the soldier coming toward him from the cabin where he had been put to bed. "That guy that's been hanging around all afternoon tried to rob me. I raised up and let him have one on the chin." "Where is he?" "Ran down toward the depot." "I'll get him," said Bill grimly, as he started walking as rapidly as his crippled condition would permit, in the direction of the station.

The next morning the sheriff brought Salliday to my office. "Old Bill nearly killed a fellow last night," he announced with a broad grin, apparently not at all displeased with his prisoner. I asked Salliday what had happened. "You heard what the sheriff said," was his curt reply, and then, with suddenly blazing indignation he added, "that G—D—— stewbum tried to rob a soldier."

The case was called for trial two days later before Justice of the Peace Pat Glasgow[86]—old Carnahan had died a few months before. The court room was filled with stockmen from the Green River Valley,

[86] James W. "Pat" Glasgow was nominated to several terms as Justice of the Peace. Kemmerer *Camera*, July 31, 1918.

who were there, as one of them told me, just in case Old Bill should need them, a bond or something of the sort, anything.

The prosecuting witness was a horrible sight as he limped into the court room assisted by a deputy sheriff. With both eyes blackened, face lacerated and a nasty cut across his scalp, he looked as though he had been run through a stone crusher. He told the jury that Salliday had come to the depot where he was waiting to catch a freight train, ordered him to get out of town at once, and when he started walking down the track, had followed him, knocked him down and kicked and beaten him almost into insensibility.

I put Salliday on the stand and asked him to tell in his own words just what happened. With a vicious look at the prosecuting witness he said, "That G—D—— stewbum sponged off of the soldier all afternoon and when he thought he was drunk, sneaked into his cabin and tried to steal his wad." He admitted that the story of the prosecuting witness was true so far as it went, but said that "he had it coming to him." The first jury disagreed, but the second, after deliberating two or three hours, brought in a verdict of guilty. There really wasn't anything else they could do.

I was on my feet in an instant to ask that my client be released on his own recognizance pending appeal to the district court. The county attorney vigorously objected, insisting that Bill Salliday should be treated just as any other man would be treated. I called the court's attention to the fact that Salliday was worth at least fifty thousand dollars and that his own recognizance was as good as gold. Anyway, why hadn't the *prosecuting witness* been arrested for attempted robbery? It was *he* that was really guilty. Why hadn't the county attorney done his duty by prosecuting this worthless derelict instead of a highly respected local citizen? The offended prosecutor was furious. Was I attempting to tell him how to run his office? How did I know that this man wouldn't be prosecuted? The argument was getting hot, which was just what I wanted. "Very well," I finally agreed, "how large a bond do you want?" The county attorney insisted on at least five hundred dollars and the signatures of two substantial property owners. Judge Glasgow was willing to give the defendant until tomorrow morning to furnish the bond, provided I would guarantee that he would not leave town in the meantime, to which I readily agreed.

"Is court adjourned?" I asked. "Yes, court's adjourned," the justice announced as he arose from his chair and the spectators filed slowly out of the room. In the excitement of the discussion concerning the bond the county attorney had forgotten to ask the Justice of the Peace to pass sentence on the defendant, which was precisely what I hoped would happen when I precipitated the argument concerning the bond. A few days before I had read a court decision to the effect that when a Justice of the Peace finally adjourns court without sentencing the defendant, he loses jurisdiction of the case, and any sentence imposed after adjournment is void. Although Bill Salliday was of course guilty of assault and battery, I agreed with his view of the matter that the fellow he called a "stewbum" got about what was coming to him, and I was determined that, if possible, my client should escape the consequence of the verdict reluctantly returned by the jury.

As we walked down the street Old Bill said, "What in the devil does all this fuss mean? I could give bond for a hundred thousand if they wanted it." At the office I tried to explain that since the justice had adjourned court without passing sentence he had lost jurisdiction of the case. "And what does that mean? I don't get it—the jury said I was guilty, didn't they?" My client couldn't see any sense in what was going on. "Well, Bill," I said, trying to make the situation clear to my confused client, "without going into the legal technicalities, it simply means that the case is finished—you haven't been sentenced—you're not going to be sentenced—you're not going to jail, and you're not even going to pay a fine." Old Bill's deeply lined, florid face wore a puzzled look.

When the District Judge arrived in Kemmerer the next morning I was ready with a petition for a writ of habeas corpus and telephoned the sheriff to come to my office to get his prisoner. Together we walked to the District Court room after I had telephoned the county attorney that I had an application for a writ of habeas corpus to present to the court on behalf of Mr. Salliday.

Judge Arnold[87] made quick work of the matter. After asking the county attorney if it was true that the justice of the peace had adjourned court without passing sentence, and having his admission that such was the case, His Honor announced his judgment: "The writ is granted and the defendant is discharged. Under our law a justice of the peace has only such limited jurisdiction as the statute gives him. When he finally adjourns court in a particular case without finishing it—in the present situation without passing sentence—his jurisdiction is exhausted. He cannot at another time pass sentence even though a verdict of guilty has been returned by the jury. It would have been otherwise, of course, if he had merely taken a recess, however long that might be, if within the time limited by the statute. Mr. Sheriff, you will release Mr. Salliday."

[87] A member of a distinguished Wyoming family noted for expertise in legal affairs, Judge John R. Arnold (1858–?) first saw Laramie a year after the Union Pacific passed through in 1869. Judge Arnold began his career working for the Union Pacific, "reading" law in his spare time. In 1897, he founded the firm of Ham and Arnold in Evanston, Wyoming. Governor Kendrick appointed him Judge of the Third Judicial District in 1915. Frances Beard, *Wyoming, From Territorial Days to the Present* (Chicago, 1935), III, p. 15.

"Well, I'll be damned." That was Old Bill's reaction when at last he came to a full comprehension of the situation at my office a few moments later. He appeared to have fully expected to pay a substantial fine and even, possibly, to spend a few days in jail.

He asked me what he owed me. I reminded him that I had said when he employed me that the fee would be one hundred fifty dollars. He made out a check and handed it to me. The check was for double the amount I had mentioned. "It was worth it," he said with a chuckle as he walked stiffly out of the office.

Chapter Fifteen

IT TOOK THE FEDERAL GOVERNMENT a long time to realize that one hundred sixty acres of land in Iowa or Illinois that will produce forty bushels of corn to the acre is worth more than the same area in the semi-arid sections of Wyoming and other Rocky Mountain states where a single range steer requires 15 to 20 acres.[88] True, even before irrigation began to be practiced on an extensive scale there were small areas of rich land along the mountain streams, but even these had to be watered by means of dams and ditches constructed at considerable cost before the land could be made productive. But the pioneers who began to migrate to Wyoming long before the territory attained statehood in 1890, and kept on coming through the years, had no thought of farming. Sturdy, rugged individuals, they had visions of great numbers of cattle, not just a few head such as many of them had known on small farms in Iowa and Maine and Missouri, but vast herds, cattle on a thousand hills, cattle grazing on vast plains and grassy mountain slopes.

A few of them had been in the cattle business in

[88] The literature on public land legislation of the United States overwhelms even the most diligent of researchers. For those hardy souls interested in what many times can be as arid a subject as the land described, one can suggest that they investigate, Paul W. Gates, *History of Public Land Law Development* (Washington, 1968).

Texas and had trailed their herds a thousand miles or more across Oklahoma and Kansas, up the dry bed of the North Platte River through western Nebraska into the short grass country of northern Wyoming. Others came with a small amount of capital from Massachusetts and Michigan, New York, Tennessee and Alabama; still others came with no capital at all, with nothing but their bare hands and a determination to get ahead in this vast new country.

But to raise cattle requires land, and lots of it, land measured not by acres, quarter sections, or even sections, but by townships and watersheds. How could such areas be acquired? Here in Wyoming was a vast area of almost a hundred thousand square miles—sixty-three million acres, practically all of it public domain, the property of the Federal Government. The Congress in 1862 had enacted the Homestead Law and the original law was still in effect, the law under which all the Mississippi Valley states had been settled and developed; but to be entitled to a patent the homesteader had to make oath that he had actually resided on the land seven months of each year over a five-year period, and no one could possibly make a living on a quarter section of grazing land. The law enacted by Congress, a law that worked satisfactorily enough wherever rainfall was sufficient to raise crops, would not work at all in the semi-arid west. Rather, it constituted an insurmountable barrier to the acquisition of land by homesteading; there was no law under which public land could be acquired by purchase from the government except in small isolated tracts; senators and representatives from eastern states had little or no understanding of conditions in the West and little disposition to enact laws under which land could be legally acquired upon terms that would make it available for stock raising, the only purpose for which it was of any use.

And so many of the men who came west to raise cattle and wanted to give permanency and stability to their business by owning at least a substantial part of the land on which they were to graze their livestock, found that they had two alternatives—they could either give up the idea entirely, or they could make an effort to evade the law by arranging to have their employees, their foremen and range riders, and even friends and relatives, make homestead filings without any actual intention of ever living on the land and often without even having seen it.

Some of them chose the latter alternative. One of these was V. Z. Starling[89] who operated a large cattle outfit two hundred miles or so from Kemmerer. Starling's ranches embraced more than a hundred thousand acres, some of which he had purchased from other ranchmen, but much of which was composed of homestead entries made over a period of many years by cowpokes, merchants, miners, bank clerks, all of whom were employees or close friends

[89]V. Z. Starling perhaps was another allonym of Rose's.

or business associates of Mr. Starling, but very few of whom, so far as anyone knew, had ever resided on their homestead entries. To all appearances most of them were simply "accommodation" entrymen. The "go-between" who had made the preliminary arrangements, none of them in writing, and had arranged for the deeds by which, after the issuance of patents, titles were conveyed to Mr. Starling, was Starling's foreman, Dennis Daugherty, a big-fisted Irishman with a ready wit, a rich brogue, a friendly manner, unbounded resourcefulness, and above all, unfaltering loyalty to his employer.

In the course of many years Starling's herds had grown to enormous proportions, his investments in bank stocks, mines and mercantile establishments were yielding large dividends, and he had become widely known in his section of the state, and justly so, as a man of wealth and influence, one whom everyone held in the highest esteem.

One day he learned that two or three inspectors from the Department of the Interior were examining his title records in the County Clerk's office, and a few days later that representatives of the Department of Justice were interviewing the scores of persons who had made homestead entries and later conveyed title to Starling. The investigation proceeded for several months until finally Starling was charged in the Federal Court with defrauding the Government of the United States, and a score of witnesses took the stand to tell what they knew of his vast holdings of public lands and the manner in which they were acquired.

United States District Attorney Burke,[90] who was conducting the examination of the witnesses, seemed delighted with the prospect of securing a conviction—delighted that is, until he attempted to match wits with Dennis Daugherty, who as the prosecutor had figured it out, was the Government's key witness, the man who had handled all the alleged fraudulent land entries, the one man whose testimony would connect Starling with the alleged fraud.

What happened when Mr. Burke put Mr. Daugherty on the stand proved to be the District Attorney's undoing and provided the gentlemen in the jury box no little amusement. So successful was the witness in his encounter with the prosecuting attorney that whatever advantage the Government had gained by the testimony of the earlier witnesses was entirely lost.

The examination of Daugherty by the District Attorney ran about like this:

Mr. Burke: You will please state your name to the gentlemen of the jury.

Mr. Daugherty: My name, Mr. Bourke? Why ye know my name as well as I do misalf, Mr. Bourke. Sure ye do, Mr. Bourke.

Mr. Burke: Yes, certainly, Dinny, I know your

[90]Timothy Burke held the office of U.S. District Attorney from 1898–1912.

	name, but just to have it in the record, will you please give your name to the jury?
Mr. Daugherty:	Sure thin, Mr. Bourke, if it will give ye only satisfaction, Mr. Bourke, my name is Dennis Mickael Daugherty, sure it is, Mr. Bourke, it is.
Mr. Burke:	Very well, Dinny, do you know Mr. Starling?
Mr. Daugherty:	Do I know Mr. Starling, Mr. Bourke? Sure and I do, Mr. Bourke, and a finer man God niver let live, Mr. Bourke.
Mr. Burke:	Now Dinny, how long have you known Mr. Starling?
Mr. Daugherty:	How long, ye say, Mr. Bourke, how long have I known Mr. Starling? Fine honest man that he is, Mr. Bourke—
Mr. Burke:	Now, Dinny, will you please just answer my questions—
Mr. Daugherty:	That I will, Mr. Bourke, I was just lettin' ye know, and these fine gentlemen here, what a good man is Mr. Starling, Mr. Bourke—and I suppose ye know that yerself, Mr. Bourke.
Mr. Burke:	Well, now—
Mr. Daugherty:	Yes, sir, Mr. Bourke, I was just goin' on to tell ye how how long I have known Mr. Starling—if I can—Mr. Bourke, if I can. Let me see—Mr. Bourke, it was back in—about thirty years ago that I landed in New York,—and I got a job there for a time, Mr. Bourke—and thin I was in Omaha for about a year, or maybe it was as much as two years—and af-

ter that I went to Kansas City and after that—

Mr. Burke: Dinny, will you *please* just tell the jury how long you have known Mr. Starling?

Mr. Daugherty: Well now, Mr. Bourke, I was just tryin' to figger that out for ye, Mr. Bourke. I want to be just exact, so to speak, Mr. Bourke—Then I was in Chicago for awhile,—will now, Mr. Bourke, fer the life o' me, I don't know just *exactly* how long I have known Mr. Starling, Mr. Bourke, fine man that he is, Mr. Bourke.

Mr. Burke: Alright, alright, Dinny, let's go to something else. You know Mr. Jenkins, I suppose?

Mr. Daugherty: Will now, Mr. Bourke, I know a *Jimmie* Jenkins in Omaha, that is I once did—and I think I know a *Tommie* Jenkins in Cheyenne. It's not thim you're speaking of? O yes, Mr. Bourke, I know a *Sam* Jenkins—he's waitin' table I think, at a little restaurant at Medicine Bow, Mr. Bourke—

Mr. Burke: Dinny, you know *Carl* F. Jenkins, don't you, who filed on a homestead now owned by Mr. Starling?

Mr. Daugherty: Will, now, that you mention *that* Mr. Jenkins, Mr. Bourke—

Mr. Burke: And you know that Carl Jenkins made a homestead entry on that piece of land and that it's now the property of Mr. Starling.

Mr. Daugherty: Will, Mr. Bourke, now I wouldn't

know onything about that Mr. Bourke, no, I wouldn't know.

Mr. Burke: And you know that Jenkins deeded that land to *you* about twenty years ago and that a month or so later *you deeded it to Starling*, and you know that Jenkins was at the time working as a teller in Starling's bank and that he *never even saw this land*. You know that, don't you, Dinny?

Mr. Daugherty: Will, now, Mr. Bourke, you say I know all those things, Mr. Bourke, yis that's a long time—twenty years is a long time. I don't think I remember that far back, Mr. Bourke. Yis, that's a long time, but if ye—

Mr. Burke: Dinny, look at this deed—is that a deed from Carl F. Jenkins to you, isn't it?

Mr. Daugherty: Will, I wouldn't be able to say about that, Mr. Bourke, that says "Dinny Daugherty." My name is *"Dennis"*— Dennis Mickael Daugherty, Mr. Bourke. And—

Mr. Burke: Let me show you another deed, *Dennis*. This seems to be a deed *from you to* Mr. *Starling* covering the same land, and the consideration in both deeds is One Dollar. What do you want to say to that, *Mr.* Daugherty?

Mr. Daugherty: Will, now, Mr. Bourke, what I want to say is the *truth*, Mr. Bourke, yes, sir, Mr. Bourke, the truth, Mr. Bourke—*not onything but the truth*—and I want to be *sure*, Mr. Bourke—

Mr. Burke: Now, Dinny, let's get right down to the truth then. Isn't it a fact that by an understanding between Mr. Starling and yourself, you had Jenkins file on this land, that you built a little shack on it, that Jenkins *never even saw* the land, that you had him swear falsely that he had actually *lived on the land* for a period of three years, that he conveyed it to *you* without any consideration, that *you conveyed it to Starling* without any consideration, and that *the whole thing was simply a scheme to defraud the Government*? Now, *isn't that the truth*?

Mr. Daugherty: Ah, Mr. Bourke, you do Mr. Starling a *very great injustice*, you do, Mr. Bourke, *fine honest man that he is*, Mr. Bourke. Mr. Starling, niver defrauded onybody out of onything in his whole life, Mr. Bourke. *A finer gentleman never walked in shoe leather*, Mr. Bourke—

And so it went on most of the afternoon, with one land entry after another under investigation. The jury were being treated to a great comedy and finally gave up all effort to restrain their mirth. The District Attorney, at last, thoroughly exasperated and giving up all hope of obtaining from the witness the least evidence favorable to the prosecution, decided upon an effort to discredit him entirely.

"Dinny," he began, "do you realize you are under oath?" "Sure, I do, of course I do, Mr. Bourke, I do." "Dinny, do you know what it means to take an oath?" "Do I know, Mr. Bourke, what it means to take an oath, Mr. Bourke?" The witness was making a great show of righteous indignation. "Sure I know what it means to take an oath, Mr. Bourke, I do. When a man takes an oath he raises his right hand, he swears before Almighty God, Mr. Bourke, to tell the truth, the whole truth, and nothing but the truth. *That's* what it means to take an oath, Mr. Bourke, yis, sir, Mr. Bourke, it is." The prosecutor ventured one more question: "Dinny, do you know what will happen to a man that takes an oath like that, and then tells a lie on the witness stand?" "Do I know what will happen to that man, Mr. Bourke?—Do I know what will happen to that man? Denny was now at his best, his deep religious conviction finding full expression in a rich brogue as he delivered the knock-out blow in a battle of wits that had been his from the opening round. "Do I know what will happen to that man, Mr. Bourke? *God will strike him dead on the spot*, Mr. Bourke, I've seen it happen mony a time in Ireland, I have."

The District Attorney had had enough. He was no match for Denny Daugherty and he knew it, and moreover he knew he had lost his case. Mr. Starling went back to his ranch and continued to prosper without further interference on the part of any Government agents.

Chapter Sixteen

I WAS AROUSED EARLY one morning by the persistent ringing of the telephone. Though it was
scarcely daylight the man at the other end of the
line insisted on my coming to the office immediately. His business was imperative, he said, and he had
to leave town as soon as it could be attended to.

No one was in sight when I reached the office a
quarter of an hour later. Within a few minutes,
however, there was a knock at the back door, and I
opened it to admit a large man, well dressed and
rather good looking. Stepping to one side so that he
would be completely out of sight from the street, he
directed me to lock the front door, pull down the
shades, and bring my typewriter into the back
room. When I had done so, he proceeded to explain the business that had brought him to my office
at this unusual hour. "I want you to write a will,"
he said. "It won't be complicated. Just sit down to
the typewriter and begin. I'll give you the necessary
information as you go along—I'm in a hurry."

Bringing a chair into the little room, I began typ-
ing, making the formal parts of the instrument as
brief as possible. There were only two or three specific bequests, and the residue of the estate was to
go to his wife. To complete the job required not
more than twenty minutes or so; and just as I was
finishing the attestation clause, there was another

knock at the back door. My visitor opened it and two men entered. "These men are to witness my signature," he said, and lifting the typewriter from the little table and placing it on the floor, he sat down, signed his name, the other two men signed as witnesses, he laid fifty dollars in currency on the table, and the three took their leave. With his hand on the doorknob, my strange client turned to me and said politely, but with an unmistakable firmness, "You will please not mention our being here."

I looked out the back window a few seconds later to see the three men untie their horses from a telephone pole and ride down the alley toward the edge of town. I couldn't have told anyone who my visitors were had I desired to do so because in the excitement incident to the unusual circumstances of their visit, to say nothing of the fact that my client's attitude and conduct had been somewhat alarming, I had entirely forgotten his name and failed even to notice the names of his friends.

Notwithstanding the peculiar circumstances and the generous fee that I had received for less than a half hour's work, I should probably have long since forgotten the incident but for the tragic fate that befell my client and but for his notorious activities which served to explain the secrecy with which his early-morning visit to my office was enshrouded. The Salt Lake Tribune a few days later carried on the front page the account of a train robbery that had occurred in Oregon the night before, and a picture—taken at the morgue—of the man whose will I had written. Under it was the name of Charles Manning. A United States Marshal, the Tribune said, was reclining half-asleep in the front section of a Pullman car as Manning entered. For some reason the bandit passed him by without arousing him, and proceeded down the aisle relieving the passengers of their money and jewelry. As soon as he had proceeded a few feet the officer fired. Manning though fatally wounded, wheeled and returned the fire, aiming at the Marshal's heart, a shot that would have produced instant death but for the fact that the bullet was deflected by a deck of playing cards the officer carried in his shirt pocket.

I had heard something of the escapades of Whitney Bros. and Manning bandits who had terrorized communities along the Short Line Railroad for a number of years, and have since learned much more from Tommie Holland who knew the two when they were teen-aged youths in Cokeville in the western part of Lincoln County.

Cokeville, before the turn of the century, was what might be called a wild frontier town. Located in the center of an extensive sheep raising area before the building of the railroad, and far distant from the nearest settlement and a hundred miles or so from Evanston, then County Seat of old Uinta County, the little community seemed for all practical purposes to be almost entirely outside the protection of the law. The sheepherders coming to town

from months on the range with pockets bulging
with a half year's wages, craved excitement and had
the cash to pay for it. A few dollars sufficed to purchase the few items of merchandise they required,
such as tobacco, overalls and shirts, and the rest was
usually spent at the bars and gambling tables in
Tommie Holland's and Henry Wyatt's saloons. After a few days and nights of revelry, with whiskey,
dancing and poker, their wages spent, the barkeep
was always willing to lend them two or three dollars
to get back to the sheep where they would work
another few months until they had accumulated
money enough to come to town again to spend it in
another twenty-four or forty-eight hours drinking,
dancing and gambling. Led by Tex Long and
Blackie Brown, who liked to be known as "bad"
men, and fairly deserved the reputation, they would
shoot out the saloon lights, and generally have an
all-round good time.

It was in this environment that the Whitney
brothers, Hugh and Charlie,[91] and Charlie Man-

[91] O. Henry's imagination could not have better inscribed
finis to the Charles S. Whitney story. One summer day in
1952, Charles S. Whitney, alias Frank S. Taylor, "modest
and remorseful," saith the press, walked into Governor
Frank A. Barrett's office in Cheyenne and confessed to robbing the Cokeville bank on September 11, 1911. Whitney
had stuffed into his pocket several letters from prominent
Montanans, including Governor Bonner, attesting to the fact
that as Frank S. Taylor, Whitney had led an exemplary life
for some forty years as a rancher in Glasgow, Montana.

According to Frank Taylor, or Charles Whitney of 1952,

his downfall had been engineered by his uncle Charles Manning, whom Whitney referred to as "that nefarious crook in Cokeville," plus a strong addition of brotherly love. The Whitney story began in 1910, when as a youth of twenty Charles came to Wyoming accompanied by his older brother, Hugh. Soon Hugh managed to get in debt to an associate, who pressed Hugh for immediate payment. Hugh's thoughtful creditor pointed out that economic salvation lay close at hand if he would only recognize the fact. All that need be accomplished was the robbing of the Cokeville bank, and economic security was his. "So" said Charles in 1952, "I sold my birthright for a few tainted dollars. . . . For my brother's sake and my love and loyalty to him."

In the fifties, Charles Whitney recalled vividly the details of the forty-year-old robbery. About high noon on September 11, 1912, Charles and Hugh hid their horses in sagebrush a mile or so from Cokeville. Near one o'clock, with as much nonchalance as they could summon, the two brothers casually walked into the Cokeville State Bank, brandished a couple of six shooters, and forced the bank-owner, A. D. Noblitt, up against the wall.

Noblitt, behaving as any respectable bank owner would, did his best to stall the youths by insisting that he did not recall the combination to the safe. His captors, rather than get into an extended debate on the matter, decided to await the appointed hour for the time lock mechanism to release. Customers sauntered in, to discover to their mortification that their business would be delayed until the Whitneys completed their business. Almost an hour elapsed, during which time the little bank became extremely crowded with patrons lining the walls. One panic-stricken woman fled, but for reasons best known to female intuition, she refused to sound an alarm.

Finally, the fateful hour arrived with the safe door slowly opening, the Whitneys scooped up the contents and ran out the door. Charles remembered that the entire community stood in the street seeing them off! "We believed a posse followed us, but we were never sure," Charles recollected in 1952. "Anyway, we saw no sign of one." Galloping off into the mountains, the brothers finally rested after putting some fifty miles between them and Mr. Noblitt. They counted their loot and decided that the better part of discretion, if not valor, required their immediate removal from the Cokeville area.

First they moved to northern Wisconsin, where Hugh's former creditor and criminal mastermind caught up with them. This time Hugh's criminal benefactor suggested the contents of the Cokeville safe might be worth a touch of blackmail. So the brothers, changing nothing but their names, headed for Montana. Hugh adopted the sobriquet of George Walter Brown; and Charles decided that Frank S. Taylor fitted his mood and mien. With their new identities they formed a partnership and went into ranching near Glasgow, Montana. When their country called for their services in World War I, they joined the army, serving in France. After their discharge (Charles left the service, but memories of his experiences at Fort D. A. Russell in Cheyenne remained), the two brothers went back to ranching in northern Montana until 1934, when they dissolved their partnership. Hugh immediately left for Canada, and died in Saskatoon in 1951.

In turning himself in, in Cheyenne, the chastened Charles opined, "If Hugh and I are not punished for our mistakes, we certainly have been punished by them. . . . We paid a mighty sum in remorse, tears, loneliness and regret." Although Wyoming authorities refrained from saying so, they must have thought, once they surveyed the legal complication of the case, it would have been pleasant had Frank S. Taylor, alias Charles S. Whitney never left Montana and gone to his grave unrecognized and unknown. For instance, in 1911 Cokeville was part of Uinta County, in 1952 Cokeville had long been a community in Lincoln County. For years, the Cokeville Bank doors had been tightly closed to robbers and patrons. The legal bramble bush was resolved with Charles S. Whitney pleading guilty to District Judge Robert Christmas, who placed Whitney on a five-year probation. Sheridan *Press*, June 19, 1952; *Star Valley Independent*, June 27, 1952.

ning[92] grew up. Tommie Holland said they were
respectable boys, at least as well behaved as any of
the young fellows in the community. Tommie went
to Cokeville in the late eighteen-seventies when a
lad of eighteen. He got a job tending bar, and soon
presided over one of his own. Young Holland made
up his mind that there'd be no shooting the lights
out in his place; and so when one night Tex Long
rode to the saloon entrance and called out, "Get
out of the way, I'm comin' in, and I'm comin' shoo-
tin,'" Tommie responded with "Come on Tex, I'll

[92]The adventures and misadventures of Charles Manning
came to a violent end in 1914, when he was killed holding
up a train in Meacham, Oregon in July. The Cokeville *Register*, with no nonsense prose, printed, "Manning had lived
around Cokeville for the past number of years and was a
professional gambler. His connection with the famous Whitney boys has been conceded and it has been charged against
him that he had taken part in some of their operations. Notwithstanding these suspicions, he has always stayed clear of
the law until the news of the train holdup—near Meacham,
Oregon. . . . Charley Manning was known by his neighbors
to be one of the most considerate of husbands, fathers and
neighbors. His wife and children were always first in his
thoughts and so far as home life and care and guardianship
of those dependent on him is concerned there are men in
every community who could profit from his example." Manning died at age 33. Cokeville *Register*, July 11, 1914. Courtesy of Mrs. Joyce Dayton, October 19, 1976. One Cokeville
pioneer remembers Charles Manning as coming to Cokeville
as a young man. "No bad habits and a fine worker. He
worked for my father in the cement work. He was in Cokeville several years and finally married a Cokeville girl, Miss
Ell Stoffers. . . . He later worked on ranches. He finally
began running with a bad crowd." Fannie Chamberlain to
Gene M. Gressley, November 20, 1976.

try to entertain you;" Tex got no more than half-way through the swinging doors when he found himself looking down the long barrel of Tommie's forty-four. "My gawd Tommie, I didn't know you felt that way about it," he apologized, pretty well frightened, and backed his horse out onto the street. The young barkeeper had no further trouble with the self-styled bad men who up to then had run things about as they pleased around Cokeville.

The Whitneys and Charlie Manning were just or-dinary hard working, fun-loving decent young fel-lows, until they fell in with Tex Long and Blackie Brown.[93] After that, Tommie told me, they were different men entirely. Their desperate career be-gan when Hugh committed some minor crime, and a deputy sheriff started with him to Evanston. Rid-ing with his prisoner in the Pullman car smoking room, the officer foolishly laid his six-shooter on the seat between them. The hot-headed youth picked it up and shot the deputy through the heart. The train conductor, hearing the shot, ran to the door, and was instantly dispatched by another bul-let. Hugh ordered the porter to open the vestibule door and leaped from the train which, fortunately for him, was going slowly up a steep grade, and made his escape. From that moment the Whitney brothers and their friend Charlie Manning were outlaws.

[93]Interestingly enough the antics of Tex Long and Blackie Brown have been entirely fogged in by the historical past.

The Whitneys were not seen around Cokeville for some time, though Manning married the daughter of one of the prosperous sheepmen of the neighborhood and built a nice home in town where he lived for a number of years to all appearances a good citizen worthy of the respect of the community. But now and then he would disappear for a few days and there would be reports in the Salt Lake and Pocatello papers of a train or bank robbery, usually participated in by three masked men. In a little while Manning would return to his home in Cokeville, and no one had the temerity to inquire where he had been.

One night one of the Whitneys walked into Tommie Holland's[94] saloon with a handkerchief tied over the lower part of his face, and pointing a six-shooter at a half dozen men at the poker table, ordered them to put up their hands. A young cowpoke whose position was nearest the hold-up, with less judgment than courage, jumped up and pulled the handkerchief from his face, whereupon Whitney, his identity revealed, pretended that he was

---

[94]Thomas Holland lived a long life in Western Wyoming, dying in Kemmerer on November 7, 1949. Noted all his life as the first white boy born in Evanston, Wyoming, in 1873, his family moved north to Cokeville in 1876. He graduated from Kansas State University at Manhattan, returned to the Kemmerer area to run his family's ranching interests. He ran for Justice of the Peace in 1916. Kemmerer *Camera*, October 4, November 1, 1916; and Cokeville *Register*, November 10, 1949. Courtesy of William H. Barton, Wyoming State Archives and Historical Society, October 13, 1976.

playing a joke on his old friends, bought a round of drinks, and took a hand in the game. When the game broke up a little before dawn Whitney had all the money anyway, though it had taken several hours longer to get it than he had anticipated.

The bandit rode out of town just as daylight was breaking in the east and wasn't seen around Cokeville until noon one hot summer day a year later, although meantime there were several bank robberies in out-of-the-way places and one in Montpelier, Idaho; all by three masked men closely resembling the Whitney brothers and Manning. Though generally suspected of the hold-ups, they were never arrested, due in some instances to the fact that their identities could not be definitely established, and in others to the fact that there seemed to be no one who cared to undertake their arrest.

Around the dozens of sheep shearing pens scattered each spring along the railroad from Rawlins, Wyoming, to Pocatello, Idaho, where the shearers made as much as thirty dollars for a single day's work, and the season would last as long as three weeks, there was always a poker game that ran most of the night; and it was not at all unusual for Manning or one of the Whitneys to drop in at one of these sessions. One night Manning happened along where a game was being conducted at the Opal shearing camp by Clint Holland, a brother of Tommie. Unmasked and with no effort to conceal his identity, Manning "stuck up" the game and after passing around a bottle of whiskey, though he never drank himself, backed out of the place with a little more than a thousand dollars in his pocket, mounted his horse and rode away. When I asked Tommie why the fellow wasn't arrested, he grinned sheepishly and drawled, "Oh, he was a pretty good guy," and then asked sharply, "would you have wanted to go out to get him?" I admitted that I would not. "Well—," he said questioningly in a manner he had of letting you infer what he had in mind instead of telling you. That seemed to be the answer.

A few months later, Manning walked into the lobby of the Kemmerer hotel a little after midnight, and stepping up to the desk said to Fred Chapin,[95] the proprietor, who was on the night shift, "Fred, I want five hundred dollars." His tone was imperative, though he made no display of fire-arms. Mr. Chapin, not mistaking his meaning, opened the safe and counted out the currency, and thinking that his visitor might possibly regard the transaction as a loan, volunteered that he could let him have more if he needed it. "No," said Manning with an understanding grin, "that's all I need." A week or so later there was a bank robbery in the upper country, and

---

[95] A couple of months after attorney Rose arrived in Kemmerer, Fred Chapin formed a hostelry cartel by leasing the Hoskins house. Within a matter of months, Chapin decided that this had been an unwise decision, and released the Hoskins establishment. Eventually Chapin moved to Idaho, then on to Texas. Kemmerer *Camera*, June 3, September 2, 1914.

a few nights after that Manning came into the Kemmerer hotel and with a broad smile handed Chapin the five hundred dollars. He had chosen himself to treat the transaction as a loan, though doubtless more for the fun he got out of it than as the fulfilment of an original design. Certainly his action in the matter could scarcely be said to be consistent with his customary way of doing business. Chapin kept the incident to himself and first told it to a group in the hotel lobby after Manning's death.

It was in the summer of 1912, I think, that the Whitneys made their first, and last, hold-up in their hometown, when a few minutes after twelve noon they rode up to the Cokeville bank, tied their horses and unmasked, walked casually inside. Hugh whispered to the two or three customers, all of whom were old friends of the bandits and one of whom was a young woman who had grown up in the house next door and with whom the Whitney boys had played when the three were youngsters, that there was going to be a hold-up and they had better get outside, a suggestion which they acted upon with alacrity. To remove all suspicion of his own complicity in the undertaking, Manning happened at the moment to be making a deposit at the teller's window and remained to share the fate of the employees of the bank. As soon as the others were outside, Hugh drew a revolver from his holster and ordered Manning, the cashier and the teller into the safe, holding his gun on them while his brother gathered up several thousand dollars, and after gagging and tying their victims, the two brothers ran out, mounted their horses, and made a hurried get-away across a field just north of the bank and into the hills beyond.

Their escape was a narrow one, however, and due to the kindness of a middle-aged woman who had known them from childhood. Henry Wyatt and his wife were at an upstairs window in the hotel which they had but recently erected next door to the bank, and had seen the Whitneys enter the building and come out on the run a few moments later and strike off across the field. Knowing the Whitneys, they did not need to be told what had happened. Wyatt, whose reputation for marksmanship was well established, lifted his rifle and took careful aim, but laid it down again when his wife begged him not to shoot.[96]

The Whitney brothers, so most of the residents say, never came back to Cokeville, although I've been told that at long intervals over a period of years they would return late at night to the home of an old friend and be gone before daybreak. After Manning's death there were no reports of outlawry on the part of the other two. Whitney brothers and Manning were the last, so far as I know, of the many

[96]The Charles S. Whitney of 1952 obviously did not recall, or perhaps care to recall, all the escapades of the Whitney boys pre-1911. Self-evidently, they never knew how close they came to ending their lives on the Cokeville street.

outlaw gangs whose escapades for more than a century extended from the Missouri River to the Pacific Coast, and, at least in the retrospect, add to the romance of the West.

Spinning along over a broad oil-surfaced highway from Kemmerer toward the Pacific Northwest, the motorist of today traverses miles of waving hayfields with here and there a cluster of ranch buildings backed by a dozen or more canvas covered sheep wagons, and finally comes to a quiet orderly village of comfortable old homes and paved streets spanned by arching trees. This is Cokeville, the wild frontier town of thirty-five to fifty years ago, where, now as then, more lambs and wool are shipped than from any other point on the Oregon Short Line Railroad, and where the old-timers, lolling lazily in the shade of wide spreading trees in summer and lounging in easy chairs before open fireplaces in winter, still speak kindly of the Whitney boys and Charlie Manning.

Courtesy of the Western History Research Center

THE FAMOUS BANK IN COKEVILLE
robbed by the *Whitney Brothers*, 1912

Chapter Seventeen

I SHALL NEVER FORGET a discussion that occurred in Kemmerer's City Drug Store in the summer of 1914. It was the same sort of conversation that was occurring in thousands of places where men were accustomed to get together to talk over the little things that interest them. The young fellows, mostly businessmen of Kemmerer, were in the habit of dropping in at the drug store after dinner, partly because they liked Charlie Christmas,[97] the owner of the place, and partly because they were certain to meet most of the other young men of town. The talk was seldom in a serious vein; and on the occasion of which I speak it was even less serious than usual.

"What's all this fuss in Europe about?" one of the fellows began. "Search me," said another, "the papers say that some crazy young guy in Serbia shot an Austrian Archduke or something." "Well, what of it?" asked a third. "A Serbian killed an Austrian down at No. 3 Camp the other night, but we didn't get all het up about it." At this sally everyone

[97] The *Camera* printed, in 1922, the departure of Mr. Christmas, "or Charlie as he is known to a host of friends, is a member of the well known Christmas family, one of the oldest in the county, his father, H. E. Christmas, having been a pioneer of western Wyoming bar." The Christmases had fled Kemmerer for the land of sun—San Diego. The Kemmerer *Camera*, April 26, 1922.

laughed. Someone got back on the subject under discussion with the remark that he supposed the archduke wasn't just an ordinary coalminer. "No better than a coalminer to me—nor as good," another said indignantly. And still another gave evidence of his gambling instinct by declaring his willingness to bet that "the old duffer never did anything in his life as useful as digging a ton of coal." Here they all laughed again. "Well, so far as I'm concerned, the Kaiser, the King, the Czar, and whoever it is that rules the French, can fight it out to their heart's content," was another's contribution to the discussion. One of them followed with this—"One thing sure—there's no danger of *our* getting into the mess—they can't cross that three thousand miles of ocean." This sage remark was made with a good deal of assurance. Everyone seemed to agree; and the discussion was about to turn to local subjects of more immediate interest.

"Wait a minute boys, I wouldn't be so sure about that." Old Doctor Hocker,[98] sitting on a high stool

[98]One of the most beloved and respected physicians of Western Wyoming, when Dr. Hocker's death was announced, "The Flag in the Triangle was at once placed at half mast and the sorrow of his old friends was voiced everywhere on the streets." Born in Kentucky, a graduate of Bellevue Medical College in New York, Hocker practiced in Missouri for five years. In 1873, Hocker moved to Evanston, Wyoming, where he engaged in general practice, later becoming the Union Pacific physician for some twenty-five years. By 1898, he had hung up his shingle in Kemmerer, when again, in addition to his regular practice, he was the

THE ROBERT R. ROSE HOME
1023 Cedar, Kemmerer

at the soda fountain, had appeared to be reading the afternoon's weekly issue of the Kemmerer *Camera*. Without taking his eyes from the paper he went on, "This ain't just an ordinary war—the whole world'll be in it before it's over, America included. Some of you boys'll cross that three thousand miles of ocean alright, with millions of others—and some of you'll never come back." The old doctor went on reading his paper. There was complete silence for a moment or two. Then, when Dr. Hocker spoke everyone listened.

Two or three of the younger fellows walked slowly toward the door with serious expressions on their faces, and went out into the night. Others sauntered over to the cigar counter. "Wonder if the old Doctor really knows what he's talking about," one of them mused in a low voice. "He usually does," said another.

"Boys, I see that John Kendrick's going to be the Democratic candidate for Governor." Delighted that the old Doctor had hit upon a more cheerful subject, we all crowded around while he made a futile effort to light the stub of a waterlogged cigar.

———
company doctor for the Kemmerer Coal Company and the Oregon Short Line.

A lifelong Democrat, while in the state legislature Hocker lobbied for the formation of the state mental hospital located, logically enough, in his hometown, Evanston. Some of the doctor's descendants' activities are chronicled in Woods Hocker Manley, *The Doctor's Wyoming Children*, (New York, 1953), and Kemmerer *Camera*, April 30, 1919.

"That's great," one of them said drily, "but who's Kendrick?"—"never heard of the man." The Republicans laughed boisterously. "Well, for one thing, he's a Southerner." "That should be enough for *you*," ventured one of the listeners. It was a daring thing to do, for no one ever took the liberty of joking with the old Doctor. Doctor Hocker smiled at this good-natured jab, for he was a little proud of his reputation as a wheelhorse in what little there was of the Democratic party in Lincoln County. "Yes, that would be *quite* enough," he agreed defiantly, "but in this case there's something more—he's a westerner—trailed longhorns from Texas to northern Wyoming in the early days—Wyoming and southern Montana—lives just outside Sheridan in a big stone mansion—'Trails End' he calls it. And I'll tell you something, boys, he'll beat your Cheyenne lawyer friend to a frazzle." "Atta boy, Doc," shouted one of the two or three Democrats in the group. He'd called the old gentleman "Doc", something no one ever did unless in a moment of enthusiastic approval of his views on politics or the south.

Doctor Hocker lit a fresh cigar. "Hate to leave you boys," he said, smiling a bit. "There's a youngster down in The Willows that's just itching to bust into this troubled old world and I've got to help him." Then a little seriously, "Funny, the first thing that happens to every human being's to get spanked, and the next thing's to squall." He hobbled on his lame feet to the door, untied his horse, and drove off in the direction of the part of town where the poor people lived on the north side of the tracks. Charlie Christmas was turning off the lights; and his customers were leaving for home, most of them seriously pondering what the old Doctor had said about the war in Europe.

Sitting at my desk the next afternoon I too was pondering what the old Doctor had said about the war. Was there something back of it beside the personal ambitions of a few kings? Some of the editorial writers had said that democracy throughout the world was at stake—that civilization itself was threatened. Could that really be true? Was it actually true that the Kaiser had set out to conquer the world? If England and France should fall, would we be next on the list? I wondered whether it was something like that that the old Doctor had in mind. But it all seemed so impossible—things were going along so peacefully. Certainly no one in our country wanted to fight—we weren't that kind of people—and what had we to fight about? And which side would we be on anyway? None of us liked the English very well—they were too cocky; and we didn't like the French much better, really knew little about them except that Lafayette had helped us out in the Revolution. As for Russia, all we knew about the Russians was that they wore long ragged whiskers and were ruled by a Czar. Really, after all, I thought I liked the Germans better than any of them—I was thinking of Old Criss, an old German hired hand on my father's farm in South Dakota when I was a small youngster. No, I guessed the old Doctor really didn't mean what he said—it just couldn't happen. The afternoon was hot and sultry, and there was little to do anyway—why not go up to his office and talk things over with Doctor Hocker? I guessed I would.

But just then the door opened and a tall slender man entered, dressed in tight gray trousers and coat of similar material that hung a bit loosely over his thin spare shoulders. There was a touch of gray over his temples. His widely separated small eyes were of an unusual dark shade with scarcely perceptible lines radiating from each pupil. "I'm John Kendrick,"[99] he said in something of a drawl as he walked slowly toward me extending a long slender hand. His manner was quiet and deliberate, almost shy. There was little about him suggestive of the cowman, unless perhaps it was the slightly weather-

[99]One of Wyoming's all-time popular vote getters, John B. Kendrick (1851–1933) was initiated into manhood in a classic western manner, when he trailed cattle up the Texas Trail in 1879. Eventually, Kendrick accumulated some 200,000 acres, spread over northern Wyoming and Southern Montana. As the "cowboy prototype of Abraham Lincoln," studying "by lantern light" while his bunk mates were celebrating "in saloons and dancehalls," Kendrick started his political career by being elected to the State Senate in 1910. Once in the political arena, he never suffered a defeat, serving successively as Governor of Wyoming (1915–1917), and as U. S. Senator (1917–1933). Casper *Times*, November 4, 1933; Casper *Independent*, January 3, 1931.

beaten dark skin, and the solemn seriousness that comes from long nights riding herd under the stars with no sound to break the silence but the long weird whine of coyotes on distant hills. Certainly there was nothing about him that was suggestive of the politician.

Sitting lazily in a chair at the end of the desk with one long leg hanging loosely over the other, his hands folded in front of him, his fingers moving nervously, he began to ask questions, first about myself, my wife, where we came from, how long we'd been married, about the cow men in the upper Green River Valley; but he said nothing about himself or his political ambitions. Suddenly a troubled expression came over his face. "You know, Rob"— he called me by my first name as naturally as though he'd known me all my life—"you know, I'm worried about this war in Europe." I was worried too. I wondered if he'd been talking with Doctor Hocker. "I'm afraid we're all treating it too lightly. Everyone seems to think it's a sporting event of some sort, something like a horse race or a cock fight. No one seems to think there's any danger of our getting mixed up in it." I was listening intently. "What do *you* think?" I wasn't prepared for the query: I didn't think anything: I was just afraid. Was I—were all these other young fellows—going across the ocean, etc. It seemed to me that he was afraid too. "This is going to be a terrible war. It will last a long time." He was speaking very solemnly.

There was an earnest, troubled look in his eyes. "It may be two years, it may be three, but we can't stay out. Isolation's a thing of the past."

There was quiet for a moment while he turned in his chair and looked out the window into the park across the street. When he faced me again there was an expression of sadness in his countenance. I thought of Lincoln. "Rob, I'm not a politician—I'm just an ordinary cowpoke. I wish they'd let me alone. I don't want to be governor, and I can't be elected anyway—probably. I can talk to the ranchmen along the creeks alright. But a man can't be elected to public office that way—he's got to talk to crowds—coalminers, railroad men, factory workers. That I can't do. I wouldn't know what to say—and they wouldn't understand me anyway."

There was another moment of silence. His manner changed, he went on: "What's got to be done's got to be done, whether we want to do it or not. My life's not been easy. It wasn't easy punching cattle in West Texas. It wasn't easy trailing longhorns a thousand miles from Texas to Wyoming. It hasn't been easy since. And *this* isn't easy. But it's got to be done, and I'm going to do my best."

His indecision was gone. "Rob, a man's first duty is to his country and state. When a man's called upon to perform a public duty he has no right to hold back. Our government is a government by political parties. We're Democrats, you and I. Ours is a party of great traditions. It's progressive. Wilson's a great leader, a great president. It's our job to back him up. We're in the minority in Wyoming—if we're to succeed we've got to do twice as good as the other fellows on a job. I think we can do it. We who've been carrying on the fight for years are getting old. We've got to have younger men. I want you young fellows to get into it." I thought I would. "By the way, Rob, I'm going to take a little trip into Green River Valley. I want you to go along."

We shook hands, and he went out. It was late afternoon. The low descending sun painted a faint pink tinge on the tops of the trees in the park across the street. Walking homeward I pondered this strange earnest man. Perhaps he was a politician after all, perhaps one of the highest type, the kind the world is always waiting for.

Standing on the steps of the Kemmerer Savings Bank the next morning, I saw Mr. Kendrick come out of the hotel a half block away and start walking leisurely in my direction. A rough looking ruddy-faced man limping heavily on a wooden leg came out of the drug store just as he was passing. "You must be John Kendrick—Dr. Hocker told me you was in town. My name's Jack Matthews," holding out a big calloused hand. "Run a shearing corral a few miles north of town." They shook hands. Kendrick's handshake, I noticed, was friendly, but no more. Chatting easily a moment about the relative advantages of machine shearing and the old-fashioned hand shears method, they seemed to be on a common footing, this cattle king and the sheep shearer. Mr. Quealy came out of the drug store, his left coat pocket bulging with the day's supply of cigars. He and Mr. Kendrick shook hands. "I'll be up for 'chow' this evening." "Fine, call for you at the hotel about six," and Mr. Quealy hurried into the bank for a directors' meeting. Dr. Hocker stopped for a few minutes' chat. He and Mr. Kendrick appeared to be old friends. They'd been talking less than a minute when a big coalminer came along to interrupt the conversation. "You John Kendrick—Me Joe Perpich." He extended a big coaldust covered hand. "Me dig coal—me and all the boys is vote for you, John—I gotta go now— good-bye John." Dr. Hocker laughed at Joe's busy exuberance, but I thought I detected a little more than his usual warmth in Mr. Kendrick's handclasp and there was a kindly smile on his face as he waved a farewell to the coal miner.

Another stopped and then another; and they were all greeted in the same friendly manner. Soon he was the center of a group of a dozen or more, each of whom would shake hands, exchange a few words, and go on. But they kept coming; and it was not until noon that he was able to make his way back to the hotel. Since he had left it two or three hours before he hadn't gotten more than a quarter of a block away. Half of the men in town had stopped to exchange a few words with him, and no one had introduced him to any of them. He didn't seem to need an introduction. He had talked briefly about everything from branding calves to the price of sugar, and no subject had been mentioned with which he did not seem perfectly familiar. When he went out on the street in the morning he didn't know more than two or three men in town. When he returned to the hotel at noon he knew almost everyone. Friendly with them all, he was effusively cordial toward none. What was it, I asked myself, that drew men to him? It was just that he liked people and people liked him, I guessed.

About noon the next day we started for the upper valley, and shortly before sundown drew up in front of Jim Black's hotel at Big Piney. Tom O'Neill and Jim Mickelson,[100] two of the biggest cowmen in the western part of the State, were there to meet him, one a Democrat, the other a Republican. Four-fifths of the stockmen of Green River Valley were Republicans, but that seemed not to detract in the least from the esteem in which they held this Democrat from the northeastern part of the state. The saloon next door to the hotel was filled with cowboys from the surrounding ranches. A moment after

[100] A rancher who was constantly being noted in the press as successful, James Mickelson (1866–1921) immigrated to America from Denmark at the age of eleven. His first stop in the United States was in Nebraska, moving on in 1895 to the vicinity of La Barge, Wyoming; shortly thereafter he found his future in Big Piney. At his death, this remarkable Dane possessed 20,000 acres of deeded land and 6,000 head of cattle. Big Piney *Examiner*, September 22, 1921.

our arrival they all poured out of the place, and Mr. Kendrick shook hands all around, taking time to chat briefly with each.

That night most of the cowmen and their "hands" came to the dance hall to hear the Democratic candidate speak. It was the strangest political speech I'd ever heard, for there wasn't a word about politics in it. Getting down off the platform he talked to his audience as though they were all neighbors. He talked about the things that interest stock raisers, about cattle, about range conditions, hard winters and feed for the stock, about taxes and how people should be willing to pay them in order to support good state and county government and provide good schools for "the kids." He said he supposed folks would expect him to make a lot of promises; that he was afraid they'd be disappointed, for he couldn't make any. He didn't know, in fact, whether he'd make a good governor or not—if he should be elected—because he'd never "tried his hand at the job." That remark seemed to strike him as being a little funny, and it seemed to strike everyone else the same way, for they all laughed. And that's where he ended his first speech of the campaign. He hadn't asked anyone to vote for him, and, while he'd intimated, as everyone knew, that he was a candidate for governor, he hadn't even mentioned which ticket he was running on.

There was an old piano in the hall, someone got out a fiddle, scraped the strings until it seemed to be at least partially in tune, and pretty soon the young folks were dancing. Mr. Kendrick withdrew to a corner of the room where he was soon the center of a group of cow men until he said it was getting late and he guessed he'd better go down to the hotel and get some sleep.

The next afternoon we went over to Pinedale,[101] another cow town some thirty miles from Big Piney. Driving along the road he noticed three men in an adjoining field putting up hay. "Rob, let's stop a minute," he said. Climbing easily through the barbed wire fence as though he'd done it a dozen times a day for years, he walked slowly toward them. "Pretty good stand of hay," he suggested, inquired how many tons they cut to the acre, how much it took to winter a critter, thought this should be a good country for dairying. In a minute or two they were talking over the problems of the cattle man, about range difficulties, how the homesteaders

[101] Pinedale's origin as a cattle entrepot was similar to that of many other Wyoming communities when the first settler in 1878–1879 made the happy discovery that cattle wintered well on the lush vegetation. The town's title, chosen by Postmaster Charles Peterson in 1899, derived from Pine Creek. Residents of Pinedale and other Wyomingites have always commented, perhaps over-enthusiastically, about Pinedale's isolation. For a time, Pinedale inhabitants insisted that they were farther from a railroad than any other incorporated town in the United States. Mae Urbanek, *Wyoming Place Names*, (Boulder, Colorado), p. 155; C. Watt Brandon, "Building a Town on Wyoming's Last Frontier," *Annals of Wyoming* (July, 1950), pp. 1–22; Pinedale *Round-up*, February 22, 1923.

were encroaching on the public domain, how the breed of range stuff was being constantly improved and Green River beef was commanding top prices on the Omaha market. The stranger told the men he'd have to be going and ambled back to the car.

That night while John Kendrick was talking with a group of cow men in the aisle of the Pinedale hall decorated with pine boughs for the occasion of his meeting, I overheard a much subdued conversation participated in by three men sitting immediately in front of me. "Why, I heard someone call that man standing there in the aisle 'Kendrick'," said one of them under his breath. "Gosh, that's the man that came over and talked with us in the field this afternoon and he didn't say a darned word about who he was," said another. "Well, dad-bust my buttons," said the third.

The Democratic candidate for governor talked about as he had in Big Piney. In the two days I had spent with him I'd learned something about politics, though I couldn't see that the education could be of any value, for no one could do it the way he did. But tomorrow night he was to speak to an audience of coal miners at Kemmerer. That would be the test.

The hall over the Lyceum bar was filled to overflowing. The miners of the Kemmerer district had turned out en masse to hear "Old Jawn", as people were already beginning affectionately to call him, although he couldn't have been more than about fifty. Joe Perpich arose to introduce the speaker and to assure him of the votes of "all the boys in the mines." The applause was scattered and stopped almost as soon as it began, which was no indication of lack of high regard for the speaker, for there is little to promote good cheer thousands of feet underground and coal miners, as I have known them, are serious minded people who are little inclined to demonstration.

Kendrick arose to face an audience of several hundred grim visaged men. "It's nice of you to say that, Joe; and I hope when I've finished talking you boys will feel as kindly toward me as Joe seems to think you do now. But before I can ask you to vote for me I think we should come to something of an understanding. There are some things about me that you're entitled to know. A railroad man over in Sheridan whom I've known for many years, told me the other day that he couldn't vote for me because he said I was a rich man. Well, maybe you boys feel the same way about it. But before you make up your minds one way or another I want to talk it over with you." There was a nervous rustling out in the audience. Some of the men leaned forward in their chairs the better to hear what the speaker was saying. Others sitting next to the aisle leaned to the side so their view would be unobstructed. None of them had heard a politician talk that way before.

"You know," the speaker went on, "what we have, whether we have a lot of money or only a little, or none at all, depends pretty much on circumstances—some people call it luck. Most of you boys were born in Europe. You came to America, and you went to work in the mines, possibly because you were miners in the old country, possibly because you already had friends here who were miners." I was afraid he was getting on thin ice. "In one sense each one of you is a better American than I am—you must love this great country of ours better than I do, because you *chose* to be Americans, while I didn't—I couldn't help it—I was born here. And down in West Texas, where I first saw the light of day, it's a cattle country—nothing but cattle. And so I began riding herd when I was pretty young. Ought to have been in school, I guess, but my parents were poor and I had to make a living. The days were long—from daylight to dark. What education I have I got by lamplight after most of the cowpokes had gone to bed—and riding herd at night under the stars. The boss put me in charge of a bunch of longhorns and told me to trail them into Wyoming. After a few trips he staked me to a herd of my own. That's where my luck came in.

"Well, boys, you know cattle have a way of multiplying pretty fast"—this was said with something of a smile and the grim faced men in front of him laughed aloud—"and I guess what my friend over in Sheridan said's true. I suppose I am a rich man—rich as we know it out here in Wyoming. After all, I suppose you and I are doing about the same thing, only in a different way. We're all trying to contribute something to everyone's welfare and happiness. I raise cattle, and you dig coal. People must have meat for food and they must have coal to cook it with and to keep them warm. Let's look at it this way: We're all one great big team, and every man and every woman that's doing honest useful works a member of the team. If we all work together we all get along better." The men by this time were sitting on the edges of their chairs, straining for every word. "After all, boys, we're all about alike—I mean those of us, at least, who spend our lives doing something useful—though we may differ a little in some respects. We all want to be good citizens; we all want to provide for our families; we all want to improve our condition in life; we all want to give our kids a better chance than we've had—Lord knows none of us is any too good."

The rich cattle man and the hardworking coal miners had arrived at the understanding he had mentioned at the beginning. He seemed to sense the fact and went on with his speech. He spoke of the privileges and duties of citizenship, the great men of his party, with particular emphasis on Woodrow Wilson and the forward-looking legislation that he had sponsored. He emphasized the necessity of everyone's allying himself with a political party because, he explained, it is only through them that the people can actually express their wishes and nominate and elect the men charged with carrying them out. There was not a word of criticism of the opposition party, nor did he even mention the name of his opponent.

When he had finished the men moved slowly down the center aisle to shake hands with "Old Jawn" Kendrick, an honor they had never paid a political candidate before. That night I knew that the man whom I had met only a few days earlier would be elected Governor.

John Kendrick's service to Wyoming and his service to his state and to the West are a matter of history. "The best possible public service is the best possible politics"—I've heard him say it dozens of times; and as often I've heard him urge young men to get into politics.

On a cold blustering winter's day a number of years ago I drove to Sheridan to attend a funeral. Senators and Congressmen were there and stockmen, business and political leaders from all parts of the State and neighboring states to do honor to the memory of one of the West's most valuable citizens. But the greatest tribute came from the scores of obscure cowpokes and workingmen who stood in silence in the cold blustering storm outside the church awaiting the opportunity, after the service had ended and the others had gone out, of passing by the bier to look for the last time upon the face of the kind friendly man whom they all loved.

Chapter Eighteen

THE LONG WINTER had come and gone. Though the narrow ravines were still lined with snow, the valleys were green, and cattle grazed on the steep slopes of the great hill north of town. It was the opening day of my first term of the district court. The little room on the second floor of the Town Hall was crowded. The sheriff and clerk were at their stations, and the lawyers in their places waiting for the call of the long docket. The hard benches outside the rail were filled with ve-niremen, litigants and spectators. It was well past the opening hour. Everyone was getting uneasy. A buzz of conversation filled the courtroom. Where was the old judge?

At last there were heavy steps on the stairway accompanied by bursts of noisy laughter, and a large strikingly handsome man appeared, his wav-ing white hair carefully combed, his large blue eyes glistening, his ruddy round face even ruddier than usual. He walked toward the clerk's office at the rear of the courtroom stopping to talk in his rich Scotch accent with a number of persons as he passed, each remark, though entirely devoid of hu-mor, punctuated with a loud laugh.

A few moments later he came out of the clerk's office, walked a little unsteadily to the front of the courtroom, and took his place at the bench while the lawyers and spectators stood until he was seated. Sheriff Hanson arose to announce the opening of the term. "Hear ye, hear ye, hear ye! The District Court, Third Judicial District, in and for the County of Lincoln, State of Wyoming, is now open. Ye who have business with the court come forward and ye shall be heard. God bless the State and this Honorable Court." Everyone sat down. "God bless this Honorable Court—I like that. Mr. Sheriff, say it again." The old judge was speaking. The sheriff hesitated, his face reddening. Certainly the judge didn't mean that he was to open court a second time. "You heard me, Mr. Sheriff! I told you to say it again." The judge's tone was imperative. The embarrassed sheriff rose to his feet. "God bless—" "No, *no, NO*, say it all." The officer started at the beginning. "Hear ye, hear ye, hear ye. The District Court, Third Judicial District, in and for the County of Lincoln, State of Wyoming, is now open—" He hesitated. The judge had opened a drawer of his desk and seemed to be fumbling for some papers. "Go, *go on*." "Ye who have business with the court come forward and ye shall be heard. God bless the State and this Honorable Court." "That's right, Mr. Sheriff. God bless this Honorable Court. Now you understand that when I tell you to do something I want it done!" The old judge hesitated an instant as though waiting for the officer to say something. "You *do* understand, don't you?" "Yes, Your Honor," Sheriff Hansen answered meekly. "All right then, don't forget it." The lawyers inside the rail sat chagrined and motionless as though glued to their chairs. The spectators looked at each other in silent amazement. I thought of the time I had stood reverently before the judge's bench at midnight in this same courtroom almost a year before!

"The clerk will read the docket." The old judge seemed to be making an effort to get hold of himself. "The State of Wyoming versus Daniel Parker," the clerk read.[102] A tall frightened negro, his thick

[102]The case of Dan Parker had the operatic overtones of a Gershwin *Porgy and Bess.* On February 21, 1915, Dan Parker, whom the *Camera* described as "colored," "had an exceedingly good reputation" as a janitor for several business houses, banks and R. R. Rose's office. Dan Parker's downfall came when he imported a woman from Denver to live with him. This act made him, gossiped the *Camera,* unpopular "with his class." All would have been well had not his lady friend succumbed to the smiles (and presumably the wiles) of one Mink Porter. Parker boldly followed Mink and Parker's fickle friend to a lonely spot (actually a blacksmith's shop). Once at the trysting place, Parker pulled out a double action 44:40 Colt revolver and "shot Mink Porter, colored, to death."

On May 14th, the jury brought in a verdict of first degree murder. The trial had lasted a week, complete with the examination of over thirty witnesses, and the pitting of the legal and forensic skills of Prosecutor Marshall Reynolds, assisted by H. S. Ridgley and J. A. Christmas, against, R. R. Rose. The *Camera* stressed that Rose had "put his whole heart and soul into his case and fought like a terrier for his client. . . . But he had a hard case." Judge Craig sentenced Parker to death; whereupon attorney Rose asked the Supreme Court for a retrial, basing his plea on Judge Craig's erroneous instructions to the jury. The Wyoming State Supreme Court reversed the decision, and ordered a new trial.

lips twitching nervously, stood up and took his place in front of the judge's bench. "Daniel Parker, you're charged with the crime of murder. This information says you killed Mink Porter—is that right?" Addressing the Court, I started to explain that I had been retained to appear for the defendant and suggested that if the clerk would read the information—"Sit down young man. The old judge is going to talk with this defendant himself." I sat down. "Dan, what did you kill him for?" The negro was silent. "If the Court please," I ventured, "this seems to be a very unusual procedure. I think I should insist that the information be read to the defendant and that he be allowed to plead." Apparently startled by what he must have thought boldness on my part, he hesitated and looked at me thoughtfully for a moment. "Guess you're right, young man. The clerk will read the information." The information was read and Parker in a quavering voice answered, "Not Guilty" and sat down.

The second trial, held in Green River on a change of venue, again resulted in a guilty verdict. Judge Arnold, having by this point succeeded the Judge Craig, accepted the jury's recommendation of life imprisonment. (Wyoming's juries could then offer a punishment recommendation.).

A new day dawned for Dan Parker in April of 1922, when Governor Carey paroled him on the condition that he leave the state. Dan did not tarry long in Wyoming, but departed as rapidly as possible for his old home in Hot Springs, Arkansas. Kemmerer *Camera*, February 24, May 19, 1915; November 22, 1916; September 17, 1917; April 12, 1922: and *Parker (Daniel) v. State*, 24 Wyo. 491, 161 p. 552 (1916).

The clerk read the next case: "State of Wyoming versus Dan Cole." A tall man with black curly hair and moustache, came forward. "Well, Dan, you back here again? What you have done now?" To which the defendant, a broad grin on his face, replied, "Well, Judge, they say I stole a cow this time." The information was read and the defendant answered confidently, "Not Guilty, Sir."

The clerk read on: "State of Wyoming versus Matthew Cirej,"[103] and the sheriff led a frail, sallow

---

[103] Jealousy again was the evil enveloping Matthew Cirej's case. An Austrian employed in the Frontier mines, Cirej, on May 21, 1915, found his wife in the company of another man on the road from Kemmerer to Frontier. Cirej, some say crazed, pulled a gun, shot his mate in the back, then in the head, concluding with a scream, "My God, I've killed my loving wife, Julia!" Previously, Cirej had complained loudly to one and all about an interfering mother-in-law and had implied that two men were plotting to alienate his wife's affections. Mrs. Cirej, in turn, had applied for a divorce. Attorney Rose decided to base his defense as not guilty by the reason of insanity. Rose claimed that nine years earlier his client, having received a blow to the head by a hammer, had exhibited "peculiar ways and actions" ever since. As substantiation, Rose marched a procession of witnesses through the witness box to testify to Cirej's erratic behavior. When the prosecution learned of Rose's defense strategy, they subpoenaed a group of doctors to consider the sanity issue; about all this produced was "a strong difference of opinion" from the physicians under oath. The jury took little time to render a guilty verdict, and Judge Craig quickly sentenced Cirej to death by hanging. As in the Parker case, Rose appealed the Judge's sentence to the Wyoming Supreme Court, on the basis of Judge Craig's instructions to the jury. So once again, the Supreme Court reversed Judge Craig's decision, ordering a new trial. On this occasion, Ci-

complexioned little man to a position in front of the bench. As he scanned the information an angry expression came over the judge's face. "Killed your wife, eh?" In a decidedly foreign accent the defendant hastened to reply to the judge's question. "She try to run away with Steve Travich. God tell me must kill 'em both. The men come—Steve git away." There was a deep silence in the courtroom. The spectators were leaning forward to catch every word that fell from the prisoner's lips. When the clerk had finished reading the information, the judge demanded angrily, "What do you say—Guilty or Not Guilty?" There was a long pause. The stillness of death filled the little room. What would he say? I didn't know. At last came the scarcely audible "Not Guilty," and there was a break in the stillness such as always comes after a tense moment in the courtroom.

It was past the noon hour, but the old judge had said nothing about a recess. The Clerk went on. "State of Wyoming versus T. Ohama."[104] A little

rej pleaded guilty to murder in the second degree and received the sentence of twenty years in the penitentiary. Kemmerer *Camera*, May 26, 1915; November 22, 1916; May 30, 1917.

[104]The third capital punishment case of T. Ohama, that Rose appealed to the Wyoming Supreme Court in 1915, met with the same fate as the Parker and Cirej cases; the Court speedily remanded Ohama to the district court. After hearing the testimony in the second trial, the jury rendered a verdict of not guilty. Kemmerer *Camera*, June 5, 1915; November 22, 1916; and May 16, 1917. *Ohama (T.) v. State*, 24

Japanese stepped forward. "Another murder!" The judge's anger was increasing. The Prosecuting Attorney explained that the man could not speak English, and the sheriff was instructed to return him to jail and get an interpreter.

For an hour or more the clerk continued reading the docket. There were five murder cases, in four of which I had been retained for the defense. There were cases involving robbery, larceny, mayhem, and stealing livestock, as well as a number of minor offenses, to say nothing of a long list of civil cases. It was time now for the judge to set them down for trial. Turning to me, he said a little severely, "Young man, you seem to have a good many cases on the docket—read 'em off to me." I began reading—Parker, Cirej, Ohama, Platos, Cole, Creadon— "That's enough—you needn't read any more. Your cases'll all be set together, the murder cases first, and then the others. After that you can take a vacation." He gave out a hearty laugh in appreciation of his own humor. In a pleasant mood now, he was smiling banteringly in my direction. I ventured to suggest that he intersperse my cases with some in which I was not interested. "Tut, tut, now you're young, you can take it. When I was your age I'd've died of joy if I'd had as many cases in one term." And laughing boisterously he walked out of the courtroom and down the stairs. When an hour or so later, the sheriff reported that he could not per-

Wyo. 513, 161 p. 558 (1916).

suade him to return, the lawyers conferred with the clerk, and though no one was certain what the legal effect would be, the clerk announced that court would be in recess until the next morning at nine o'clock. A few moments later the old judge was seen standing at the hotel bar with his arm around Cole's shoulder. "Tut, tut, Dan," he was saying in a voice loud enough to be heard by everyone in the room, "the jury ain't goin' to convict you of stealing that cow—just leave it to the old judge." Dan ordered another drink.

Promptly at nine the next morning the judge took his seat at the bench. "There's a long docket," he began. "Court will convene each morning at nine. There'll be an hour's recess for lunch, and an hour and a half for supper. Then we'll work until— well, until you lawyers get tired." He smiled at this bit of spontaneous witticism. "The first case is State versus Parker. Mr. Clerk you will call the jury." And for the next three weeks the old judge held court from nine in the morning until, frequently, near midnight, except on two or three occasions when it became necessary for the clerk to announce a recess as he had done on the first day.

The unfortunate negro had a slim chance. Prejudice is a vile thing which, born of the frailties of human nature and nourished on unreasoning suspicion, grows to huge proportions, and usually attacks with ruthless fury those who are least able to resist it. Parker was a negro; but he was the only one of the five or six of his race living in Kemmerer who attended to his own business and earned his living by honest labor, the only one who enjoyed the respect of the community. But the reputation for decency and thrift, which had until now stood him in such good stead that his services were in demand for odd jobs in the best homes in town and at both the banks, was of little value when trouble came upon him. People suddenly remembered that they didn't like the nervous twitching of his lips, or the way he hurried about from one job to another, or his superior attitude as though he thought himself better than the other negroes because he had spent two or three years in a negro college in the deep South; and they remembered that after all he was "just a nigger anyway." Besides all this, was he really married to the attractive wench he was living with in his neat little home down in The Willows? Perhaps it was over this woman that the shooting had occurred—why not?

And so, by the time some two or three dozen men had arrived from remote sections of the County to serve on the jury, the current of public opinion was running so strongly against the defendant that scarcely could they be expected to fail to absorb at least a part of it. Equally unfortunate for the defendant was the fact that the old judge had heard most of the comment that was going on about him. And so Parker's chances of getting "a fair and impartial trial" were not good.

The only witness who, by any stretch of the imagination, could be claimed to have seen the homicide, was a youth by the name of Wheeler, universally known by the nickname "Butch." Wheeler testified on direct examination that when the defendant came out of the First National Bank after finishing his work there and started down the street, he followed and watched him as he started across a vacant lot in the direction of his home. A fight ensued, he said, when Porter came out the back door of the Jack Piz saloon, in which Parker was the aggressor. The defendant he testified, knocked the other man down and shot him as he was attempting to get to his feet.

I was certain that he could not be telling the truth, for I myself had been less than a block from the scene of the tragedy when the shot rang out; and I knew that it was so dark that from the position where the witness said he was standing he could not possibly have distinguished one of the men from the other, if indeed he could have seen them at all. On cross-examination he admitted that he didn't see Dan after he entered the vacant lot, and, though he claimed to have been only a few yards behind the defendant when he crossed the street under a bright light at the bank corner, he was unable to say whether Parker wore a light or dark suit, whether his shoes were black or tan, whether he wore an overcoat, and even whether "for sure" the man he saw was Parker.

At this point the judge came to the assistance of the prosecution. "Now listen, Butch, it's the old judge that's talking to you," he began. "You *know* it was Dan Parker that you saw walk across the street under the light." The witness hung his head. He said he wasn't sure. The judge was insistent. "Now Butch, don't try to fool the old judge—answer that question again." The witness seemed to be very nervous, hesitated a moment, and, still hanging his head, said he guessed it was Dan Parker alright." "That's right, Butch, tell the truth." The judge continued the inquisition. "And you know you saw Parker knock Porter down and shoot him while he was trying to get up." At that the witness balked. "No, Judge, it was too dark—I couldn't see—" "Now Butch, it's the old judge you're talkin' to now—it ain't one of these lawyers." The witness was still unwilling to give the desired answer. "Butch, listen to the old judge—" The witness interrupted him. "Guess you're right, Judge, guess it really wasn't so awfully dark." I was watching the men in the jury box. It seemed evident from the expressions on their faces that they were impressed—the old judge had succeeded in "dragging the truth" out of an unwilling witness!

The sheriff's deputies testified that when Parker was taken into custody immediately after the shooting his face was badly bruised and he was bleeding freely from the mouth and nose, while the face of the dead man was unscarred. That should have been enough to prove that it was Porter and not the defendant that was the aggressor. Parker, of course, testified that the shot was fired in self-defense. Four or five of Kemmerer's leading citizens testified to the defendant's good character, and then there was, of course, the instruction concerning presumption of innocence and reasonable doubt. But nothing could overcome the prejudice that had gripped the minds of the jurors and their conviction that the old judge was convinced of the defendant's guilt.

"It is the sentence of the Court that you be hanged by the neck until you are dead." It was the first time I had heard the death penalty pronounced. A strange pallor came over the negro's face, and his lips twitched violently. It occurred to me that he would look like that when he stood on the gallows with a rope around his neck.

The Cirej case was next. The frail little man appeared even more emaciated than on the first day of the term. There was a grim look on the faces of the men who had been selected to try the case. Three coal miners from the Frontier camp were called to the stand, one after the other. Their testimony was in complete agreement. They were returning from their shift in the mine, they said, when passing the Cirej home they heard a woman scream. Running toward the house they heard a shot—and then another. As they entered, Steve Travich was just disappearing through the back door. Matt's wife was lying on the floor, the blood gushing from a horrible wound in her neck. Cirej, his left hand over the woman's heart, was raising the gun to his right temple. One of the men, their entrance into the room unnoticed, quickly seized Cirej's hand, and the bullet made a deep wound in his left arm. Another picked the revolver from the floor. Without a word to indicate he was conscious of their presence, Matt pressed his face against the face of the dead woman, and between sobs kept saying over and over again, "God keep telling me I must do it . . . God forgive you now . . . God forgive you now." Pretty soon, the witnesses said, the Sheriff and the coroner came and took them away, one to the morgue and the other to the county jail.

One of the officers exhibited a note which he had found in Matt's coat pocket, written by Steve to the defendant's wife. They were to have run away together that night while the unfortunate woman's husband was on shift thousands of feet underground.

At the jail, the deputies testified, the defendant sobbed continually, ate almost nothing, slept little, and kept repeating over and over again, "God tell me I must do it . . . God forgive you now." Two or three physicians, called for the defense, testified that the defendant was temporarily insane at the time of the uxoricide, his insanity caused by his conviction that only by her death could his wife atone for the sin of her unholy relations with Steve Travich. They expressed the opinion that he was not accountable for his act. It took the jury a long time to agree upon a verdict of guilty.

"It is the sentence of the Court that you be hanged by the neck until you are dead." There were tears in His Honor's eyes as he pronounced sentence. This responsibility discharged, he came down from the bench, laid his hand sympathetically for a moment on the defendant's shoulder, and walked unsteadily out of the courtroom. Again the Clerk recessed court until the following morning.

There was little of interest in the Ohama trial. The shooting was the culmination of a fight that had occurred in a Japanese boarding house at the Oakley mine. Both men had but recently come from Japan, where as nearly as could be learned from their reticent countrymen, they were members of opposing factions that had been for generations warring with each other. The jury required not more than an hour to find the defendant guilty; and for the third time in less than three weeks the old judge pronounced the sentence that meant death to the unfortunate man at the bar.

However, none of the convicted men were executed. In each of the cases the judge had given an instruction containing a palpably erroneous definition of murder in the first degree in which the necessary element of premeditation was completely omitted, and they were all reversed by the Supreme Court. I have often wondered whether the error was not intentional on the part of the old judge for the purpose of making sure that the defendants would eventually be given the fair and impartial trials which, as he must have realized, had been denied them.

When the last of the homicide cases had been disposed of, the old judge recessed court and walked slowly out of the courtroom. There was a serious, troubled expression on his face. All the next day he spent alone in his room at the hotel; and when he took his place at the bench the following morning the kindly dignity, the even-handed fairness to counsel and witnesses, the fine judicial demeanor that had marked his many years of service on the bench had returned.

One morning a year or so later the old judge was found dead in his room at the hotel.[105] In spite of his one weakness he was beloved in his lifetime by all who knew him, and to this day his memory is revered by the lawyers who are old enough to have practiced before him.

[105]The old judge, with the age-old problem, came to the United States in 1880 from Ireland, where he started life on December 5, 1860. A series of domicile changes followed; he found Danville, Illinois, to his liking. After laboring in a flour mill for a couple of years, he read law in the offices of Robb and Bradberry, from 1882–1885). He passed the Illinois Bar in 1885 and headed for Rawlins, Wyoming. Two years elapsed and Craig entered politics, first winning an election as county prosecuting attorney; then in 1894 he went to the State Senate. Governor W. A. Richards appointed him Judge of the Third Judicial District. Winning three elections, he held his judgeship until his death in June of 1915. Kemmerer *Camera*, June 30, 1915.

Chapter Nineteen

IN A LARGE HOUSE at the edge of Kemmerer Dr. DiGiacama lived alone. That he was the solitary occupant of the house was not the result of his own choice, but rather of the deliberate decision of the other members of the family—his wife, two sons and a daughter—that the terrible temper, the arrogance, the abuse which the doctor constantly heaped upon them could not longer be endured.

They may have been moved also by considerations for their own bodily safety; for, though the doctor was a small man—scarcely five and one-half feet tall and not more than 110 pounds in weight— he usually carried in its holster a large revolver, and was in the habit of amusing himself almost nightly with a half hour of target practice in the basement of the family home. And so most of the time I knew him the doctor lived alone in the big house.

If he was arrogant and abusive to the members of his own family, he was no less so to his patients, most, if not all of whom, were Italian coal miners and their families. And to the unpleasant qualities already mentioned he added, in his dealings with them, a greed as insatiable as it was unconscionable.

When called to a home where sickness had entered, the first thing to be attended to was the matter of the doctor's fee, which he always fixed at an amount so large that it would keep the entire family impoverished for months to come. And no matter how desperately ill the patient might be, DiGiacama's ministrations were withheld until the amount demanded was placed in his hand. And even then he would extend the benefit of his boasted skill, or refuse to do so, as might at the moment happen to suit his whim.

Nor was he above magnifying a mere cold into a disease of the most serious character in order to extort an exhorbitant fee, and upon the restoration of the patient to normal health, he would boast to the family and all the neighbors of the magic skill of "Zie Great Docteur De Giacama," his habitual way of speaking of himself.

It might be supposed that his insolence, his temper, and his greed, would have made him the object of the hatred of his countrymen. But these same qualities seemed to win him their confidence.

I was sitting in my office early one summer morning but a few months after I had entered upon the duties of Prosecuting Attorney when a young Italian rushed into the office, evidently in the greatest distress. He was able to speak almost no English. I finally made out that he was trying to tell me that Dr. DiGiacama had killed his wife. Seeing at once that it would be necessary to have an interpreter, if I were to get any sort of understanding of what had happened, I telephoned John Griff[106] whose saloon

[106] John Griff's emporium for inebriants was named "The Belmont."

a block or so distant was patronized mostly by Italians and whom I knew to be able to speak their language.

With John's assistance I was able to get the story which Billie Inglese was trying to tell me. He and his young bride had been living for about a year past in the neighboring town of Diamondville where he was employed in the coal mine. Expecting the birth of their first child he had a few days since visited the office of Dr. DiGiacama and at heavy cost engaged his services.[107]

The night before he had hurried to the doctor's office and told him that he was needed at once. Together they returned to the Inglese home to find that the doctor's arrival was none too soon.

Within a few minutes the baby was born; but, to Billie's horror, his wife was suffering from a most severe hemorrhage.

Indignantly upbraiding the young husband for

[107] Attorney Rose left few details out of the DiGiacama case, as previously supplied by publisher Rose to the *Camera*. The crux of the case arrived with a deadening finality when Rose called to the stand three local doctors, Marquis, Stafford and Buss, all of whom unequivocally testified that the "hemorrhage could have been easily checked by the ordinary methods employed by physicians in such cases, and the death of Mrs. Inglese (a beautiful young Italian girl of eighteen) was due to the negligence of Dr. DiGiacama." After the medical showdown in the courtroom, the verdict was automatic. A bail of $10,000 was set, and Dr. DiGiacama was free to be murdered. Kemmerer *Camera*, June 20, 1917; March 20, 1918; June 26, 1918.

his frantic expressions of anxiety, the doctor treated his wife's condition with cruel unconcern and made no effort to check the hemorrhage. When Billie timidly suggested that another physician be called, DiGiacama departed in a fierce rage, saying that he would return in an hour.

He did. But just as he entered the door the young woman expired. She had bled to death.

To the heartbroken young Italian it was a clear case of murder, and he insisted that the doctor ought to be prosecuted. I was inclined to agree with him; but the case presented obvious difficulties. I knew nothing of the situation from the medical standpoint.

Clearly the unfortunate woman had been left without the professional care which it was the duty of the doctor to provide. But *with* such care, could the fatal result have been avoided? An autopsy and consultation with competent physicians satisfied me on this point.

Then there was the question of precedent, to which we of the legal profession usually yield slavish obedience. I was unable to find in the books an analogous case. This, I finally concluded, was because in the history of modern medicine no physician had ever been guilty of such gross infidelity to the ideals of the profession.

And so I determined to make the effort. Particularly because I knew that DiGiacama, continuing in the practice of the noble profession which he so shamelessly prostituted to his miserable purposes, was a menace to the health and lives of those who trusted him.

Within a few days an Information charging the doctor with the crime of manslaughter was filed in the office of the Diamondville Justice of the Peace, and the case was set down for preliminary hearing.

It was the first prosecution of a licensed physician on such a charge in Wyoming, and, so far as I know, in any of the Western states.

Meantime, T. S. Taliaferro,[108] a very able trial lawyer from Rock Springs, who had been retained for the defense of the case, called at my office and made every effort to dissuade me from prosecuting. His arguments seemed plausible. No physician, he pointed out, had ever been prosecuted on such a charge in the history of the State. There was no chance of securing a conviction, and the only result of my action would be to antagonize every physician in Wyoming, make myself ridiculous in the eyes of the public, and ruin my prospects as a "rising young lawyer." Mr. Taliaferro, who died a few years ago, was a fine gentleman of outstanding posi-

[108] Attorney, banker, livestock grower, T.S. Taliaferro, Jr. (1865–1940), joined the Union Pacific in 1883, becoming an agent in 1888. After enrolling in a law course, Taliaferro began practice in Rock Springs in 1900. Quickly he achieved a prominence as one of Wyoming's most respected attorneys. For years he served as counsel for the Union Pacific railroad in Wyoming. His financial acumen surfaced in banking, real estate, and ranching. Kemmerer *Gazette*, August 2, 1940.

tion at the bar. Moreover, most of what he said seemed to me to be true, although I was convinced that a prosecution in this particular case should and probably would enhance the reputation of the medical profession and that I would incur no displeasure from that source. I told my caller that however that might be, and although I valued his friendship, respected his ability and years of experience, and appreciated his genuinely friendly interest in my welfare, I was convinced that a crime had been committed and was determined to proceed with the prosecution.

It was not without some misgivings that I undertook this unusual case. The practical difficulties in securing evidence upon which a conviction, if obtained, would be sustained by the Supreme Court, were not to be overlooked. Undoubtedly expert witnesses could and probably would be found to testify that, regardless of what might have been done, the woman would have died. Moreover I had not yet tried more than a very few really important cases, and in charge of the defense would be the most prominent, the most aggressive, and perhaps the ablest and most resourceful lawyer in the Western part of the state.

But in the very difficulties involved there was a challenge, and I found myself thrilling to the scent of the battle. No one will doubt that experience is a great advantage in the practice of law or in any other line of endeavor. On the other hand, youth, with its zeal and enthusiasm; with the hope of success which means much more to a young lawyer than to the older man who has perhaps hundreds of successes to his credit, if coupled with the willingness and the capacity to work—youth may be and sometimes is quite formidable. My reputation was to be made, and I was willing to work hard to make it. I might lose the case. If I did it would be no discredit provided I did the job well. I might win; and if I did it would be a notable success. Anyway the man ought to be prosecuted.

The defendant took a change of venue to Sweetwater County. That, as it seemed to me, was his first mistake, for he had practiced medicine in Rock Springs, the largest city in that county, for a number of years before coming to Kemmerer, and because of the bitter feeling against him there he had found it advisable to leave. Throughout the trial, which lasted several days, the courtroom was filled with Italians from Kemmerer and Rock Springs, every one of whom most earnestly hoped for the defendant's conviction.

The State's case was closed early in the afternoon of the third day; and the doctor took the stand as his own first witness. I shall never forget his appearance. All the confidence, all the arrogance, which had been so evident from the moment of his arrest, now was gone. The sneer which his pinched features had worn was no longer in evidence as he made his way unsteadily to the witness stand; and perspiration stood out on his countenance as he faced a courtroom filled with his own countrymen whom for years he had abused and robbed.

Dr. DiGiacama's voice was scarcely audible as falteringly he began answering the questions propounded to him by his counsel. At first they were designed to permit the witness to recover his lost composure. He told of the degrees that he had won from medical schools in America and abroad and of his years of ministering to the sick first in his native Italy, then in New York City and finally in Western Wyoming. At last getting around to the real issue in the case, and asked to state the cause of the woman's death, he said that she died of heart failure—at that point the witness was turned over to me for cross examination.

I can recall only one question that I asked, although, of course, he was under cross examination for an hour or more. The question was, "What was the matter with Mrs. Inglese's heart?" To which he replied, "One side beat faster than the other." With that question and answer the testimony of the defendant was concluded. Other witnesses were called to the stand by defense counsel; but after that answer no amount of evidence could have made any difference.

Then came the Court's instructions to the jury, followed by arguments of counsel for the State and for the defense, and the jury retired for deliberation. Within less than ten minutes, scarcely sufficient time to elect a foreman and take a ballot, the jury returned a verdict of guilty as charged. DiGiacama was sentenced to ten years' sentence in the State Penitentiary.

It was an easy victory. Almost too easy, I thought, for it seemed to me that had a defense of insanity been interposed he might just possibly have been acquitted.

Then came the second mistake on the part of the convicted doctor. Upon appeal to the Supreme Court a bond for stay of execution was given and he was released pending the outcome of the appeal. As it developed, he would have been safer in jail, for had he remained within the protection of its walls his life would not have come to so speedy or so tragic an end.

A few weeks after the doctor's release Billie Inglese came to my office in an obviously excited state of mind. "I must kill that man—I *must* kill him." After I had talked with him a few moments he became somewhat calm, but not less determined. "I *must* kill him," he said. And by now he had mastered English to the extent that he had no difficulty in making himself understood. "Every time I see him he make faces and spit at me—I must kill him— I *must* kill him."

As well as I could I tried to explain to the distraught young man that to do such a thing would only mean the most serious trouble for him, that the best thing to do would be to keep out of the doctor's way as much as possible, that the conviction would probably be affirmed by the Supreme Court and DiGiacama would before long begin serving a ten-year sentence in the penitentiary.

Before he left the office he gave me his promise. But somehow I doubted that he had entirely given up his plan and suspected that unless the doctor should change his attitude toward the young Italian he might come to a sad end. I therefore ventured to talk with DiGiacama on the telephone about the matter, only to be told in the most emphatic language to mind my own business.

Again and again in the course of the next two or three weeks, the young man came to my office, with always the same story, "Every time I see him he make faces and he spit at me. I must kill him—I *must* kill him." Always before leaving he would give me the same promise, but each time I was less certain that he would be able to keep it.

It was no surprise to me therefore when two or three weeks later the sheriff called me on the telephone one evening a little before dusk and excitedly announced that Dr. DiGiacama had been killed. A little later he drove to my house and took me to the doctor's home. Together we entered the front room of the house.

Immediately we noticed a bullet lodged in the sill of the front door. There was blood on the bench at the player piano and on the floor just beside it. Blood spots led from there into a hall and thence into another room. There sprawled on his back lay the little doctor in a pool of blood. Instantly we noticed a gruesome thing—his right ear had been cut off. We knew that meant that the job had been done by a member of the Mafia, a secret Sicilian society pledged to avenge harm to their members and friends and whose custom it was to cut off the right ears of their victims.

Angelo Molinar, who followed us into the house, told us that a few minutes before he had seen a young Italian enter the house through the front door. I was greatly relieved when the description convinced me that it was not Billie Inglese. Molinar said that the doctor was at the time operating his player piano. The music had stopped when the man entered and almost immediately Molinar, who at the time was sitting on his front porch about a hundred feet from the DiGiacama home, heard a shot. He had thought nothing of the incident at the time because of the doctor's habit of practicing target shooting in his basement. Two or three moments later, however, he had observed the man whom he had seen enter the front door, go out at the back and run up over the hill to the south. It was then that Angelo had telephoned the Sheriff.

A hasty examination of the house disclosed that robbery had not been the motive, for a wallet containing a considerable sum of money was in the front room where it could not have been overlooked.

The Sheriff, who had been in office only a week or so and was entirely without experience, appeared to have no idea as to what steps might be taken in an effort to apprehend the murderer. I suggested that it might be well to send a mounted posse up over the hill and that unless the man had a horse, which was unlikely, he might be apprehended before darkness. I suggested also that telegrams be sent to all officers along the railroad east and west with the idea that the culprit might be captured while attempting to board a freight train.

The Sheriff paid no attention to the suggestion regarding a posse but sent the telegrams, overlooking however, the little town of Opal about eighteen miles east of Kemmerer.

Early the next morning the Sheriff telephoned me that DiGiacama's murderer had been caught, and I drove immediately to his office, where he recounted the interesting story of the man's apprehension, the credit for which was due entirely to the alertness, the presence of mind and courage of the woman who was employed by the Oregon short line railroad as its ticket agent.

Although no telegram had been sent to Opal, the agent, who was also the telegraph operator, heard the message as it went over the wire to Rock Springs about seventy-five miles farther east. About midnight a man answering the description she had heard over the wire came into the station and asked for a ticket to Denver, inquiring at the same time when the next train would be through. Recognizing the man, she told him that there would be no passenger train until morning, but he could get a ticket that would be good on a freight that would be along in a few minutes. She explained that she was only the telegraph operator, but if he cared to wait, she would go across the street and get the agent who could sell him the ticket. He said he would wait. She went out and in a moment returned, not with the ticket agent, but with the deputy sheriff.

The man was placed under arrest, handcuffed and brought to Kemmerer where he was placed in a cell especially constructed on the second floor for dangerous prisoners.

When he had concluded his recital of the man's capture I told the Sheriff that I wanted to talk to the man, and together we went to the cell door. Try as he would he was unable to unlock it. After he had spent two or three minutes in the effort, I said, "Let me try it." Unable to turn the key, I took hold of the handle and casually attempted to turn it. To the astonishment of us both the handle turned without the least difficulty—the door wasn't locked. This killer had spent the night in an unlocked cell. Fortunately, he had supposed, as did the Sheriff, that the door was firmly fastened. Had he tried it, his escape would have been easy.

I asked the Sheriff to bring the man to his office. I thought he might be willing to talk, but he wasn't. I could get nothing out of him. I then asked the officer to remove the man's coat and let me look through the pockets, thinking only that they might contain possibly letters or papers that might prove of interest.

I was little prepared for what I found. Putting my hand casually in the right side coat pocket I felt something that made me shudder. I asked the Sheriff to feel in the pocket, which he did—and pulled out Dr. DiGiacama's right ear!

There could, of course, be no possible doubt that we had the right man. Why he should have kept the damaging evidence I have never been able to figure out. Perhaps it was to be the conclusive proof which, when presented to his employer, if indeed he had one, would entitle him to be paid for his terrible deed.

Still, even with this "exhibit" in our possession, the man wouldn't talk. So I went to work to gather the evidence which I hoped would make it impossible for him to escape conviction. I wanted to know who he was, where he came from, his motive for the killing, and, most of all who his accomplices were, if he had any.

Secretly and most earnestly I hoped that Billie Inglese would not prove to be involved. And so it came out, although it developed that a member of his family probably had something to do with the crime, and in truth there was some suspicion in my own mind that Billie had also, although before the inquiry got to that point there was no need for further investigation because the man was long gone.

It took only a short time to get at least a general outline of what had happened. Shortly after Billie's last visit to my office, his father had gone to Denver. A few days later he had returned bringing with him another young Italian—or rather Sicilian as it later developed. The newcomer got a job in the mine. It was customary for a new man to be put to work with an experienced miner. So, naturally enough, the newcomer was placed under the instruction of Billie Inglese. Just as naturally he went to live at the same place where Billie and his father lived and he and Billie roomed together.

One day the man got "sick" and it was quite natural that he should consult the Italian doctor. Molinar had seen him enter and leave DiGiacama's house a number of times before the afternoon of the tragedy. I was prepared to prove that the man hadn't actually been sick at all, and the inference was clear that his visits to Dr. DiGiacama were merely for the purpose of getting the lay of the ground and finding the most favorable opportunity for the performance of the task which had been assigned to him.

Whatever additional facts it might have been possible to develop, further investigation suddenly became unnecessary. As I opened my office door one morning about a week after DiGiacama was killed, the telephone was ringing. It was the Sheriff. "Well," he said, "We had a jail break last night.

The Sicilian got away." He seemed to me to be quite unconcerned, if not indeed greatly relieved.

With the doctor's murderer went a Japanese and a man who went by the name of "Slim" Creedon. The Jap, who was serving a short jail sentence for a petty misdemeanor, had been trusty around the jail and, as I learned that morning for the first time, had been permitted to serve as night jailer, and, of course, had possession of the keys. It was a very simple thing; he had only to unlock the cells in which Creedon and the Sicilian were confined and the trio easily made their escape.

Disappointed as I was on account of the escape of the murderer of Dr. DiGiacama, I was scarcely less disappointed at Creedon's get-a-way, for he was confined awaiting trial on a serious charge. As for the Sicilian, I doubt that the Sheriff ever made the least effort to apprehend him or that he had any desire to do so. He understood, of course, that members of the Mafia society were sworn to wreak the most extreme vengeance upon any officer who might be instrumental in meting out punishment to any of the members of the society. So did I. Perhaps it was best for the health of both of us that the murderer escaped, though I hadn't thought of it in that light. The Sheriff probably had.

For a long time I didn't see Billie Inglese and heard nothing of him. Our country had gotten into the war, and many of the young men of Kemmerer and the surrounding coal camps had gone "over there" to fight the "Hun." Billie, I supposed might be one of them.

He was. After the Armistice was signed and the boys were coming home, as I was sitting at my desk one afternoon a dark complexioned young fellow stepped into the office, wearing a snappy khaki uniform and a military cap. He gave me the impression that he was proud of our country, proud of his uniform, and glad to be back. "You don't know me," he said, calling me by name. I said, "Take off your cap." When he did so I recognized Billie Inglese. As we shook hands warmly tears rolled down his cheeks, and, I confess, mine too.

We spent the afternoon talking. It was he who did most of it. He told of the two years he had spent at the front and in the army of occupation, and it was quite evident to me that he was proud to have served with the American army under the American flag. Nothing was said of Dr. DiGiacama or of the man who killed him or how it had been arranged. If Billie had anything to do with it I didn't want to know it.

Before he left the office he opened a package that I had noticed under his arm when he came in. It was a sort of scarf made crazy quilt fashion, too big and too gaudy to be of any use. There must have been no fewer than a thousand pieces of silk in it, and, it seemed to me, of a thousand colors, all embroidered neatly together. In each corner there was an American flag, and in the center a legend "To

Mr. Rose From Billie Inglese With my Deepest Gratitude." With some embarrassment he confessed that all his spare time in the trenches and in camp throughout the two years of his service he had spent making the scarf so that when he returned he could bring it to me to show his appreciation of what I had done. Which of course was no more than any man in my position would have done.

It was only another bit of evidence of what I had already learned of the characteristics of our foreign born population, at least these living in the coal mining districts of our State. Once you do them what they consider a favor, their gratitude and that of all their friends never ceases. Not long ago while stopping for gas at a Diamondville filling station, an old Italian, Rocco Canoso, came out to fill my tank. Recognizing me, although the incidents related occurred more than twenty-five years earlier, he almost crushed my hand as he said, "You know, I remember what you did for Billie Inglese." Billie, he told me, had for many years been running a business of his own in Los Angeles. He has never remarried. The baby who never saw her mother now has several children of her own, and Billie every year returns to the Diamondville cemetery to decorate the grave of his bride of more than a quarter of a century ago.

Chapter Twenty

IN A DEEP RAVINE a mile or so east of town hidden from view except from the railroad a short distance to the south, stood a large green frame building, the first seen just before entering Kemmerer and the last upon leaving the town. Surrounding it were none of the sheds, fences or corrals always associated with a ranch house; and it was entirely too large for a private dwelling. Though it was an hour before sundown a great electric light burned over the entrance. I wondered as I saw the building from the car window on my first trip over that railroad what it might be, as I suppose thousands of passengers had done before and other thousands have since.

A few days after my arrival I mentioned the place to a friend. "Oh, that's the Green House," he said— "Old Isabel's place." He spoke as though I ought to have known, forgetting that I had arrived but a few days earlier. Before long I observed that it seemed to be known to everyone and that it was spoken of as casually as one would mention the drug store or the corner grocery. I knew, of course, that in the city where I had grown to manhood there was the "red light district," but it was a section of town seldom mentioned and never supposed to be frequented by respectable people.

It had not occurred to me that such a little town

as this would have its segregated district. But there it was, housed in a single large building discreetly hidden from both the town and the road leading into it, far enough away to excite as little resentment as possible but close enough to be conveniently accessible to these who might be in search of the kind of entertainment it afforded. Here under the protecting wing of Old Isabel lived a half dozen or more women of the underworld.

But no one ever spoke of them as such. One of the things that I found it difficult to understand was the entirely tolerant, if not even somewhat friendly way in which people seemed to regard the place. Public indignation might be stirred now and then over the condition of the streets with their mudholes here and there making necessary the use of chains for weeks at a time even on Pine Avenue; and a furor of excitement might be aroused over a city election, though it made no difference at all whether the candidates on the Citizens ticket or those on the Progressive ticket should be elected. And a few of the townspeople might even be stimulated at rare intervals to the point of demanding that the saloons be closed at midnight and on Sundays and that gambling be eliminated or at least required to assume an air of moderate respectability. But no tide of reform ever turned in the direction of Isabel's place.

The "Green House" appeared to be sort of an "institution," not, to be sure, to be boasted of, but

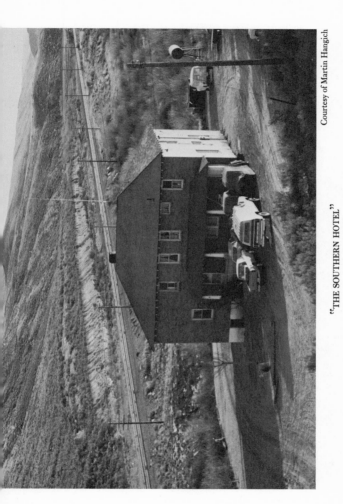

"THE SOUTHERN HOTEL"
formerly known as the "Green House"

not on the other hand to be spoken of with disparagement. Though perhaps "necessary," no one seemed to regard it as an "evil." It had been there for a long time, ever since the town started, and would probably be there a long time to come. It seemed to have a definite place, not actually as a part of the community itself, but rather as an adjunct to it. In fact, it may be said to have had a certain "character," a character given to it by the woman who conducted the place; for Isabel, whatever her faults, was indeed a kindly and charitable old woman. If a poor family down in "The Willows" was in need of groceries, they were delivered at the door. If there was sickness in a home where the head of the house was out of work and unable to pay for the services of a physician, medical care was provided. If there was poverty or distress anywhere in town Old Isabel seemed to be the first to learn about it and relief usually came promptly, though from what source few of the recipients of her bounty ever knew. Even one of the churches which was finding it difficult to pay the minister's meager salary received a cashier's check now and then, though no one but Isabel and the cashier of the bank knew that the money came from the Green House. I grew to feel that, despite the business she was engaged in, Old Isabel could not be altogether bad.

Early one morning during my term as prosecuting attorney of Lincoln County,[109] Sheriff McMinn

[109]Rose had achieved the office of prosecuting attorney by

called at the office and said that one of the girls at
the Green House had been shot. Going at once to
the place where the tragedy had occurred, we found
Old Isabel at the door waiting for us.[110] She was a
small woman, perhaps fifty-five, with soft skin, deli-
cate hands, gentle voice, and a certain air of refinement that seemed strangely out of place in a woman
of her position. Something about her reminded me
of someone I had seen somewhere in years past, but
who and when I couldn't recall. The thought was a
little puzzling.

   With scarcely a word she led us through the ball

-----

a majority of 19 votes in 1916. Kemmerer *Camera*, November 22, 1916.

   [110]If a visitor to Kemmerer has the temerity to mention
Old Isabel and the Green House, the usual reaction today is
a blank stare, or a knowing twinkle, but in either case little
comment follows. After all, in contrast to a tent revival
meeting, one does not offer personal testimony about houses,
green or otherwise. Located between Kemmerer and Diamondville, business flourished for years, until a reform wave
swept over Kemmerer, slamming shut the doors of the Green
House on February, 1920. The indestructible madam re-
opened her popular parlor, only to be closed down again
and then re-opened. If nothing else, Old Isabel had admira-
ble persistence. In April, 1921, a raid, unfairly conducted
without warning, flushed both patrons and proprietress into
the bright glare of the office of Justice of the Peace, all occu-
pants receiving appropriate fines. After undergoing a series
of revolving door openings and closings, the Green House
burned partially down in June of 1926. Shortly after the last
ashes of the fire were extinguished, the madam expired—
from burns received in the holocaust. Glen Barrett, *Kemmerer, Wyoming, The Founding of an Independent Coal Town,
1897–1902* (Kemmerer, 1972), pp. 75–77.

room, up the wide stairway and into a large room at the south end of the building, and then told us what had happened. A little after midnight, she said, two men entered the place; one tall, slender, well-dressed, and in his late twenties, the other much older, short and rough in his appearance. They herded the girls who were downstairs into this room where the others were already lounging. There were no men in the place. While his companion stood by apparently unarmed and having little to do with what was going on, the tall man command-ed the girls to get to their knees. For what Old Isabel said seemed ages, but was probably not more than a minute, he walked, with a revolver in his hand, in front of first one of the girls and then an-other and another and looked sharply for an instant at each. Their screams and entreaties, Isabel said, would ring in her ears to her dying day.

At last he stopped in front of the girl Isabel called Helen, who throughout the ordeal had knelt motionless with head bowed as if in prayer. Seizing her roughly by the hair he pushed her head back until they were facing each other and then moved a step or two backward. A few seconds they looked steadily into each other's eyes. Slowly he raised his revolver and fired. The girl fell to the floor. Laying the smoking revolver deliberately on a small table near where he stood, he gathered the girl in his arms, gently lifted her to a couch at the end of the room, carefully smoothed her clothing, looked down at the lifeless body for a moment, and turned slowly away.

At the sound of the shot the other girls had escaped to a room in the north end of the building and locked themselves in. Isabel, she said, stood frozen in her tracks. The two men walked unhurriedly out of the room, down the stairs, through the hall, out under the bright light over the outside door, and Isabel through an upstairs window saw them disappear into the darkness in the direction of town.

Sheriff McMinn later in the day brought the men to my office. The taller of the two, who gave his name as Tom McCluskey, the other called himself Jim Ford, appeared to be more or less overcome with emotion, though he expressed no regret for his inhuman deed. Refusing to say whether he had ever seen the murdered girl before, he recited the story of the tragedy exactly as it had been told to us by Old Isabel. The only excuse or explanation that either of the men made was that they had been drinking. The sheriff told me that upon receiving Isabel's telephone call he had hurried downtown, and seated at a table each with a glass in front of him in the first saloon he had come to, were the two men perfectly answering the description Isabel had given him. They had made no effort to escape and offered him no resistance when he took them into his custody.

Beyond telling how the crime was committed,

they would say nothing. Who they were, where they came from, whether either of them had actually known the girl before, what motive actuated the brutal murder, we never learned; for on the afternoon of the same day the men entered pleas of guilty to charges of murder in the first degree and later in the evening were aboard the eastbound train to begin serving life sentences in the State Prison at Rawlins. No further investigation of the case seemed necessary.

As Isabel, the sheriff and I were descending the stairs from the room in which the tragedy had occurred she said that she wanted to talk with me privately. While McMinn waited in the hall below the old woman and I sat down on a bench at the stair landing and she told me one of the strangest stories I have ever heard.

Speaking in a very low voice and obviously under emotion she was not able to entirely to subdue, she told me that years before, she had lived for a long time in a large house at number 100 on "Q" Street in Denver. She hesitated for an instant, and I got the impression that in her mind what she had said should convey more than was in just the words themselves, I knew the neighborhood, of course, and that it was in one of the most exclusive sections of the city not very far from where I had lived while attending law school. Nothing could have startled me more than what came next. "I was Mrs. J— S—," she said, and, as though that were enough, said no more.

It was enough—enough to bring to mind a flood of recollections, chiefly of the years when I was a student at the University. Life then had been very different from what it is today, particularly so at Denver University, at that time what we would now regard as an exceedingly straight-laced institution. Whether we would be right I'm not at all sure. Dancing on University property or even under the auspices of the fraternities or sororities was strictly forbidden.

While the students could not be prevented from attending dances downtown—as we frequently did, though nowhere except at the very exclusive Cotillion Hall at the foot of Capitol Hill—we were not permitted to sell the tickets on the campus or even to sell tickets for the theatre parties that always followed after the big Saturday afternoon football games.

Yet I'm sure we had as much fun as the college students of today and, I'm inclined to think, more. But it was a different sort. There were parties galore, generally at the homes of the young people, with auction bridge, and usually music, followed by a supper that was always over early enough so that we could take our girls home and be home ourselves before midnight. My older brother was an excellent singer, which made him very much in demand. I played his accompaniments, so that almost always we went out together. "Bendemeer's Stream," "O Promise Me," and the like, as well as selections from several of the operas, were in his repertoire, and seldom was I able to get away from the piano until he had sung at least five or six songs. They were very pleasant evenings, and there were never any headaches the next morning.

How well I remembered the big house on "Q" Street, for it was in that house that my brother and I had attended more than one of these delightful parties. And now that I knew who she was, I could recognize in Old Isabel's face the features of the very charming and elegant Mrs. J— S—. But how she had changed!

Old Isabel talked to me of her life in Denver, where, as everyone knew at the time, she was socially prominent as the wife of one of the city's leading businessmen. She told me of her husband's indifference and of her own indiscretions which had led to the separation. She had gone abroad for a time, then returned to a Pacific Coast city where, for reasons which she made no attempt to explain, she had conducted a house of prostitution, coming from there to the little town of Kemmerer where for a number of years now she had been the "madam" at the Green House.

Through the long, long years she had never permitted her whereabouts to be known even to her own daughter. She told me that she was waiting for the end, hoping that it might not be too long delayed, and that she had been able through the years of degradation to get some degree of happiness by being kind to all the girls in the House and relieving distress among the poor wherever she found them. Old Isabel wasn't altogether a bad woman. If she has been called to give an account of her stewardship I hope she has received credit for the good things to offset, to an extent at least, some that were not so good.

Isabel also told me what little she knew of the murdered girl. She had come to the Green House only a few weeks before and had been "working" there ever since. She was a beautiful girl and unusually intelligent, bearing no resemblance to the type usually found in such places.

As to who she was and where she came from Isabel knew nothing. She had received no mail except that about once a week a letter had come in an envelope bearing the engraved name and address of a Chicago lawyer. Isabel had noticed that the letters had been mailed to an address in Salt Lake City and forwarded from there to Kemmerer. She had thought little of this and said nothing to Helen about it—she had the habit, she said, of never inquiring into the personal affairs of the girls in the house.

Other papers found in the dead girl's trunk told the rest of the story. The baby, born in San Francisco, had been adopted into a nice family and the young woman, perhaps as she viewed it, forever disgraced, perhaps utterly overcome with grief at the loss of her child, or it may be yielding to impulses that defy human understanding, had come to live at the Green House.

At Isabel's suggestion I sent a telegram to the Chicago lawyer advising him of the girl's death. Two days later he arrived in Kemmerer. He was her brother. Overwhelmed with grief, he asked me to tell him just the bare facts. I told him what Isabel had told me and that his sister's murderer, with his companion, was already serving a life sentence in the State Penitentiary. "What did this McCluskey look like?" he asked. I said he was tall, slender, light, perhaps twenty-seven or twenty-eight, apparently well educated. The muscles of the man's face grew tense and there was a cold hard look in his eyes. "Are you sure he'll never be released?" I told him it would be a long, long time if ever.

Two or three moments later he asked me if I'd go with him to the morgue. The dead girl's face was as white as the pillow upon which it rested in the casket, her features as perfect as though they had been chiseled out of marble by the hand of a master. So skillfully had the mortician done his work that the wound in the center of her forehead was scarcely visible.

A half hour later the man stood looking out of my office window at the great high hill that rose from the edge of the river valley a mile north of town and extended far to the east and to the west like a huge wall, as it often seemed to me, separating Kemmerer from the vast country beyond. A heavy rain came out of the low hanging clouds that almost hid it from view. I had seen the great hill in all its varying moods, but never in a drearier one than this.

Presently the man at the window began to sob and the shaking of his large frame rattled the trinkets on my office table. "My poor little sister—if I had only known!" Over and over again he repeated the words. At last he began talking, very much as though I were not there and he were talking to himself. Their father had died when Helen was a child, leaving a considerable estate including the somewhat elaborate family residence. There he and Helen had grown up. Several years older than she, he had been father as well as brother to her. A year or two after his admission to the bar he had married and brought his bride to live at the family home. A few months later Helen, having completed her studies at an Eastern University, returned to find their invalid mother suffering from serious complications from which she died within a few weeks.

Helen's grief over her mother's death had seemed to her brother to be mixed with some other anxiety, the nature or cause of which he could not at the time understand. He now remembered that some months before her return to Chicago she had written that she was in love with a young man in the engineering department and that they planned to be married as soon after graduation as he could get a position; but since her references to him became less and less frequent and finally stopped altogether, he had concluded that there had been a falling-out, and gave the matter no further thought.

One day Helen had said she thought she would like to go to San Francisco to visit a girl who had been in her graduating class. Her frequent letters from there had been cheerful from the first, and her brother became convinced that it was only her mother's death that had been the cause of her own extreme grief. She seemed to have found complete relief in the post-graduate work she said she was taking at Stanford. The letters in the past few weeks had come from Salt Lake City.

That evening the brokenhearted Chicago lawyer boarded an eastbound train with the body of his murdered sister in the baggage car ahead. I have never since heard from him. Ford and McCluskey, so far as I know, are still confined in the Wyoming State Penitentiary at Rawlins. Some years ago the old green frame building was burned; but a new modern brick structure arose on the site to house a new generation of women of the underworld; and Old Isabel, though she disappeared from the local scene more than a quarter of a century ago, is still remembered not unkindly by the old residents of Kemmerer.

Index

INDEX

List of The Lakeside Classics

The Lakeside Classics